Whan I haik't up to Craigie Hill
And lookit east and west;
'In a' the world,' said I to mysel',
'My ain shire is the best.'

Whan I haik't up to Craigie Hill
And frae the hicht look't down;
'There is nae place,' said I to mysel',
'Mair braw nor our borough-town.'

And a' by mysel' on Craigie Hill
I spak in the Lord's ear;
'O! whan the haly bugles trill
Let me wauken up richt here'.

                    William Soutar

*To the memory of my late mother and father
to whom I owe everything and to my wife Wilma
for her constant encouragement*

NAE PLACE MAIR BRAW

A Social History of Perth's Craigie and Cherrybank

Donald N M Paton

Foreword by Willie Wilson,
former Depute Provost of Perth & Kinross Council

First published 2022
by Rymour Books
45 Needless Road,
PERTH
PH20LE

© Donald N M Paton 2022
ISBN 978-1-9196286-9-1

A CIP record for this book is
available from the British Library
BIC Classification HBJD1

Book and cover design by Ian Spring

Printed and bound by
Imprint Digital
Seychelles Farm
Upton Pyne
Exeter

CONTENTS

ACKNOWLEDGEMENTS

Whilst researching and writing this book, I inevitably had to draw on the work of a number of authors for information, quotations and opinions which appeared relevant to the purpose of this book. I have tried to give full credit to these sources but over the long period between collecting and using the information, I may have neglected to give full attribution where due. If so, I offer my apologies to those concerned.

Thanks are due to Ron Harkess, Mike Brocklebank, Michael Clark, Ian Macpherson, Mark Bousie and Jim Galloway for permission to use their photographs. Neal Mathers, who was born next door to me in Needless Road and is now a retired minister in Canada, kindly provided me with photographs and newspaper articles relating to his father's time as the minister of Moncreiffe Church.

Where photographs and illustrations have not been credited they have mainly been taken by myself or are from my personal collection. However, in the few instances where I have been unable to trace the source of a photograph, I apologise for failing to acknowledge.

Extracts from William Soutar's poems are reproduced by permission of the Trustees of the National Library of Scotland. Uncredited poetic quotations are my own.

Also thanks to Ian Spring who designed the book and the cover and for the reproduction on the cover of a painting from his private collection.

During the years of the book's preparation and also that of my earlier book on the history of Needless Road, there are several people deserving of personal acknowledgement. Particular thanks are due to Jess Smith for kindly permitting me to reproduce the story of the Broxden Curse from her book, *Way of the Wanderers*– a tale which Jess said deserves to be shared; Alan Brotchie for sharing his vast knowledge of Perth's old tramcars and buses; Alexander S Hay for allowing me access to his private collection of Perth Livestock Mart memorabilia; Robert Wilson and the late George Macdiarmid for making records and photographs of the West End Bowling Club available to me; Ken Bruce for information regarding the 'flying circuses' at Cherrybank and Lawrence Read for information about the Bernard Holt School.

Special thanks are due to Gordon Hynd, David Macdonald, Elizabeth Gray, Ian Macpherson, Sheila Walker, John Annat and the late Alan Cowan for taking time to submit contributions of their own personal memories – in some cases from as far away as Australia, Canada and the USA.

Countless other people must be thanked for their invaluable advice, suggestions and interest in the project including my Cherrybank 'lunch bunch' of Jim McNeill, David Bertie, Stewart Bousie and Keith Rezin – all who have remained my close friends since primary school days.

The local studies and archives departments at the A K Bell Library were paramount in my research. Perth is extremely fortunate in having such excellent research facilities with such a patient and helpful staff.

In these days of modern technology the internet is a valuable source for any author`s research and there were many Google searches which revealed informative information. I found the Auld Perth Bairns website particularly useful for clarifying many relevant matters which had become hazy with the passage of time, for discovering new leads and for enabling me to contact people who were willing to share their memories.

I wish to acknowledge the support of the Jimmie Cairncross Charitable Trust for assistance received in financing the book`s production and for the support of those who contributed to the funding by placing advance orders.

FOREWORD

I was delighted to receive Donald Paton's request to write the Foreword for his latest book, *Nae Place Mair Braw*, dealing with the social history of Craigie and Cherrybank.

I have known Donald for a great many years and he has been a long term friend of my wife Margaret. Donald's commitment to the local area speaks for itself with his previous book, *Twixt Castle & Mart* outlining the history of Needless Road constituting an excellent taster to this new publication.

Craigie and Cherrybank are rich in history and Donald's book explores this from very early days right up to the present time.

My own links with both communities have been real and lengthy but my introduction to Craigie was a personal one. After leaving Perth High School, Margaret and I met regularly, became engaged and subsequently married. We did our courting in Craigie. In those days it was a much quieter suburb with lots of different shops which you will read about in Donald's book and had far fewer cars than at present!

It is still great to walk the highways and byways of Craigie and Cherrybank and take in the richness and diversity of the area. Getting to know Cherrybank was even more straightforward. I was first elected to Perth & Kinross District Council in 1980 when Cherrybank and a big chunk of Craigie were included in the ward. There is no better way to find your way into the very sinews and bones of a community than being a local 'Cooncillor'. I got involved very quickly in local life and many of the issues which are reflected in the book.

We moved in the 1970s up to Oakbank, but Craigie and Cherrybank were visited virtually daily. Donald describes in his book so much of the wonderful tapestry of life in these communities. He highlights many special occasions, tells us about lively personalities and describes the wonderful areas to walk in and explore.

Both Craigie and Cherrybank have changed hugely in the last fifty years. The communities have had to face a new set of challenges including a decrease in local shops, reduction of Post Office services, a huge increase in the volume of traffic, new housing and schools and changing work patterns. Many of the true gems remain however – the Buckie Braes, St Magdalene's

Hill and the Community Woodland, Craigie Knowes and Craigie Hill Golf Course.

We need to cherish our open spaces even more and respect them in totality. Donald paints a wonderful picture, often from personal experience, through each of the chapters in the book and describes in detail how many things have changed and developed over the years.

I thoroughly commend the book to everyone who lives in the city of Perth and much further afield. The book forms a serious part of our developing. It is a vital social history of and for the generations and should be essential reading for everyone.

Willie Wilson
Former Depute Provost of Perth & Kinross Council.

Donald Paton grew up in and still has a home in Craigie. Educated at Craigie School and Perth High School, most of his working life was spent in the world of advertising with the Dundee publishing company of D C Thomson & Co. Ltd.

An enthusiast of the social history, traditions and culture of Scotland, he is a founder member and an honorary president of The Perth Burns Club. During a period of thirty five years when he served as the club's secretary, he was the instigator of events such as Perth's Day of Scottish Culture and the annual Schools Festival.

He is the author of two earlier books on Perth. His first, *Twixt Castle and Mart* published in 2005, was a history of Needless Road followed in 2014 by the anthology *Perth: As Others Saw Us*.

In 2015 he was the recipient of the prestigious D K Thomson Award for his services to cultural activities within Perth and Kinross.

A Fellow of the Society of Antiquaries of Scotland, he currently divides his time between Perth and West Vancouver in Canada.

INTRODUCTION

Today, the days of Queen Victoria seem astonishingly close when people now in their seventies, eighties and nineties can recall with clear memory grandparents and, in some cases, parents born during her reign. I once had an elderly neighbour who remembered the collapse of the Tay Rail Bridge in December, 1879. The first chapter of this book goes back even further but, for the main part, it tells of the Perth suburbs of Craigie and Cherrybank for the century and a half which followed the arrival of the railway system to Perth around 1850 spiced with the memories of a few people born before, during or shortly after World War II.

After the first year of the twentieth century Queen Victoria was dead and with her a social and moral way of life which had actually been on its way out for fifteen years and her son, King Edward VII, was already into his declining years by the time of his coronation. The second decade of the century belonged to World War I followed by an armistice which brought relief from the carnage of the male population and left a generation of girls to contemplate life without marriage.

The book tells how the 1920s and 1930s were a time of social improvement before the country was again plunged into another world war in which everything was in aid of it, in spite of it, or because of it. A period of change followed World War II when the re-structuring of national reforms, new housing developments and greater attention to the well-being of children paved the way to a new strata of society. By the 1960s new freedoms lessened certainties and there were as many views of life as people to hold them. The later years of the twentieth century until the present times of the twenty first century are included but these really belong to another era which will be remembered by the elderly of the future.

Whilst researching material for *Twixt Castle and Mart*, my 2005 book on the history of Needless Road, it was inevitable that I would unearth a lot of interesting information on the surrounding areas of Craigie and Cherrybank. Although it was always my intention to use this information in another book, other diversions (including the publication of an anthology on Perth) took over and the material gathered lay largely untouched.

It was not until 2020 and the periods of self-isolation caused worldwide by the Covid-19 pandemic, that I decided to make use of unexpected free time to resurrect the project. However, I make no apology for re-using some of the material which appears in my earlier book on Needless Road but altering, amending, abbreviating or extending the copy as I saw fit.

Social history is almost like family business with the good, the bad and the ugly, as well as the shameful and embarrassing, all revealed. Discussing it in public can lead to arguments as it is an amalgam of facts and opinions as the writer sees them. That is what makes it so fascinating and engaging for there is nothing like a genial and constructive argument!

One of my first decisions was to define the area which constitutes both Craigie and Cherrybank. I decided eventually to mainly use the parameters of an area bordered by Glasgow Road, Graybank Road, Glover Street, Craigie Cross and St Leonard`s Bank, Priory Place, Glenearn Road, Glenlyon Road, Quarry Road, Glenlochay Road, Callerfountain Hill and part of the M90 motorway to Broxden, whilst making occasional detours into Moncreiffe, Friarton, Viewlands and Oakbank – areas well deserving of a history of their own.

The content of the book has varied from personal reminiscences to information gleaned from books, magazines, newspapers and the internet. There have been countless hours spent researching Dean of Guild records, Council Minutes, street directories and electoral registers and many happy connections have been made with people with stories to tell and memories to share and who were, I think, glad of the opportunity to share them.

This account includes some of the lively personalities who lived in the area, their working lives and the recreation they sought. What I hope emerges is a strong social history of two districts of Perth, each with completely different backgrounds and stages of development, but which have gradually merged together over the years to become a major part of western Perth.

The very recent past, populated as it is by people still alive, is hard to write about in the context of a social history book. Denied the filter of distance and time, characters and events can sometimes appear too close and too personal. The passage of years allows a sort of lens, enabling us to focus clearly and, until enough time has elapsed, the stuff of just a few years ago seems hopelessly blurred.

If this book can revive memories for older generations or let younger and future generations understand and appreciate the changes over the years in the community life of Craigie and Cherrybank, it will hopefully have served its purpose.

And the title? Well, it comes from 'Patriotism', a poignant poem by a famous son of Craigie, William Soutar. As another Craigie lad from a later generation and one who always relishes his trips home from western Canada, I have to agree with Willie that, to me anyway, there is still 'nae place mair braw'.

Donald N M Paton, FSA Scotland, 2022

THE EARLY DAYS

The Romans, following from afar
Agricola to northern wars,
In Tay and its fair banks beheld
Their Tiber and their Field of Mars.
That landscape stopped the veterans' march
Till admiration gazed its fill;
Their shouts resound along the Tay,
And up the slopes of Craigie Hill.

From 'Craigie Hill' by William Clyde (1791-1873)

The beginnings of the modern Craigie, as we know it today, began in the mid-nineteenth century when the railway came to Perth and cut through the rising ground above the South Inch altering the original topography.

However, before the arrival of the railway, part of the area was known as Craigie-mill and an entry in Nicholas Carlisle's *Topographical Dictionary of Scotland* of 1813 refers to Craigie-mill as being 'a pleasant and populous village half a mile south of Perth and situated on the site of the old castle of Craigie (which formerly belonged to the family of Ross the proprietors of the Barony of Craigie) and that a great brewery had been established there'.

In these days, the area around Craigie-mill would have been mainly open farmland with 'bonny corn-rigs and rigs o' barley' mellowing in the sunshine. The only buildings being a few thatched cottages. However, by the end of the nineteenth century, the railway station and its associated activities had made this the fastest expanding area of Perth.

Cherrybank was originally a weaving hamlet built on the lands of Pitheavlis. It was originally by-passed by the old south road to Stirling which travelled from Perth up what was later to become known as Needless Road and then continued up the Necessity Brae. Low Road in Cherrybank is part of that old route.

The Topographical Dictionary of Scotland published in 1851 by Samuel Lewis of London, lists Cherrybank as being 'a village of 157 inhabitants'. It is recorded that in the middle of the nineteenth century Dr Pringle, minister of the North U P Church in Perth, regularly spent his summer holidays in what was then a rural retreat.

The need to increase the city's housing base in the early part of the twentieth century, combined with the location of the western tramway terminus, soon brought rapid expansion to what had previously been a peaceful rural community.

But the history of the entire area of Craigie and Cherrybank actually stretches back many centuries.

The Priory and Hospital of St Leonard

The Priory of St Leonard and its adjoining buildings were situated beside an ancient route which, before the construction of the railway, led from the South Street Port through Pomarium to Carr's Croft (Cat's Croft) and Craigie. The main building appears to have been situated in what is now St Leonard's Bank immediately beyond the north side of the present railway bridge. The chapel stood at a little distance to the east on rising ground overlooking the South Inch. The site of the Priory was well selected commanding a sweeping prospect over the South Inch to Kinnoull, Moredun, St Magdalene's and Craigie Knowes.

A plaque on the side of the red brick building on St Leonard's Bank reads: 'In this vicinity stood the Priory, Hospital and Chapel of St Leonard founded before 1296 – gifted by James I to the Prior and Convent of the Charterhouse in 1429 – suppressed in 1434'. Archaeological finds in the area have included human remains, a brooch enclosed in a full-size stone cist and medieval pottery. The burial grounds included the victims of a 1608 plague.

By 1296, the Priory had become fully established and was occupied by nuns of the Bernardine or Cistercian Order conforming to the rule of St Benedict but following certain private constitutions. The Cistercians had thirteen monasteries and thirteen nunneries in Scotland.

The habit of monk and nun was white but when the Order arose, the black monks reproached their new brethren with wearing a garment fit only for a time of joy, while the monastic state was one of penitence. However, the white monks answered that the life of a monk was not only one of penitence but was like that of the angels and therefore they wore white garments to show the spiritual joy of their hearts.

The Saint of the dedication was Leonard (sometimes spelt as Leothenard or Lithenari) a favourite saint of the middle ages who was made patron of many churches and chapels. He was a nobleman of the French Court of King Clovis the First and who became a monk and hermit. He built for himself an oratory in the Forest of Nobilac near Limoges where he lived only on fruit and herbs. To some extent, the nuns of the Priory of St Leonard perpetuated this lifestyle supplied by the produce from their own pleasant crofts which extended to the Craigie Burn, the Thorney Croft (Croft Bank) and Cat's Croft (Carr's Croft) and over the land occupied by the present railway lines.

The Leonard institution comprised a nunnery, a hospital and a chapel and was ruled by a Prioress. In 1296, the 'Prioress of St Leonard, near the town of St John of Perth' swore fealty to Edward I of England for her lands in the shires of Perth, Edinburgh, Haddington and Fife and her seal is appended to the deed of homage. The other prioresses of the same order in Scotland also swore fealty that same year.

From 1327 (and probably long before) The Prioress of St Leonard appears to have received an annuity of £5 out of the King's fermes of Perth and the Home possessed a considerable portion of the surrounding lands, besides other sources of income, from annual rents in the town and elsewhere. About the year 1396, Gilbert Taylor, Burgess of Perth, granted an annual rent of forty pennies to the Hospital of St Leonard out of a tenement on the south side of the North (or High) Street.

Until the beginning of the fifteenth century, the Prioress bore rule over the whole establishment at the Leonards but, by favour of King Robert III, a temporary change took place and a Master was appointed to the Hospital. In 1403, the annuity of £5 was paid to 'the Master of the Hospital of St Leonard's, John Brown, son of Robert Brown, who holds the Hospital for life, by grant of the King under the Privy Seal.' Brown's tenure of office was short for in 1411 the Master was Robert Clark who, on 23rd November that year resigned his membership in the hands of Robert, Duke of Albany, the Governor of Scotland on condition of being paid an annuity of thirteen merks. This resignation enabled Lady Elizabeth Dunbar to be appointed the Prioress 'as the said Hospital should commonly be governed by ladies, or devout women religiously associating.'

Lady Elizabeth Dunbar was the last to hold the title of Prioress of St Leonard and held that office until the transfer of the Priory to the Carthusian Monastery by grant of King James I. On 24th April 1438, Lady Elizabeth, as Prioress, resigned to the Carthusian Prior and Convent 'all right, claim and title of right to the Hospital of St Leonard.'

The Priory was now suppressed but the Chapel was maintained for divine worship and appears to have been used up to the period of the Reformation when it shared the fate of other ecclesiastical buildings. The Scottish Reformation of 1560 was the process by which Scotland broke with the Papacy and developed a predominantly Calvinist church which was strongly Presbyterian in outlook. The previous year, on 11th May 1559, John Knox preached a sermon on the sin of idolatry in Perth's St John's Kirk which led to four monasteries and religious houses in the city being destroyed during a two-day rampage.

The Reformed faith claimed the altarage, chaplaincy and endowments and retained the name and title of Chaplain with the consent of the managers of King James VI Hospital. In the early seventeenth century the chaplaincy was held by John Davidson, Notary Public, in Perth who, on 20th June 1634 resigned the position in favour of his son John Davidson, a student in Perth, who later followed his father's profession and became Notary Public and Fiscal of Court in Perth. This John Davidson took a leading position among his fellow citizens during the Cromwell invasion of Scotland in 1651 and he was appointed Lieutenant of the contingent of one hundred men raised by the town of Perth to support the force based at Inverkeithing to oppose Cromwell. The Scots were defeated and Davidson returned to Perth with the remnants of his men and shut the gates of the city but the English army advanced to Perth on 1st August and the town surrended next day.

In the eighteenth century, the lands of Leonard's Ley, Leonard's-hall or haugh which were now held by the Barony of Craigie were purchased by the Glover Incorporation. This acquisition effectively saved the South Inch from becoming the site of the new railway station in the mid-1800's although no doubt some good resulted to themselves in the disposal of the St Leonard land. The Craft fued out the land around Glover Street, named after the Incorporation of Glovers who were chartered in the fifteenth century and at one time were Perth's greatest land owners. Thus commenced the suburban development of Craigie with the ancient priory now remembered by the nearby streets of St Leonard's Bank, Priory Place, Abbot Street, and Friar Street.

In 1880, while a number of the old thatched cottages at Carr's Croft were being demolished to be replaced by new dwelling houses, it was found that many hewn stones, which must have belonged to ecclesiastical buildings, had been used in their construction. It is believed that the stones came from the Hospital or Chapel of St Leonard as one of the stones was finely sculptured and may have been the capital of a pillar or the base of a baptismal font.

The Hospital of St Mary Magdalene

Situated in the location of today's Glenturret Terrace in the Moncreiffe housing estate, the Hospital of St Mary Magdalene stood about a mile south from Perth and was probably near the homestead of the Magdalene's Farm, past which went the old road from Edinburgh. The date of its foundation and the name of its founder (probably some royal personage) are unknown. All writers on the ecclesiastical antiquities of Perth call this a nunnery but there is no trace that such was its character. On the contrary, it is designated as a hospital, being evidently intended for the casual reception and entertainment of poor and weary travellers. No doubt, however, a small chapel would have been attached for religious services.

In the earliest of the Exchequer Rolls of Scotland, 'The Master of the Hospital of St Mary Magdalene' is entered. From 1327 he appears as being in receipt of an annuity of twelve shillings out of the King's fermes or rents in the burgh of Perth. At the beginning of the fifteenth century, the Master was Thomas de Douglas. The house was well endowed with a portion of the lands lying around it, certain annual rents in the town and the salmon fishing of Poldrait on the North Inch.

After King James I founded the Carthusian Monastery, he gifted to it the Magdalene's Hospital and the Priory of St Leonard, both of which the monks suppressed, but continued the chapel of the latter house. Up to 1434, the annuity of twelve shillings was paid to the Master of the Magdalene's but after the Hospital closed that year it was paid to the Carthusians.

Being the feudatory possessors, the Carthusian friars became the superiors of Craigie and the small village of Freertown or Friartown (now Friarton), with a farm annexed, was built on the Magdalene land near the River Tay.

It is recorded that near the site of the Hospital 'there is a most excellent spring of living water, one of the best in the country' and Henry Adamson in *The Muses Threnodie* speaks of 'Mourning Magdalene, / Whose crystal fountain flows like Hippocreme.'

In 1591 at Holyroodhouse, Edinburgh it is recorded that King James VI 'disposed to John Ross of Craigie and Agnes Hepburn his wife, the lands of St. Magdalene's, in the lordship of the Charterhouse of Perth, which formerly were part of the patrimony of the priors of the said Charterhouse.'

The Rise and Fall of the House of Ross

The ancient family of Ross, much identified with the history of Perth, were the proprietors of the Barony of Craigie from the reign of Alexander the First (c 1078-1124) and for centuries thereafter. There is no certain record of when this family had its beginnings but they are believed to have been around at the time of the Norman Conquest and they were certainly a flourishing family during the reign of Robert the Bruce. The original family seat of the Ross family appears to have been at the castle of Craigie on the elevated site above Craigie-mill where the Craigieknowes Care Home is now situated.

The Barony of Craigie covered nearly all of south and western Perth. Between 1552 and 1570 the Ross family acquired the lands of Pitheavlis and built the tower house now known as Pitheavlis Castle which meant that the Barony at that time stretched eastwards from Pitheavlis to the New Row and the lordship of the Charterhouse in what is now the King Street area of Perth. Southwards, the Barony incorporated the Friartown village (Friarton) and reached all the way to the lands of Mailer and the River Earn.

There are no Charters in Register House regarding the Rosses before the sixteenth century but Robertson's Index of Rolls, which was lost in Cromwell's time, mentions four of the Ross Charters:

King Robert Bruce to John de Fortune of the lands of Craigie and West Mailer; David II to Adam Blaircradock of the lands of Craigie and West Mailer which John de Fortune forfeited; David II to Godfrey Ross of Cunninghamhead of the Mill of Craigie; Robert III to Hew Ross of Kinfauns of the Barony of Craigie and West Mailer. Hugh Ross received from King Robert Bruce a Charter of the lands of Kinfauns about 1316.

In 1541, the Lyon King-at-Arms gave a patent for a coat-of-arms and armorial bearings to John Ross, younger of Balgregie, son of George Ross descended from the family of Ross of Craigie. The Ross family were governors of the Spytower of Perth until 1544, when the keys by order of the Regent Arran were surrendered to Provost Macbreck and the Town Council under protest by John Ross. Provost Macbreck was married to a member of Perth's ancient Mercer family.

Although the Ross family was closely associated with Perth for at least five centuries, their history is disappointing and at times fragmented. None of them appear to have held the position of Provost of Perth although one of them, Patrick Ross of Craigie, was Sheriff-Clerk of Perthshire and his son had a successful career as an advocate in Edinburgh. They were certainly a flourishing family in the fourteenth and fifteenth centuries and can boast some distinguished members. Two of them were killed at the Battle of Pinkie near Musselburgh where so many of the Scottish nobility were slain in 1547. Among the county families with which they were connected were the Charteris of Kinfauns, Patrick Ross having married Beatrix Charteris.

Despite their honorable background, several members of the Ross family featured discreditably in the official records of sixteenth century Scotland, some of them even being executed for their crimes. John Ross of Craigie and his brothers James and William along with over one hundred others, who included Lord Ruthven and Lord Methven, were charged before the Justiciary on one occasion with besieging and breaking into the House of Dupplin. This was one of the deadly feuds which were so prevalent in Scotland at that time.

In 1541, John Ross of Craigie was Usher of the Chamber to Mary of Guise, the consort of King James V, and was one of the Council who opposed the meeting of James and his uncle. On January 8th, 1543, Ross signed an open document with nine others asking King Henry VIII of England to take possession of the young Queen Mary and her realm. He also signed a secret paper which stated that if she died, Henry was to seize her crown. It is evident from this that John Ross of Craigie, although a confidential member of the household of James V, became a traitor after the King's death and we know that he was imprisoned. Henry VIII, up to the day of his death, acted on Ross's suggestion and made many unsuccessful attempts to capture the royal infant and this is why the child (later to become Queen Mary) was taken to France at the tender age of six years. What Ross's reason for becoming involved is unclear but it is possible that he was bribed by King Henry as the Rosses were never very plentiful of money. Some insight into this is provided by the following entry in the Hamilton Papers in 1543 when John Ross of Craigie was in trouble in England and presented the following petition to King Henry VIII whilst imprisoned in London:

> Would it please the King's Majesty to write to the Governor that he is advised that a certain John Ross of Craigie whose enemies have written letters on him and his friends to underlie the law for certain lairds coming furth of the realm and other crimes, and that his grace desires a letter to the governor that I may have his discharge and pardon to me and my friends as contained in the summons, and to restore us to our lands and goods.

This was the reply of King Henry VIII to the Governor:

> We have been advised that John Ross, laird of Craigie, and his friends have sustained great damage since his arrival here as our prisoner, by means of certain persons in Scotland who have pursued divers matters against them which would not have been if he had been there to defend himself. Therefore he and such of his friends who have suffered for him shall be restored to their liberty, lands, and goods, and you shall act for us.

King Henry's intervention secured the release of John Ross and it is recorded that in 1543 at Linlithgow, John Ross signed Cardinal Beaton's secret bond, the object of which was to join together and protect themselves in the event of persecution by the authorities. The following year John Ross along with a John Charteris of Kinfauns were named as being on the Queen-Dowager's Council.

In 1547, at a meeting of the Privy Council at Stirling, it was ordained:

As to the lands of Craigie and John Charteris, the Commissioners shall cause them either to enter into ward or pass out of this country, and there to remain during the Governor's will between this and 28th April. If they do not obey the said lords, Lord Ruthven and his friends shall put the laird of Craigie and John Charteris furth of the bounds and take part with them no further. As to the teind fishings of the Kirk of Kinfauns, they shall be administered by John Christison and John Marshall, burgesses at Perth, until the said 28th April. The Governor shall give to the laird of Craigie and John Charteris to that effect that they may enter into ward or pass furth of the realm as they please. The minute is signed by Patrick, Lord Gray; James Charteris; William, Lord Ruthven; and David, Lord Drummond.

A bond of caution was executed by Archibald Ruthven in 1573 when he obtained permission to raise sixteen hundred men and go with them to Sweden to assist the King. The cautioners to this bond, who became bound for its due performance, were John Ross of Craigie; William, Lord Ruthven and William Moncreiffe of Moncreiffe. In 1584 a summons for treason was raised against John Ross of Craigie, brother and heir of the late James Ross of Pitheavlis. The Scottish Parliament gave sentence of treason in terms of this indictment and declared James Ross and his name, memory and honours to be extinct. His arms to be deleted from the book of arms so that his posterity would never have place nor would he be able to hold any office or dignities within the realm. John Ross of Craigie protested that whatever was done to James Ross of Pitheavlis, his brother, should not prejudice him in his lands, reversion and rights as he knew nothing of his late brother's doings or proceedings. The request was granted.

John Ross of Craigie was closely identified with the parsonage and vicarage teinds of Perth – teinds being the tenth portion of the produce of a parish. In 1591, King James VI and Queen Anne granted a lease of certain teinds to John Ross and Agnes Hepburn (his wife) for life and after their decease for the space of two nineteen years' tacks for the sum of £20 per annum. This was granted as John Ross and his predecessors were respected managers or tacksmen of these teinds. This tack was afterwards assigned by John Ross to his son, James, as a provision against his father and mother's death and for his education along with the teinds of the lands of Tarsappie and the salmon fishings called 'the Garth'. This was all ratified in the King's Charter of Confirmation of 1600 and a note of Ross's properties were listed in one of these papers as being as follows: Barony of Craigie with the Mill therof; the lands of Henrihall; Wester Mailer; salmon fishing in the river Earn; the lands of Kirkton, Jackston, Logiebride; Rushley; Balmacalie; Blelock and Inchstruie; and fishings in the Tay, as also the vicarage teinds.

On 23rd July 1598, the minister son of John Ross of Craigie, also called John Ross, was denounced a rebel for having failed to appear in court regarding an infamous libel written by him against John Boig, the King's master painter.

At the beginning of the seventeenth century there are some curious entries regarding the Rosses in the Register of the Privy Council. In 1601, there is a complaint by Alexander Peebles, advocate, that 'Robert Ross of Craigie remains unreleased from a horning of 19th November for not paying seven hundred merks and one hundred merks of expenses and decreet was granted in absence'. In 1602, there is a bond by Robert Ross of Craigie for John Pitscottie of Luncarty for one thousand merks, not to harm William Young the minister of Luncarty and a similar bond by Ross for William Young of Redgorton and ten others of £500 each not to harm John Pitscottie. There is a complaint by Eviot of Balhousie 'that Agnes Hepburn, relict of John Ross of Craigie, claims right to the teind sheaves of parsonage and vicarage of Perth'. Letters had been granted arresting the teinds in the hands of the tenants and The Lords ordered the suspension of the letters. In 1606 there is a complaint against Robert Ross for not paying four hundred merks principal and £40 expenses and in 1607 there is another complaint that Robert Ross and three others had not paid the pursuer one thousand merks plus one hundred merks of yearly interest and one hundred merks of expenses. Similar decreets were issued against John Ross by John Howe and David Rhynd, both burgesses of Perth, for one thousand and two thousand merks respectively.

All the above entries show that the family were rapidly getting into serious financial trouble but worse was to follow.

It is recorded in Fleming's Chronicle for 1608 that Patrick Eviot, the brother of the laird of Balhousie, was shot dead in his bed by his wife Janet Ross, who was heir to the estates of Craigie and Kinfauns and her lover, a James McNair. Janet Ross and McNair were apprehended, tried and executed, their bodies burned in the Playfield of Perth on 17th May 1608 and McNair's head and arms put on the gate of the Castle Gable.

On 11th September 1618, Thomas Ross, who had been a minister in the parish of Cargill and was the third son of John Ross, was executed at the Mercat Cross of Edinburgh for the crime of libel. His crime was that he had affixed to the main gate of his college a libel on the conduct of Scotsmen in England likening them to the seven lean kine of Egypt and describing them in other less than flattering terms. In his defence he said that necessity had driven him to do this in order 'that he night procure some benefit from the King'. The King was unsympathetic to his plea and following his imprisonment in the Tolbooth of Edinburgh and his subsequent hanging, his right hand was cut off and affixed to the West Port and his head removed and affixed to the Netherbow. Drastic punishment for libelling the Scots!

It also alleged that one of the Ross family, was among the conspirators involved in the Gowrie Conspiracy of 1600 and the plot to assassinate the young King James VI who had gone to Gowrie House, apparently at the invitation of Alexander, the Master of Ruthven. It still remains one of Scotland's great mysteries and the story rests on the testimony of the King who claimed that Ruthven and his associates threatened to kill him. The King's supporters came to his rescue and the Master of Ruthven and the Earl of Gowrie were killed. Given the close association of the Ross family (particularly John Ross) with the Ruthvens, the involvement is quite conceivable.

Over the centuries, various members of the family appear to have been restless, troublesome and insubordinate, fighting for their rights, violating the laws of the realm and occasionally being confined in the Tolbooth. Although they were landowners and proprietors of various properties besides Craigie, that does not appear to have modified their predatory habits. Although they appear to have been disinclined to take any part in public affairs, it is clear that they were a family that had to be reckoned with before any proposed schemes could be carried through.

How the Rosses originally acquired Craigie is not known but it is clearly evident that they eventually lost it by extravagant living and it appears to have been seized by creditors and sold in 1620 to the Moncreiffe family. But the decline of the family really began in the sixteenth century when, as quoted in the Hamilton Papers: 'several members of the family figured discreditably in the official books of the time, and others of them suffered death for their crimes.'

Pitheavlis Castle

At number 58 Needless Road, the A-listed Pitheavlis Castle is a fine example of a sixteenth-century castle or fortalice. Three storeys tall with an attic, it is built on the L-plan and is harled and grey-washed, sometimes seven feet thick, with arched chambers for strength and, if need be, subterranean passages for escape. Despite its once strategic situation outside the city, Pitheavlis appears to have escaped recorded historical involvement but remains one of Perth's intriguing gems of past times.

Peter Baxter in his 1928 publication, *Perth: Past and Present*, states: 'Do not disparage Pitheavlis for its looks – it had its day when knights and retainers crowded its courtyards, gallants and gay ladies danced in it and slept in it, as Prince Charles is said to have done; had a ghost for a time – a lady spirit; saw the Great Montrose sweep the Covenanters before him in 1644 at the Battle of Tibbermuir; Pitheavlis Castle may still see other days and better days. Meanwhile, it is the old time sentinel and reminder of a past that looks out on a fair prospect.'

When Bonnie Prince Charlie was in Perth from 3rd September to 11th September 1745, the Jacobite ladies of Perth and the surrounding neighbourhood arranged a ball held in Charles's honour. The Prince attended but he incurred the wrath of his hosts by leaving after the first dance, maintaining that his military duties and the inspection of his sentry posts on the North Inch were of greater importance. It has been said that the

An old view of Pitheavlis Castle from the Craigie Hill direction. (Photograph courtesy of Perth Museum and Art Gallery).

ball was held at Pitheavlis Castle and this is highly likely, taking into account the strong Jacobite connections of the Oliphants who owned the castle at that time. There were certainly

Pitheavlis Castle today from Needless Road.

few other buildings in the immediate vicinity of Perth at that time which could have hosted such an event and society balls are known to have taken place at Pitheavlis. It is also recorded that the Prince breakfasted one morning at Gask House, a home of the Oliphants, and he would have passed Pitheavlis Castle as he rode out from Perth and back again.

In a 1535 Act of the Scottish Parliament it is stated that: Each man possessed of lands valued at 1000 pounds in the inland or upon the bordouris to build a barmkin or enclosure for the resett and defence of him, his tenants and their gudes in troublos times, with ane toure in the saymen for himself gif he thinks it expedient.

And so, as a result of that Act, between the years of 1552 and 1570, the then prominent family of Ross of Craigie Barony built the Tower House of Pitheavlis. The family's part in the 'Raid of Ruthven' and the kidnapping of the boy King James VI terminated the influence of the Rosses and the Barony passed to the Murrays of Tibbermuir who later disposed of it to the Moncreiffs. The Barony originally extended as far as the New Row in Perth.

In 1587, a Gilbert Oliphant had purchased Bachilton, near Methven, from Gilbert Moncreiff, the King's Physician. William Moncreiff had a Charter of Craigie and Pitheavlis in 1621. Another Oliphant, John, purchased Bachilton in 1628 but resided mainly at Pitheavlis.

By 1636, Patrick, son of Laurence

Pitheavlis Castle's distinctive pepperpot turrets.

Oliphant of Bachilton 'was served heir in the lands and quarry of Pitheavlis'. The same Patrick Oliphant perished during the rout which followed the Battle of Tippermuir on 1st September 1644 whilst attempting to reach the safety of the castle's defensive walls.

Further generations of Oliphants succeeded in Pitheavlis until David inherited the estate in 1744. Apprenticed to an apothecary by 1721, he went to Jamaica and married the widow of a wealthy plantation owner. He prospered well and with some validity claimed the title of Lord Oliphant of Dupplin and Aberdalgie before he finally died in London in 1770. His son, John, born in Jamaica, succeeded to Pitheavlis and was established there on his father's death. The last of the Pitheavlis Oliphants, his daughter Janet, married Alexander Murray, Younger of Elibank and their descendants owned Pitheavlis until 1921 when Sir Robert Usher, Bart. purchased the property from M. F. Oliphant-Murray, Viscount Elibank. The Murrays, who spread from Tullibardine to Machany, got their name and possessions from the part of Scotland which still bears the name of Moray – surname spelling varied in these far off days as it still does. Their families stretched from Moray in the north, to Atholl and the Carse of Gowrie and from Perth to Elibank in Peebles-shire. The Murray name is preserved today in nearby Murray Crescent and Murray Place.

The Usher family, once one of Scotland's great brewing companies, sold the castle to John Fraser, auctioneer, of the MacDonald, Fraser Mart who had for a number of years been the tenant of the Pitheavlis farmlands. The Valuation Roll for 1903-04 shows the following entry:

Farm of Pitheavlis: Proprietor – The Right Hon Lord Elibank per W & F Haldane, WS., 41 North Charlotte Street, Edinburgh. Farm – John M Fraser, Auctioneer. Ground at Pitheavlis – The Perth Curling Club. House and garden - William Dawson, gardener.

In the olden times it was the custom for houses to be built around a castle. The castle gave protection to the houses, as the retainers who lived in them helped to give protection and strength to the lord of the Manor. And so it was with Pitheavlis. It once had its own village of thatched-roof cottages with white washed walls which have long disappeared and been replaced with the houses and tennis courts of Murray Crescent and Orchard Place. The small sheltered housing development of Pitheavlis Castle Gardens was built during the 1960s.

Pitheavlis eventually passed into the ownership of Perth & Kinross Council and during this time was used as clubrooms by the Perth Society of Model and Experimental Engineers and the Perthshire Art Association.

During the 1960s a society, the Pitheavlis Castle Club, was formed with a view to restoring the castle to its former splendour but met with limited success. Today, the castle is in private ownership and consists of four apartments.

The Battle of Tippermuir

A little to the east of the rather dreary expanse of Methven Moss and about four miles west of Cherrybank, lies the hamlet and parish of Tibbermore. The name derives from Tober-mhor, which in Gaelic means a great well and at one time there was a Lady Well behind the church but which was destroyed in the mid-nineteenth century when the land was drained. To the east again, at Tullilum, there was once a Carmelite priory and chapel attached to the bishopric of Dunkeld. The last prior thereof, Alexander Young, embraced the reformed faith and became the first Protestant minister of Tibbermore.

At the end of 1642, when the Civil War in England had reached stalemate following the Battles of Edgehill and Brentford, both sides (parliament and king) sought the assistance of Scotland for military aid. The Scots, realised that this was an opportunity to export Presbyterianism and bring English worship and ecclesiastical harmony into line with those of Scotland and, in 1743, presented the English commissioners with the draft of a Solemn League and Covenant. This was both a religious treaty and military and civil pact. In exchange for Scottish intervention in the Civil War, the Scots would attack the Royalist positions from the North. The English parliament would guarantee preservation of the religious settlement in Scotland, reform religion in England and Ireland, extirpate popery and confirm the 'firm peace and union' of Scotland. To the Covenanters, this was the realisation of their ultimate dream – the establishment of a single Presbyterian Church based on the Scottish model to unify religious practices in the three kingdoms. The English accepted the military part of the Solemn League and Covenant and a powerful Scottish army crossed the border and played a crucial role in the defeat of the

Royalist forces at Marston Moor in July 1644.

However, the religious aspect of the Solemn League was less clear-cut. Although the English parliament had pledged itself to accept the principle of Church unification, there were many in Scotland who doubted this. Among them was James Graham, the Earl of Montrose who suspected, correctly, that the English were deviously using the Scots' Presbyterian crusade for their own political ends and to ensure, at all costs, that the Scots were on their side in the Civil War. Montrose, although himself a moderate Covenanter, was by birth and instinct a Royalist and could not bring himself to disown his king. King Charles I made Montrose a marquis and appointed him lieutenant-general of the Royalist forces in Scotland, thus bringing the Civil War north of the border.

The summer of 1644 saw Montrose join forces with a giant and fearsome Irish adventurer named Alasdair McColla MacDonald, a heroic legend at the age of twenty-one, who brought with him two thousand well-armed troops from Ireland who were quickly joined by a thousand Highlanders. MacDonald's men rampaged and looted their way through the Campbell territory of Argyll while Montrose slipped into Perth with a couple of companions, disguised as Covenanter troopers. In late August, Montrose and MacDonald met up at Blair Atholl where Montrose combined his force of cavalry and Highland foot soldiers with MacDonald's troops.

On 1st September 1644, the Royalists' formidable army, under these two inspired commanders, James Graham, 1st Marquis of Montrose, and Alasdair MacDonald arrived at Tibbermore, then known as Tippermuir, to begin their campaign against the Covenanters for Charles I. Their target was the reclamation of Perth.

The Royalists fell upon a much larger Covenanting force under the command of David Wemyss, Lord Elcho, who had around seven thousand men, largely composed of the inhabitants of Perth, and seven hundred cavalry, shepherded by coveys of attendant ministers. They were also in possession of cannon and better equipment than the Royalists but on both sides the troops were undisciplined, the Covenanters especially so.

The site of the battle was Lamberkin Moor on Cultmalundie Farm, near Broxden (originally Brock's Den) on the outskirts of Perth. Montrose had reached the area with a slight strategic advantage. MacDonald positioned his men centrally, flanked by Montrose's men and cavalry, armed with swords, Lochaber axes and long clubs with Montrose leading his own right wing. Lord Elcho led the right wing of his troops, Sir James Scott of Rossie, an experienced soldier, the left and the Earl of Tullibardine led the main body. When the advancing Covenanters were within a hundred yards of their enemy, a section of their cavalry raced ahead to draw the fire. However, MacDonald's Irishmen had developed a devastating new battle-tactic – the 'Highland charge' – where the infantry, armed with muskets, advanced to within a hundred metres of the enemy, fired a single volley, then dropped their muskets and charged with their broadswords. Such a ferocious attack caused Elcho's raw recruits to lose their co-ordination and hundreds were killed. Panic and great confusion spread throughout the entire Covenanting forces and they fled the field.

The Covenanters' horse fled, it is said, at the first shower of stones but more probably, it has been alleged, by the treachery of Lord Drummond and Lord Oliphant who joined with Montrose after the affair was over. Among those killed were Patrick Oliphant of Bachilton, George Halyburton of Culross and David Grant, captain of the Perth men.

The slaughter of Covenanters was not confined to the battlefield and in the rout that followed, two thousand men died and another two thousand were captured, putting Tippermuir at about the same level of post-battle massacre as Culloden.

The lands around Cherrybank and Craigie were very much a part of these killing fields, being the route taken into the city by Montrose's victorious army. An Irish officer is alleged to have said that there were so many dead lying in their blood that a man might have walked on them all the way into Perth.

That same night, Montrose entered and took possession of Perth where he levied a subsidy of nine thousand merks and stipulated free quarters for his army for four days. He then went on to Dundee but that city refused to surrender and he pushed onwards to Aberdeen, as he knew that he was being pursued by Argyll. Perth now belonged to King Charles I and the military genius of Montrose had brought triumph, despite the odds, for the first of many times.

A plaque on the gable wall of the house on the western corner of Needless Road and Wilson Street refers to the battle and, in particular, to the Covenanters Stone which at one time stood on the battlefield and marked the spot where much of the carnage occurred.]

The story of the stone and the plans for the erection of the memorial tablet is described in the *Perthshire Advertiser* of 11th June 1927:

Covenanters' Stone: tablet for Needless Road cottage

Interest attaches to a report by the Burgh Surveyor to the Property and Works Committee of the Town Council, that Mr David Beat, builder, has offered to insert a tablet in the gable of the new cottage at the corner of Needless Road and Wilson Street. This tablet, which will bear a suitable inscription will be in lieu of the Covenanters' Stone, which for so long had a prominent place in the wall of Granny Peat's Cottage, Needless Road. For a considerable period the stone remained on the site of the battle in which the Marquis of Montrose defeated the Presbyterian forces, but it was subsequently removed and built into Granny Peat's Cottage, where it remained until the house fell into a state of disrepair some years ago, and finally had to be demolished to allow of Mr Beat building houses. It was next taken to Craigie Haugh, but the surface is now so decayed that the lettering has become obliterated. The committee decided to approve of Mr Beat's suggestion.

A TOMBSTONE WHICH STOOD AT ONE TIME IN THE FIELD TO THE NORTH OF NEEDLESS ROAD MARKED THE SPOT WHERE MANY COVENANTERS FROM FIFE WERE SLAIN IN FLIGHT AFTER THE BATTLE OF TIBBERMUIR ON 1ST SEPTEMBER 1644

Needless Road and Necessity Brae

Although the original Craigie was mainly hilly and wooded grazing land with the few scattered thatched cottages and crofts eventually giving way to the steeper slopes of the surrounding hills, it was an area bordered by significant routes *The plaque on the gable wall of the house on the corner of Needless Road and Wilson Street.*

out of the city.

Perth in those early years was small, compact and mainly confined to the area around High Street and the Shoegate (now South Street) with very few houses west of the present Methven Street or north of Mill Street.

The old road to Edinburgh, Falkland and Fife, before the opening around 1770 of the present route through the South Inch, followed a line from the South Street Port and through Pomarium to the north end of Carr's Croft (Cat's Croft) at Priory Place, then along the high ground by the St Magdalene's bridle path or packman's road before leaving the city by Craigclowan (the Cloven Crags) to Bridge of Earn and Dron then over the Ochil Hills by the Wallace Road to Kinross.

The present Glasgow Road was not made until the early 1800s. Until then, there were two ancient exits out of Perth to the south and west. One left Perth by the High Street Port and Longcauseway, continued through Jeanfield (then known as Gin Field) to the high ground at Burghmuir and along the old Gallows Road to Tibbermore and Crieff or to Gask and Auchterarder.

The other route, known as the south road to Stirling, was also the road to Dunfermline and Queensferry. From the South Street Port it followed the line of Hospital Street, Kinnoull Causeway (Cow Causeway) and Earl's Dyke, once the historical boundary of the lands of the Earls of Kinnoull, before cutting across what is now the Perth-Inverness railway line and continuing up what was to become Needless Road to the hamlet of Cherrybank and thence up Necessity Brae.

It was the route taken by travellers and carriers and would also have been used by some cattle drovers as part of their journey to the great cattle markets, or trysts, at Falkirk. At one time no fewer than fifty-three carriers' carts plied to and from the city from various parts of Scotland every week. Before the arrival of the railway in 1847-48, some fourteen stagecoaches arrived at or departed from Perth each day, many using the old south road to Stirling.

But why the strange names of Needless Road and Necessity Brae? Old maps of Perth clearly show that at one time there was a property called Needless which stood near where Wilson Street joins Needless Road today. It was occupied until around 1904 and known locally as Maggie's Cottage or Granny Peat's Cottage. After falling into a state of disrepair, it was eventually demolished and replaced in 1927 by a bungalow.

It is this house which gave its name to the street but what was its importance and how did it get its name?

The popular story is that Needless was the first place of refreshment for the carters and their horses or oxen after leaving Perth. However, it was felt that there was not any requirement to stop there for a drink so early, as a mile further on was the pleasant hamlet of Cherrybank and its hostelry. Old maps certainly show the existence of a well on the site of Needless and this was possibly the watering place of the legend.

The inn at Cherrybank dates back to 1761 and, according to Perth tradition, served well in assuaging the thirst of both man and beast before the long haul up the steep hill which lay ahead. They would then have continued past Aberdalgie to the Earn Valley and Dunning. From there, they would have headed over the Ochil Hills to the Yetts of Muckhart and Dunfermline or continued through Dollar to Falkirk. Alternatively, they would have travelled from Dunning to Auchterarder, Stirling and the west of Scotland. What was needless on the gentler slopes of Craigie became a necessity at Cherrybank. The steep hill became known as Necessity Brae and the earlier halting place was named Needless.

Another variation of the story is that an extra horse was required at Cherrybank to pull the carriages up the steep Necessity Brae. It was needless to go to such an expense for the earlier part of the journey out of Perth but it was certainly necessary at Cherrybank.

There is, however, another point of view regarding the name and it is thought that the area around Needless Road was once known as the Nowt Leas or Neat Leas, which simply means cattle pastures. The old Scots form of the word for cattle was 'nowt,' as used in the Robert Burns poem 'The Twa Dogs' which mentions the Scottish gentleman on the Grand Tour indulging himself by fighting 'wi' nowt' (in the bullring presumably).

Or by Madrid he takes the rout,
To thrum guitars an' fecht wi' nowt…

Interestingly, in 1753, *The Scots Magazine* records the phrase 'drawn by oxen or neat cattle' which shows that the English form of the word was current in the north during the eighteenth century. The Scots word for meadow and pasture land is 'lea' and certainly in former times, before the development of Craigie for the railway and for housing, the area bordering the south road to Stirling consisted of fields and fallow ground used for the grazing of oxen, cattle and sheep. We also know that there were cattle byres beside the property at Needless. Perhaps 'Needless' is purely a derivation of 'Nowt Leas' or 'Neat Leas' and also a bit of tongue-in-cheek humour from the travellers of long ago.

A further opinion is that once the Glasgow Road was built as the main western route out of Perth, it was unnecessary to use the old route as it had become a 'needless road'. However, the toll road to Glasgow was not planned until the late eighteenth or early nineteenth century and Necessity Hill is clearly marked on Stobie's 1783 map of the Perth area with the position of Needless also shown on the same map. It is not clear if the cottages were a croft, or perhaps a drovers' check bar, but the map appears to confirm the Needless/ Necessity connection and shows that the property at Needless or Neat Leas must have been of some importance.

A drovers' check bar which was situated on the path between Craigie and Cherrybank close to where Woodside Crescent and the modern homes of Craigie View are today. The roof of the building collapsed during a snow storm in 1922 while it was still occupied as a dwelling house.

It would probably have been a fairly humble dwelling. Until around 1780, the vicinity of Perth was in total contrast to its present appearance. Outside the city boundary, apart from the house of Balhousie, the castle of Pitheavlis, the old palace of Scone and perhaps the aforementioned House of Ross, there was scarcely a slated or two storey house to be seen.

In 1758, the east side of New Row was partially built by a linen manufacturing company and, about the same time, the proprietors of lands in the vicinity of Perth began to feu their property for building. The suburbs soon extended and more commodious houses were built. A row of clay houses was built up the south side of the Laigh or Cow Causeway, which eventually became Kinnoull Causeway, and then turned round onto the west side of the south road to Stirling at Earl's Dyke. The Glover Incorporation, the proprietors of the lands of St Leonard's, feud out a great part of them. Leonard Street was built, as were Cross Street and Pomarium Street.

The Hillend Jail

Although situated just slightly out of Cherrybank, the farm of Hillend deserves mention. It is believed that the farm steading was originally a military prison and the surrounding farmlands were military property used as headquarters for government troops as early as the seventeenth century, possibly for keeping rebellious clans under

Hillend Farm. (Photograph from The Courier).

control.

In 1901, Hillend Farm was bought by Danish immigrant farmers. In a 2006 article in *The Courier*, Mrs Jean Christie, a descendant of one of these farmers, recalled her grandfather Karl Christian Yde showing her graffiti left by French prisoners held at Hillend during the Napoleonic Wars. The farmyard had been the exercise yard for the prisoners.

Perth Prison was built to accommodate the prisoners when the buildings at Hillend could no longer cope with the increasing numbers and the buildings then ceased to be used as a military jail.

The farm was sold to Hay's, the agricultural auctioneers, in 1939 and the land was used for grazing with a shepherd occupying the farmhouse. Hay's sold the land in the 1980s and the farm buildings and steading which were situated at the top of Oakbank Road near the present day Alder and Cedar Drives were demolished.

The Perth Poorhouse and the Playfield of Perth

In the middle of the nineteenth century, the Poor Law Act of 1845 and the establishment of Parochial Councils gave an impetus to the provision of institutional accommodation for the homeless and destitute.

As a result of this social change, the Perth Poorhouse was built on a site at the south western corner of Glasgow Road and Glover Street which had previously been part of the Playfield of Perth which had flourished throughout the Middle Ages. After the erection of the Poorhouse, a surviving relic of the Playfield was a curling pond which was built over by the later development of Glover Street and Gray Street.

A high and forbidding wall enclosed the grounds of the Poorhouse which was entered from a gatehouse and porter's lodge on Glasgow Road and the administration of the home was carried out by a governor, matron and gardener.

A transformation of the premises at the close of World War I

Rosslyn House.

resulted in the demolition of the prison-like adjuncts. Improvements were made internally and externally and the building was re-named Bertha Home. Some years later there was a further name change to Rosslyn House but by then the pattern of social work had radically changed and the house never really fitted the mode of present day care.

For a few years the building provided office accommodation for some local authority departments before being turned into the private luxury apartments of the present day.

A plaque on a boundary wall of Rosslyn House acknowledges the former existence of an amphitheatre and the aforementioned Playfield on the site. The plaque reads:

On lands extending northwards were the playfields or bow-butts – the amphitheatre of St Johnstoun – where King James V witnessed plays in 1539 AD.

It is widely believed that William Shakespeare (1564-1616) performed in the amphitheatre around 1589 as part of a troupe of travelling players. Dunsinane Hill, which features in Shakespeare's famous play Macbeth, can be seen from the area. Could it be that Shakespeare wandered around Craigie and Cherrybank gaining inspiration and picking up stories for his play about the Thane prepared to murder his King and guest in order to obtain the throne? As the play predicts that Banquo's descendants, the Stuarts, would take over the crown of

Scotland, did Shakespeare see the Stuarts as aspiring to be the Caesars of Scotland?

Historical Figures

Perth's strategic location between the Highlands and Lowlands ensured its importance as a military fortress and it is interesting to speculate upon the historical figures who may have travelled through Craigie and Cherrybank along a track which at one time was the main southern route to and from Scotland's ancient capital.

The Roman legions are believed to have passed through Perth on at least three occasions to establish their camps on Tayside and four Roman roads led into Perth from different quarters. Only vestiges of a chain of watchtowers, signal stations and of the fort at Bertha, near the confluence of the Rivers Almond and Tay, recall the efforts of the Romans to bring the region within their so-called civilisation. Maps show that a line of signal stations, or more likely watchtowers as they were only one mile apart, stretched from Ardoch, near Braco, to Innerpeffray and then along the Gask Ridge by Ardunie and Muir o' Fauld to Aberdalgie and then Bertha.

Henry Adamson, a native of Perth, wrote about the Romans in Perth in *The Muses Threnodie* (c1620), a poetical effusion on the history of Perth and its antiquities:

And there, hard by a river side, they found
The fairest and most pleasant plot of ground
That, since by bank of Tiber they had beene,
The like for beauty seldome had they seene
…which, when they did espy,
Incontinent they Campus Martius cry,
And as a happy presage they had seene,
They fixt their tents amidst that spatious greene,
Right where now Perth doth stand…

Leading figures in the emergence of the kingdom of the Scots were associated with the Perth area, the first being Kenneth MacAlpine who was perhaps animated by stories of Rome as a seat of power. He is believed to have been an adventurer who led some Norse Vikings in seizing power in the Hebrides in 836 AD, then usurped the throne of Dal Riada in 840 AD. Thereafter, in 847 AD he defeated Durst, the King of Picts, at Forteviot which had become his secular capital. He divided up the relics of St Columba, formerly laid to rest in Iona, half going to Ireland and half to Dunkeld. He probably led his war bands through Cherrybank and Craigie on raids that some see as efforts to unite the Scots and Picts in a new kingdom of Alba.

It is said that Kenneth held a banquet at Scone after his succession as the first King of the Scots and murdered seven earls of Dal Riada who might have disputed his position. Kenneth MacAlpine died at Forteviot after a reign of fifteen years and was buried on Iona. He was succeeded by his brother King Donald I who extended Dalriadic law into Pictland and who died of natural causes near Scone in 862 AD.

Afterwards there were many struggles between two collateral branches of the royal house of MacAlpine seeking to control Scotland. Success in this effort was achieved by the last MacAlpine king, Malcolm II (1004-34), who killed Kenneth III in a battle near Perth and made his daughter's son, Duncan I, his heir. Duncan was killed by his cousin, Macbeth, in 1040 and the murder was avenged in 1057 by Duncan's son, Malcolm III (Canmore). Thereafter a line of descent from his marriage to the saintly Margaret, sister of Edgar the Atheling, brought settled kingship of the Scots through primogeniture down to Alexander III (1249-86). Alexander fought off the Norwegian threat in 1263 and ruled wisely until his accidental death at Kinghorn in Fife plunged Scotland into a crisis over succession, exploited by the English king, Edward I, the infamous Longshanks.

King James VI travelled through Cherrybank and down Needless Road into Perth on the occasion of his state visit to Perth in 1617. It is documented that the King's route into the city passed Pitheavlis Castle, then the seat of the Oliphant family, and entered Perth by the south road to Stirling with the bells of St John's heralding the approach of the royal cavalcade. The journey was well described by R S Fittis in *Chronicles of Perthshire* (1877):

> The royal cavalcade descends at proud pace the hilly slopes where trees are but thinly scattered. As it advances towards the Castle of Pittheavlis (the seat of a branch of the Oliphant family) the King's eye dwells dreamily on a lovely landscape, which he had oft viewed with delight in the days of langsyne. Before him the broad valley of the Tay, bounded by heights diverse in cloud and aspect; but strath and hills combining to form a scene of surpassing beauty and grandeur. Across the northern horizon, where snowy cloudlets

hung becalmed, stretches the blue range of the Grampians, looming through the sultry film of the summer day. Nearer in the east, appears the venerable Palace of Scone, embowered among its thick woods, and invested with the glorious reminiscences of Scotland's dear bought freedom. Yonder the skyline is broken by the bluff summit of Dunsinane Hill, still crowned with the fire-blackened ruins of a pre-historic stronghold which has given a witching theme to garrulous tradition and romantic history. Straight in front rises the hill of Kinnoull, whose breast is variegated with grey rock, brown furze, and green vegetation. Almost at its base the old city spreads itself out, like its own imperial eagle, on the level plain washed by the Tay, a portion of whose silvery flood is seen to the right, lying, like a mountain-girdled lake, which storms never ruffle, in the hollow between Kinnoull and Moredun – Moredun, the glory of Scotland, which fills in its majesty the south-eastern prospect; and the Craigie hills, rounded and pastoral, extend to the west. This is a day of triumph. The procession winds down the Pittheavlis road and the causeways, and reaches the Highgate port of St Johnstoun, amid deafening acclamation, the peal of joy-bells, and the crash of martial music. The King enters the gateway, and now the ceremonial of his reception begins.

Perth was both a centre of English rule and a fierce resistance to it. William Wallace and Robert Bruce were in action in and around the city and their efforts finally threw the English back. The independence of Scotland was established in King Robert's reign by the Declaration of Arbroath in 1320. Bruce's son, David II (1329-71), was childless but his daughter Marjorie's marriage to the 6th High Steward, Walter, brought the Scottish crown to their eldest son who ruled as Robert II (1371-90) and founded the Stewart line.

Voltaire once called the Stewarts (Frenchified as Stuart) the 'most unfortunate house in Europe' and the ebb and flow of their power had associations with the Perth area. The strong king, James I, was assassinated in the house of the Blackfriars of Perth in 1437 and the queen mother and the six-year-old son had to be hurried to Edinburgh as Perth was no longer safe for the royal family. Mary of Guise and her daughter, Mary Queen of Scots, were in Perth in 1559 attempting to thwart the approaching Reformation and when the daughter travelled to Dunfermline in 1565 with her husband, Lord Darnley, they would probably have taken the track which led from Perth along Needless Road, through Cherrybank and up the Necessity Brae.

The royalist cause of Mary's grandson, Charles I, was upheld by the Marquis of Montrose. He and his following were certainly here in the vicinity of Perth, as the battlefields of Methven, Dupplin and Tippermuir can testify. Afterwards came Oliver Cromwell, General Mackay on his way north from Stirling to Killiecrankie and the Earl of Mar on his way to the Battle of Sherriffmuir.

As we have already read, Bonnie Prince Charlie was here and Sir Fitzroy McLean, in his account of the life of the Prince, refers to him as leaving Perth by the Stirling road on September 11th 1745 with an army of two thousand men in his march south in his fruitless attempt to regain the throne for the Stuarts. It was the subsequent battle the following year on the Drumossie Moor near Inverness by ill-equipped Highlanders against the full might of the House of Hanover that marked the end of Jacobitism and the tradition of personal rule and the divine right of kings.

Cherrybank and Craigie were no longer to be a gateway to dynastic recovery but to commercial development. No more would they see the march of troops on their way to battle but cattle rolling along to the trysts and marts.

With the arrival of the railway, a cattle mart was to become established on the lower part of Needless Road. The nearby hill farms bred cattle, some for local consumption and some driven south to feed the growing urban population of eighteenth century Britain.

It can be argued that the story that unfolded in Craigie and Cherrybank was the transformation of Scotland from a country where castles were required to defend a pastoral people and maintain an aristocracy in power, to one with a market economy focused on agricultural and industrial products. Then followed a post industrial economy where the primary location need of people was for housing and schooling, relatively close to the sites of their service and micro-industrial occupations.

THE CREATION OF A COMMUNITY

Every house where love abides
And friendship is a guest,
Is surely home, and home sweet home,
For there the heart can rest.

Henry Van Dyke

In 1828 Craigie had its beginning as a recognised suburb of Perth. That year the city architect, William Mackenzie, acquired land for St Leonard's Bank from the Glover Incorporation and had it laid out for building.

An article in the *Perth Courier* of 30th December 1830 reports a draft plan for development which projected turning a large semi-circular hollow of Craigie Park at the top of the South Inch into pasture field, similar to the Inch itself, with the sloping bank which encircled it along the south side to Craigie village to be feued for an extensive range of villas. The remainder of the article makes interesting reading:

These villas are to be laid out in the form of a crescent, fronting the north, with gardens reaching down the bank towards the level ground, betwixt which and the gardens, bounded on either side by hedgerows and shrubbery, a gravel walk to be the private property of, but common to, all the feuers, from the entrance at the mineral

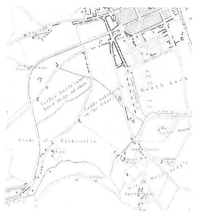

An 1832 map showing Craigie and Cherrybank prior to the arrival of the railway. The houses of St Leonard's Bank are shown beside the South Inch. The new Glasgow Road is in place with a toll house and in the centre of the map the south road to Stirling (later to become Needless Road) connects with the city centre by way of Earl's Dyke and Kinnoull Causeway. Lower and Upper Craigie are both shown and the hamlet of Cherrybank is on the bottom left. There is another toll house on the track between Cherrybank and Upper Craigie.

well, to its termination at Craigie bridge. It is also contemplated that the public access to the villas should be from a carriage-way to be carried round behind. Were this affected, and the feus of St Leonard's Bank built to its southern extremity, there would be a complete and beautiful range from King's Place, now building in a line with Marshall Place, all along the west and south sides of the South Inch and Craigie Park to the Depot. In this case, the plan comprises an extension of the carriage-way above mentioned, by a semi-circular sweep from Craigie bridge, along the western side of Provost Ramsay's property, till it joins behind the new villas of St Leonard's Bank, which, with the road in front of King's Place and Marshall Place, joining the Edinburgh, or the avenue along the east side of the Inch, would form a beautiful and pleasant drive, uninterrupted by toll-bars or any other obstruction, for an extent of more than two miles.

When it was eventually decided to locate the new railway station on the lands of St Leonard's, instead of on the South Inch itself as was originally proposed, this ambitious plan for St Leonard's Bank was modified. Another report in the same newspaper in April 1853 read as follows:

CRAIGIE TOWN – Mr Falshaw's new town of Craigie is rising a-pace and promises to supply a great deal of additional accommodation for the upper as well as middle classes in a beautiful and delightful situation. Five or six of the cottages are already roofed in, and four of the superior class of dwelling-houses are at the upper storey, the views from which will be perhaps unrivalled. The pipes for the supply of water and for sewerage are quite new here, being of fire clay, glazed like stoneware, which are said to answer their purpose admirably. The whole bank promises soon to be feued out and unless the Glovers bestir themselves, the promised New Town in that quarter may prove another Tay Street.

The ornate nineteenth-century detached villas of St Leonard's Bank with their substantial front gardens sloping down to the South Inch were soon to prove highly popular with Perth's business and professional classes. As the years progressed they were to undergo many changes and styles of ownership which would include two schools (the Misses Hindmarch's Academy and the Bernard Holt

TOP: *A nineteenth-century map of Perth and the Craigie area after the arrival of the railway in 1848. It shows the lower half of what was to become Needless Road with the property Needless marked in the centre. Craigie Mill, Priory Place and the railway workers' houses on the east side of Glover Street are also shown.* BOTTOM: *One of the original villas in St Leonard's Bank which became the Atholl Hotel (later the Inch Park Hotel) and underwent a £1 million restoration in 1991 to become the award winning Parklands Hotel. (Photograph from Perth & Kinross Libraries)*

School), the Atholl Hotel, the Royal Army Service Corps Memorial Club, the Railway Athletic Social Club, a doctor's surgery and the headquarters of the Perth & Kinross Society for the Blind.

During World War II, the 1925 Neo-Greek B-listed classical villa at Number 7 became a headquarters for the 51st Highland Division. The army maintained a cover story that the building was an officers' mess but in fact it served for several years as 'a secret remote emergency command/control centre'.

The arrival of the railway in 1848, the decision to house the railway terminus in its present position, the associated activities of the railway and the need for housing in excess of two thousand railway workers, made Craigie the fastest expanding area of Perth. Houses, primarily for railway workers, quickly appeared along the eastern side of Glover Street from the Craigie railway bridge to what was then the south road to Stirling and then shortly after, with the arrival of the livestock mart

At the same time, development continued towards Craigie Mill with the creation of Priory Place (which incorporated the Carr's Croft weavers' cottages) and the construction of Queen Street, Abbot Street and Friar Street.

Housing and Development

In 1885, Glover Street in Craigie is listed in the *Perth Street Directory* as having one hundred and ten residents, Priory Place (including Carr's Croft) as having sixty seven residents

Priory Place looking towards Craigie Cross with the old weavers' cottages of Carr`s Croft and Stirling's bakery shop on the right. (Photograph from Perth & Kinross Libraries).

and there were fifty families living in Queen Street. The flatted-homes of Friar Street were by then well established with forty seven residents. Sections of that street were named St Jane's Place, Wolseley Place and Kilmartin Place along with two private houses, St Catherine's Villa and Craigie-Lea Villa. In Abbot Street, twenty one families were living in the area between Glover Street and Friar Street.

Many of the people living in these homes were railway workers, varying from engine drivers and guards to ticket collectors and porters, but the directory also lists people from other occupations, trades and professions such as joiners, plumbers, teachers, clerks and dyers.

An interesting article in the *Perthshire Advertiser* described the later demolition of the Carr's Croft cottages in Priory Place:

By the demolition of the thatched roof cottages at Carr's Croft, Perth is shortly to lose another of its historical and picturesque landmarks.

Two hundred years ago, the cottages were built alongside the old road to Edinburgh which, before the advent of the railway, extended in continuation of Leonard Street. The present roadway leading to Priory Place runs at a higher level to allow traffic to pass over the railway at St Leonard's Bridge.

Originally the cottages extended further south than the shop now

LEFT FROM TOP: *Glover Street, Friar Street, Queen Street, Looking up Abbot Street from St Leonard's Bridge. All photographs by W L Hampton, Perth. For many years Hampton owned the newsagent business on the right on the last photograph. His main shop was in Scott Street.*

occupied by Mr James Stirling, baker. Some years ago, The Croft passed into the hands of the late Baillie Forgan who demolished a portion of the old cottages and built the houses in Priory Place to the north of Croft Park.

By the mid-nineteenth century the area around Upper or High Craigie above the waterfall at Craigie Mill and around the rocky and wooded outcrop of Craigie Knowes was already established for residential development. Substantial detached and semi-detached stone built homes were now established there and proving popular with the business and professional classes of Perth. Moncreiffe Terrace, Brunswick Terrace and the beginnings of Evelyn Terrace were in place by 1885 but most of the Victorian villas in Upper Craigie simply went under individual names such as Ivybank, Craigiebank, Northbank, Earlybank House, Viewbank House, Moncreiffe Bank and Mount Craigie.

Craigie Park House, a distinctive house of black whinstone, dates from the early nineteenth century and early residents include General George William Lennox and the 1880 Lord Provost of Perth, Kirkwood Hewat. The house has since been used as a nursing home, a funeral home and a nursery for pre-school children.

One quaint and distinctive house in St Magdalene's Lane is South

Esk Bank which is believed to have been erected around 1845 and provided accommodation for the domestic staff of Earlybank House situated in Craigie Place. This grade B listed villa built in 1828, is associated with

South Esk Bank

General Alexander Lindsay (1785-1872) of the East India Company and with Hugh Barclay (1799-1884) a judge and writer on legal issues.

Further Development

Between 1903 and 1912, the steep, narrow and winding lanes of Upper Craigie were turned into new streets (some of them still steep, narrow and winding) but most of the Victorian villas incorporated within these new streets still chose to retain their own individual names. Craigie Knowes Road, which led into Upper Craigie from Queen Street, was formed with David Squire Young, a joiner from Craigie Bank House, building a picturesque row of cottages next to Craigie Knowes which he named Squire's Cottages.

The villas of Brunswick Terrace became part of upper St Magdalene's Road. Other established villas such as Dunvorist, Viewbank House and Mount Craigie were incorporated into the new streets of Moredun Terrace and Verena Terrace.

The steep hill of Quarry Road, named for obvious reasons, was also now in place and Murrayfield House was added to it around 1910. The house, lodge and cottages of Craigie Park became the beginning of Craigie Road which, by 1903, had thirty five homes listed in the street directory. Kinnaird Bank and Clifton Bank, leading from Moncreiffe Terrace to Craigie Knowes Road, were in place by 1911 with ten homes. The south and east sides of Moredun Square were completed around the same time but it was the early 1970s before the other two sides of the square were developed. This included Craigiebank House, a modern block of nine apartments on the western side built by A & J

Stephen Ltd in 1981.

RIGHT: *A 1920s photograph of Mount Craigie in Verena Terrace. This was one of the early detached villas built in Upper Craigie and was the family home of the author's mother.* LEFT: *Looking up Wilson Street from Queen Street. Craigie Parish Church is in the background. (Photograph from Perth & Kinross Libraries).*

By the end of the nineteenth century and with the arrival of Western District School, Abbot Street had continued up the hill with an off-shoot into a new street alongside the school, Young Street, in 1894. Wilson Street, named after Lord Provost George Wilson (1890), was now developing at the top of Abbot Street with its lower section connecting with Queen Street.

With the building of a new toll road out of Perth to Glasgow in the early 1800s, there had been little use for the old stagecoach and carriers' track route once known as the south road to Stirling. The building of the railway station in the mid-nineteenth century finally ended the road as a direct link in and out of the city centre although it

Squire's cottages on Craigie Knowes Road

RIGHT: A George Sievwright property advertisement from 1951.

continued to be much used once the livestock mart was established in 1886.

As Craigie rapidly grew along Priory Place, Queen Street, Friar Street, Abbot Street, Glover Street and Wilson Street, it was not long before the old Stirling road with its proximity to the railway station and the livestock mart attracted the attention of the developers. In its new form, it was to become Needless Road and is first mentioned in the 1890 edition of *Leslie's Directory* with Isla Cottage, Needless Road being occupied by Robert Stewart, coalman; Mrs Lilias Robertson; and Thomas Paterson, engine driver. Further up the hill, apart from Pitheavlis Castle, the only other properties mentioned are the cattle byres and dairy at Needless occupied by Mrs John Peat and John Angus a dairyman.

MAINTAINING PROPERTY

CAN PRESENT MANY PROBLEMS TO THOSE WHO HAVE THIS RESPONSIBILITY

CONSULT

SIEVWRIGHT

FOR

WOODWORK JOINERY and CARPENTRY

and be sure of sound workmanship and close personal attention

HOUSE BUILDING—We have long experience in complete House Building and can show examples of our work and possible sites

GEO. SIEVWRIGHT & SON
Joiners and Contractors
TULLYLUMB, 60 GLASGOW RD.
PERTH
Telephone (Office and Residence)
325

The first semi-detached houses appeared in the street by 1901 and by 1904, much of the lower half of Needless Road was in place with more semi-detached houses and the flatted homes of Castle Terrace on the south side and Kinfauns Crescent on the north side. A variety of local builders were involved – E & W Gray; Fraser & Morton; David Squire Young (the builder of Squire's Cottages in Upper Craigie); John Marshall; and James Gowans. Another local builder George Sievwright, the builder of one of the early semi-detached homes in lower Needless Road, was meantime building a

1904 photograph of early housing in Needless Road with their first residents. From right to left – numbers 55, 53, 51 and 49 which were re-numbered in the 1940s as 73, 75, 77 and 79.

TOP: *Kinfauns Crescent in Needless Road from the end of Darnhall Drive. The horse and cart in the centre of the photograph is probably delivering coal. (Photograph from Perth & Kinross Libraries).* BOTTOM: *Gray Street and some of the early inhabitants. (Photograph from Perth & Kinross Libraries).*

cluster of semi-detached homes on the upper half of the road and in 1910 built a row of semi-detached houses on the western side of a new street, Murray Crescent, which linked Needless Road with Glasgow Road.

Between 1902 and 1904 the firm of Fraser & Morton, builders of the Castle Terrace flats in Needless Road, were also building around the corner on what was to become Darnhall Drive and Clyde Place (named after Gavin Morton's west of Scotland background). Three terraced houses and a double villa were built in similar red sandstone to the Castle Terrace flats with the builders retaining ownership and renting the properties to tenants at an annual rent of £19.19/–. A further row of sandstone villas were built on Darnhall Drive between Clyde Place and Park Place. In 1903, Fraser & Morton had plans approved for two large red sandstone villas in Needless Road on the upper side of Pitheavlis Castle near the junction with Glasgow Road.

By 1901 the Glasgow Road was well developed along both sides. It was an area favoured by many of the professional classes of Perth with the owners of the substantial stone buildings having views towards the city across the open farmland which stretched almost all the way to Craigie and the railway station. In 1903 a new street, Gray Street, was to appear in these fields at the lower end of Needless Road and parallel to Glover Street which was now being extended to meet up with Glasgow Road.

Gray Street is named after Colonel Stuart Gray of Kinfauns who at that time was the owner of the land and also acknowledges two former Lord Provosts of Perth – Andrew Gray (1635) and William Gray (1760). The street directory of 1904 shows the street as having six semi-detached homes, a row of flatted dwellings and Bon-

LEFT: *Darnhall before development.* RIGHT *Pitheavlis Cottages on Necessity Brae under construction in 1928. (Perthshire Advertiser photograph).*

Accord Terrace with four houses. One of the home owners in this new street was John Craik of Thomson Craik Ltd. the aerated water manufacturers who lived in the house named Turfechie. Part of Gray Street (numbers 14-16) was named Dewar's Terrace and initially built to house some of the staff from the nearby Dewar's Whisky factory.

Whilst most of the new house building during the late nineteenth and early twentieth centuries had been concentrated around Lower and Upper Craigie, Cherrybank was also beginning to change from a weaving hamlet and an outpost of Perth to an area of residential potential. The construction of the Glasgow Road in the early nineteenth century had made Cherrybank much more accessible from the city and attracted a number of new residents and their families which led to the establishment of a school in 1864.

The 1903-1904 *Perth Street Directory* lists properties such as Pickembere Cottages, Viewfield Cottages, Sunny Brae, Pitheavlis Bank,

1901 map showing the first four semi-detached houses in Needless Road. Glover Street and the livestock mart are top right. Also can be seen the bowling green, railway station and beginnings of Gray Street. Friar Street, Abbot Street, Young Street, Craigie School and part of Wilson Street are on the bottom left. The Glasgow Road and its substantial dwellings are off the map to the left

Cherrybank in 1908. McVean's Buildings are on the left of the photograph behind the lamppost. The shop on the left is now a private dwelling. (Photograph from Perth & Kinross Libraries).

Oakbank Cottage and Whitelaw Cottage. Low Road, formerly a part of the old south road to Stirling, is shown as housing fifteen families most of whom would be living in the Perth Shepherds' Friendly Society Buildings which were built in 1903. Six families were living at the Burnside and seven homes had been built in Oakbank Terrace. The mansion house, lodge and grounds of Cleeve (formerly Oakbank House) were also a prominent part of Cherrybank at that time as was the nearby house and farm of Woodlands.

On what was then called Main Street but was actually a part of Glasgow Road, a large stone building called McVean's Buildings (later known as McKinlay's Buildings) housed several families in 1904, the occupants being: Mrs Peter McKinlay; John Edwards, ironmoulder; George Sharp, spirit merchant; Mary Kidd; Thomas Heggie, labourer; Peter Gillies, machineman; and John Pritchard, labourer.

New home building continued

LEFT: *Queens Avenue. (Photograph from Perth & Kinross Libraries) and Pre-1929 thatched cottages at Pickembere. Later demolished and replaced by new cottages erected by Lord Forteviot. (Perthshire Advertiser photograph).*

BELOW *Cherrybank in the early twentieth century with the school on the extreme right. (Photograph from Perth & Kinross Libraries).*

until 1914 when the onset of World War I saw the end of house building throughout the country. When hostilities ceased in 1918, most of the earlier building firms were no longer in business and it would be a new generation of builders who would continue the development of Craigie and Cherrybank.

The immediate aftermath of World War I, with the return of many citizens from active service, sharply focused the attention of Perth's town council on the necessity to expand the burgh with the provision of municipal housing. The 1919 and 1924 Housing acts saw the introduction of local authority housing in Scotland. These new council-owned houses began a radical change in living standards throughout Perth with most of the building being concentrated on the Muirton, Hillyland, Friarton and Darnhall areas.

Development around Darnhall began in 1920 with sixteen houses and was completed in 1930 with the addition of another one hundred and fifty two houses. The plans were drawn up by the architects Messrs Smart, Stewart and Mitchell. The name Darnhall comes from Darn Hall near Eddlestone in Peebleshire which was the family seat of the Elibank family. In 1803, Janet Oliphant of Pitheavlis had married Alexander Murray the 8th Lord Elibank.

Between 1924 and 1930. Murray Crescent was extended south of Needless Road and Darnhall Drive towards Queen's Avenue, a street of stone-built semi-detached homes. Council homes also appeared in Park Place, Darnhall Crescent and Knowelea Terrace.

An article in the *Perthshire Advertiser* of 3rd December 1924 supported plans for an extension of Queen Street to Darnhall Drive for the convenience of both pedestrians and motorists:

A movement is afoot for the opening of a new road between Darnhall Drive and Queen Street and not a few in that particular part of the district will follow the developments with a considerable amount of interest. I may say that many subordinates will appreciate any developments in this connection. A new road would avoid a great deal of trespassing. It is a well-known fact that many people proceeding from High Craigie towards Darnhall Drive, or vice versa, adopt a short-cut by going over what is known as the Sheppie's Field. Vehicular traffic, too, would find a new road very convenient. For a long time a barrier has existed at the top end of Wilson Street and all traffic which wishes to go from the Darnhall

Drive neighbourhood must proceed by Glover Street which is a very 'round about' road. I have no doubt I am voicing the opinion of many in the city, and particularly in the Craigie district, when I hope that the Town Council will give Sir Robert Moncreiffe's petition the consideration which it deserves and get on with the road.

One week later, the same newspaper reported that the Town Council had granted a warrant for the construction of the new road which used part of the Queen Street allotments. A short time later the gates which had closed the Needless Road end of Wilson Street were removed.

Housing subsidies offered in the 1920s led to various new developments throughout Perth by both individuals and organisations. In 1928, at Necessity Brae in Cherrybank, Lord Forteviot (the Dewar's Whisky magnate) built Pitheavlis Cottages, a group of single-storey cottages in an English Arts & Crafts style, for his workers. He also arranged for the thatched cottages at nearby Pickembere to be replaced by new cottages and after his death, the Forteviot Trust built further cottages and a hall at Pomarium in Perth.

The subsidies offered to private developers marked the appearance of the prolific new building firm of David Beat & Son of Fues Road, probably the first of Perth's large-scale developers. David Beat's homes were soon to radically change the appearance of Craigie and Cherrybank with their distinctive detached and semi-detached bungalow style dwellings. Beat-built homes were to spread all over Perth and beyond during the next thirty years with the Craigie, Viewlands, Burghmuir and Muirton Bank districts being particularly popular. These Beat homes were an indication of an increasing desire on the part of householders to become owner-

1925 map of Cragie and Cherrybank.

TOP LEFT: *The old bridge over the Craigie Burn at Windsor Terrace before the construction of Glenearn Road. This was the terminus for the Craigie trams and their overhead cables were connected to the two upright poles in the centre of the photograph. (Photograph from Perth & Kinross Libraries).* TOP RIGHT: *The tenement homes at Craigie Place which were demolished in the 1950s for the new Glenearn Road. The beginning of Queen Street is in the background. (Photograph from Perth & Kinross Libraries).*
BOTTOM: *On the edge of Craigie, this 1950s photograph shows the Edinburgh Road at Friarton before joining with Glenearn Road. The coal hopper in the railway marshalling yards is prominent to the right of centre. (Photograph courtesy of Elizabeth Gray).*

occupiers and an early Beat home could be purchased for £475. By 1957, Beat's were still building on sites at Pickletullum and Rhynd Road.

In 1928, Cavendish Avenue, named after Lady Rachel Cavendish, the daughter of the Duke of Devonshire, was built to run parallel with Needless Road. At one time, the lands running from Needless Road to Burghmuir Loaning were part of the Moray Estates to whom the householders paid fue duty and Lady Cavendish married a son of the Earl of Moray around the time the street was built.

The Beat-built homes of Pitheavlis Terrace and Pitheavlis Crescent also appeared around this time although it was to be the late 1940s and early 1950s before all these streets were finally completed. Stuart Avenue was not built until the mid-1950s. Until then, the triangle of land between Cavendish Avenue, Pickletullum Road and Pitheavlis Terrace, remained as a large open field and was a popular play area for the youth of Craigie. Pickletullum (originally Pickletillum) takes its name from Pickletillum

House and farm which until the mid-1830s was part of the loaning to Burghmuir and sometimes known as the Packman's Rest. The name is said to have been derived from a one-time 'pickle' of lint-land added to a nearby small hill known as a 'tillum'.

It is interesting to look at the house prices in both Craigie and Cherrybank in 1939, just before the country was plunged into another world war. For example, a modern semi-detached house in Evelyn Terrace in Upper Craigie could be purchased for £525 with a deposit of £37 and weekly payments of 18/8d per week. In the Oakbank area a four-apartment semi-detached villa would cost £650 but when looking at these prices one has to consider the average wages of that time. A bank clerk after three years' service was paid £50 per annum and any man who earned £5 per week was considered to have a well-paid job. Youngsters leaving school at fourteen, the statutory leaving age at that time, entered the commercial world at 7/6 to 10/– per week. At the end of an apprenticeship, a well-trained seamstress or milliner could expect 30/– to 35/–. A journeyman joiner would have earned about £2 per week.

Post-war developments

The outbreak of war in 1939 halted all further building activity but the end of World War II saw the beginning of great change. Throughout Britain, massive housing programmes in the mid 1940s were transplanting people from decaying tenements to new homes with modern amenities. A re-structuring of education was opening doors to a new strata of society and, at the same time, discarding some of the old social groupings. In this time of urban re-generation, Perth, although it had survived the bombings encountered by many British cities, played a major role in the post war housing boom.

There were eighteen hundred people on the waiting list for a council house in Perth at the beginning of the war. This number was expected to rise when hostilities ceased as, in the four years up to June 1943, there had been over two thousand marriages in Perth. The majority of these couples had a spouse still serving in the forces and all would expect to be housed when war ended. As many of the city homes were overcrowded and unfit dwellings, this contributed to a shortfall of three thousand houses. By careful acquiring of land in areas such as Letham, Tulloch, Muirton and Friarton the council by 1955 had built around two thousand four hundred and fifty of the estimated requirement of three thousand houses.

In Upper Craigie, a new housing development of over five hundred local authority homes was built on the Moncreiffe land with all the roads and streets named after the glens of Perthshire. I can just recall the beginning of building on Glenlochay Road, the steep brae leading up to Callerfountain Hill, with some of the early labouring being done by German prisoners of war prior to their repatriation. The new streets of the Moncreiffe scheme joined neatly with those of Upper Craigie – Glengarry Road with both St Magdalene's Road and Craigie Road; Glenalmond Terrace with Verena Terrace; Glenlochay Road with Craigie Knowes Road.

The name Moncreiffe is widely thought to have come from 'Monadh Craiobh' which is Gaelic for 'Hill of the Tree'. However, Moncreiffe is actually a habitational name and originally came from the name of the lands granted to Sir Matthew de Muncrefe by King Alexander II of Scotland in 1248.

As part of the new Moncreiffe housing estate, Glenearn Road was developed to connect Priory Place with the Edinburgh Road and to take some pressure off the use of Craigie Road. There had been a proposal to link the Edinburgh and Glasgow roads with a connecting road between Glenearn Road and Cherrybank and, with that in mind, Glenearn Road was made wide enough to allow for a length of dual carriageway. An alternative plan saw Gleneagles Road being made capable of taking another dual carriageway but neither plan was implemented.

In the 1950s, improvements to Glenearn Road involved the demolition at Craigie Haugh of the old tenement homes at Craigie Place which had deteriorated into slum properties. Extensive road alignment meant the building of a new concrete deck over the Craigie Burn with improved pedestrian access to the walkway leading to the South Inch.

The Darnhall development of the pre-war years continued in 1947 with the emergence of one hundred and fifty council housing homes in Woodside Crescent, Orchard Place, Glamis Place and Balmoral Place on the fields surrounding the Craigie Burn.

Cherrybank, although not included in the local authority housing programme, continued to develop with the introduction of new

TOP: *Cleeve House under renovation in 1959. (Photograph from Perth & Kinross Libraries).* LEFT: *Perth tourist advertisement for the Cleeve caravan park.*

homes in Oakbank Road, Oakbank Crescent and Fraser Terrace. Streets such as Murray Place, Viewlands Road, Viewlands Terrace and the lower part of Oakbank Road were by now well established.

In the late 1950s, part of the Cleeve estate was developed by the building firm of A & J Stephen into the residential homes of Cleeve Drive, Francis Road, Norie Terrace and Miller Avenue – all in tribute to Sir Francis Norie Miller, the previous owner of the Cleeve estate and

Woodlands House before demolition.

founder of the General Accident Insurance Corporation. It was Sir Francis who changed the name of his residence from Oakbank House, one of the homes of the early Ross family of Craigie, to The Cleeve. The remainder of the estate was purchased by the Perth Council and for over forty years was a popular caravan park

TOP: *An aerial view of Craigie and Cherrybank around 1950. The South Inch is in the bottom left corner with the Moncreiffe housing estate immediately above. Needless Road and Cavendish Avenue are right of centre above the railway station with Necessity Brae stretching upwards through the then undeveloped countryside. (Photograph by Valentine and Sons Ltd., Dundee).* BOTTOM: *This 2004 aerial view of a section of Craigie and Cherrybank shows Needless Road and Cavendish leading upwards from Gray Street and Glover Street. Craigie Hill golf course, the houses of Woodside Crescent and the Darnhall tennis courts and bowling green are top left with part of the Glasgow Road top right. (Photo courtesy of Kenbarry Marketing).*

for tourists before being sold in the early twenty first century to Stewart Milne Homes who developed the site into the modern homes of Cleeve Park. Cleeve House itself, built in 1902, was purchased by the Perth Council following the death of Norie-Miller in 1947 and converted into a children's home. It only operated as such for five years and in 1959 underwent conversion into apartments. The attractive entrance lodge to the Cleeve estate dates from 1911.

THE CREATION OF A COMMUNITY

The neighbouring Woodlands House with its adjoining farm first appeared as 'Perth Wood' on Macfarlane's 1792 map. In 1813, The *Perthshire Courier* advertised for sale: 'the House and Grounds of Woodlands, near the Auchterarder Turnpike Road, containing about 34 Scots Acres of good ground' and by 1858 Woodlands was listed in the *Post Office Directory* as a 'Gentleman's Seat' owned by W Devas.

Woodlands House appears on the first edition Ordnance Survey map with large tree-lined formal gardens and a good-sized walled garden. A coach house is shown to the west of Woodlands and a courtyard steading with a circular structure which was probably a horse mill. The farmhouse was a gabled building which was reworked during the later nineteenth and twentieth centuries. West Woodlands Coach House remained and is now part of the Westerhill residential development situated off Oakbank Road.

In the early 1900s, Woodlands House belonged to the grain merchant James McDonald of the Perth City Mills before passing into the ownership of the Fraser family of the Macdonald Fraser Mart. The house then lay empty after the Frasers moved to Fields on the upper part of Oakbank Road which was still on the Woodlands estate. It gradually fell into a state of disrepair mainly due to dry rot and was finally demolished in the late 1960s following a fire. The next door farmhouse was owned by the Wood family of the bakery business in Perth High Street.

Another private housing boom during the late 1950s and 1960s would see the creation of further new homes in Cherrybank Grove, Braeside Gardens and east of Viewlands Road at Athollbank where an architect-designed detached house could be built in 1965 for around £7000. This was all part of the beginning of the huge development of Oakbank and Burghmuir into Perth's western edge by progressive building firms such as A & J Stephen, Thain, Dunbar & Cook, Bett Brothers and George Wimpey.

House prices began to rapidly increase by the 1970s – the first sign that the light at the end of the tunnel was, in fact, a train! The age of the monetarists came in the 1980s with properties being bought for investment as well as for private ownership and the Thatcher government offering incentives which encouraged the renters of local authority houses to become the owners of their homes.

SHOPS, SERVICES AND SOCIALISING

Streets wi' shops and houses stand
Where once was open farmland;
Now there's pubs and schools and kirks
Instead o' woods wi' bonnie birks.

As Craigie and Cherrybank began to develop it was only natural that shops and services would soon follow to serve this growing population. Craigie Cross became the shopping hub of the area with a variety of independent shops of high quality. In these pre-supermarket and pre-refrigeration days, food shopping was almost a daily habit and although Craigie was relatively close to the centre of Perth it became so much more convenient for housewives to shop almost on their doorsteps and, as a result, a social camaraderie and community spirit soon developed between traders and their customers.

The City of Perth Co-operative Society opened a store on the upper side of the Abbot Street/Friar Street corner before moving diagonally across Abbot Street in 1890 to the ground floor of the flatted building at the Raeburn Place corner with a butcher shop next door in Abbot

The original Co-operative shop at the Abbot Street/Friar Street corner. (Photograph from Perth and Kinross Libraries).

Street. The Perth Co-operative Society was formed in 1871 with ninety members, £85 capital and annual sales of £704 and thrived until the decline of the co-operative movement in the 1960s. A carved relief on the building reads: 'CO-OPERATIVE SOCIETY MDCCCC – EACH FOR ALL & ALL FOR EACH'. The premises became

The butcher's shop of A D Lamond at the corner of Glover Street and St Leonard's Bridge. (Photograph from Perth & Kinross Libraries).

the Abbotsford Lounge in 1971 but the upstairs flats still remain. The original Co-operative shop has remained as a general store to this day and now also houses the Post Office.

Despite being within walking distance from Perth's city centre, a village atmosphere soon developed in Craigie. It became a thriving place with a great variety of shops and businesses and, apart from the Co-operative store, all under private ownership. There was the grocery business of A L Darling at the corner of Glover Street and Abbot Street and across the road, on the Priory Place/Abbot Street corner, a branch of Peter Thomson, Perth's popular grocery, wine and spirit merchants. The butcher trade was well represented by Lawson's shop (later George Handyside's) at the corner of Friar Street and Abbot Street; A D Lamond's shop at the Glover Street/St Leonard's Bridge corner and the Co-operative on Abbot Street. There was the Craigie Post Office owned by J K Taylor; at least four newsagents – Hampton's (later Campbell's and then Hepburn's) on St Leonard's Bridge, Bert Alexander and Stephen's on Glover Street and another on the upper Abbot Street/Friar Street corner (the original Co-op) which was also a grocery and general merchant. Stirling's Bakery had a shop in Priory Place and another on St Leonard's Bridge; there was Helen Bartie's ladies' dress shop; two chemist shops; a fishmonger (Dow's and later Tainsh); Harrower's electrical shop in Abbot Street; Miss Crichton's knitting and sewing shop in Abbot Street; Fordyce the cobbler; Hynd, painters and decorators; Sorlie's confectionery in Priory Place; John Johnson & Sons joinery works on Priory Place and two plumbing firms – Miller's and Smart's. Ramage & Cooper builders and Mason the coal merchant were on St Leonard's Bank and Player's the ladies' hairdressers on Glover Street is still a hairdressing salon. Many of these shops and businesses still existed well into the second half of the twentieth century, some with second and even third generation owners, some with new owners, some as completely new businesses and some in new locations.

In 1933 and a short distance from Craigie Cross, Alexander Muil opened a popular grocery shop at the corner of Darnhall Drive and Park Place. It later passed into the ownership of the Forsyth family followed by David Sands of Kinross and is still trading as a modern Co-operative convenience store. Until the early 1950s there was a similar shop (Taylor's) above the waterfall on Craigie Knowes Road. The former Cadzow's Dairy at Craigie Place became an 'open all hours' store run by the popular Jimmy Forbes but is now sadly closed.

For many years the Stephen family ran a small grocery and newsagents shop on the site of a former dairy at the corner of Glover Street and Needless Road. It was later owned by the former Perthshire cricketer Arthur Dewar and is now a pet shop.

Over the years new businesses emerged in Craigie as social changes took place. In the 1940s, the Giulianotti family had established a popular fish and chip shop on St Leonard's Bridge and later a small café/restaurant which was eventually incorporated into today's popular 'Craigie Chippy'. Another fish and chip shop in a wooden hut on Glover Street across from the junction with Needless Road was later destroyed in a fire. Sorlie's shop has seen several owners and uses and is now one of five Craigie hairdressing businesses. The Craigie Post Office on St Leonard's Bridge moved to smaller premises next door and the premises became a branch of Kennaway's a long established Perth bakery company. It later became Tower Bakery and for a short time was a community café. For a number of year's what had been Fraser's pharmacy in Abbot Street was a popular confectionery business owned by Mr Irvine with his delightful selection of handmade sweets and chocolates before becoming a second-hand bookshop. Another butchery (David Ballantyne's) opened in what had been Miss Crichton's sewing shop and John Duncan took over

A railway employee looks up at the wreckage that was once the Craigie Pharmacy on St Leonard's Bridge. (Perthshire Advertiser photograph).

On the morning of Saturday, 11th September 1948, I was walking with my mother to the shops of Craigie when, as a small boy, I was excited to see from the top of Abbot Street a fire engine on St Leonard's Bridge. The floor and one of the walls of the Craigie Pharmacy on the south side of the bridge had collapsed and the owner, Alexander Macgregor, had to be extricated from the debris. Fortunately, Mr Macgregor who lived at 44 Abbot Street, although severely shaken, suffered only slight cuts. A message boy, Charles Ireland of Glenbruar Crescent just got out of the shop in time when a loud cracking noise gave warning of the collapse. In common with several of the neighbouring shops on the bridge the rear of the pharmacy on the railway side was built on stilts. The shop was never re-built.

Laurence Lamond's butcher's business which later became Mannion's convenience store. Harrower's electrical business became a launderette and the shop next door became a ladies' fashion business and is now a laundry. Peter Thomson's grocery and wine and spirit shop became a hairdressing salon and remains so today. The shop of A L Darling is now a private dwelling as are the butcher shops of Handyside and Ballantyne and Taylor's grocery store on Craigie Knowes Road. The former premises of Mason's coal yard on St Leonard's Bank was a car dealership for Arnold Clark until 2018.

In addition to the excellent choice of shops in Craigie, street trading was prevalent and up until the 1950s many deliveries were still made by horse and cart. The sound of early morning milk bottles from the Perth Creamery and the Perth Co-operative Society landing on doorsteps was as good as any alarm clock. The glass-sided horse-drawn Co-operative grocery van was popular but sometimes just as popular as the van's produce were the deposits left by its horse! Somehow, when the horse-drawn delivery carts were replaced with motor vehicles the roses in the Craigie gardens never seemed the same!

In those pre-central heating days there were regular coal and firewood deliveries from various local coal merchants and familiar throughout Craigie and Cherrybank was the horse and cart of the one-armed William Dawson with fruit and vegetables from his market garden in the grounds of Pitheavlis Castle.

There were several bakery vans and for many years Jessie Cargill brought fresh fish on the train from Arbroath and, in all weathers, sold it round the doors from a pram. Later she and her brother acquired a van and increased their number of customers.

For several decades until the 1960s the 'Onion Johnnies' from Brittany with their bicycles and black berets brought a piece of the north of France to the area as they cycled round the doors selling their distinctive pink onions.

Most of the local shops had their own message boys delivering butcher meat, groceries, etc, on heavy message bikes with a metal basket in front. The newsagents employed boys to ensure that households had their newspapers delivered breakfast time. Postal deliveries were twice daily and a posted letter was almost guaranteed to be delivered the following day. Telephones were regarded as a luxury and lot of quick communication was done by sending a postcard!

For many years a Saturday evening ritual for the men folk of Craigie was a visit to the news vendor at his stance in the doorway of Kennaway's the bakers for a copy of *The Sporting Post*. It was the main way of keeping abreast with all the local sports news of the day (particularly the football) until modern technology and instant sporting coverage gradually eased the popular paper out of circulation in the 1980s. In its heyday it was not uncommon for a Perth man heading out for a Saturday night at the pub, the pictures, the theatre or the dancing to have a copy of *The Sporting Post* sticking out of his pocket!

Today Craigie still bustles but with many more changes. Fast food takeaway shops such as China China are situated around the Craigie Cross triangle along with a property business. A florist now occupies the shop which for many years was a thriving newsagent business on St Leonard's Bridge.

The Craigie Clock

One lasting and familiar feature of Craigie, perhaps intended as a status symbol for the district demonstrating Craigie's individuality as a distinct suburb of the city of Perth, is the Craigie Clock (popularly known as The Lollipop) which stands on the triangular island at Craigie Cross. The money for the clock was partly raised by the children of Craigie School in 1924 from the proceeds of £30 from a school concert.

The following article appeared in the 'Tayside Echoes' column of the *Perthshire Advertiser* of 17th December 1924:

> Craigie's Clock. I sincerely trust that our good friends of Craigie are finding the public clock for which they clamoured so long is serving the purpose. It unfortunately cost a lot more than the amount collected by the school children, but the balance is being made up by the Common Good Fund so that the rest of the community will now have an interest in the punctuality, or otherwise, of suburbia.

The Craigie Clock.

Cherrybank, while not having the same variety or quantity of shops as nearby Craigie, was also growing as a community in its own right. The old main road from the south west which had approached the city by way of Aberdalgie and Necessity Brae was, by the early 1900s, bypassed by the present Glasgow Road. The two roads converged at Cherrybank with part of the old road, now known as Low Road, at a lower level from the junction with the new road. A line of buildings, which included the post office, made the most of the situation with their lower floors facing Low Road and the upper floors facing the higher-level Glasgow Road.

The tram terminus for Cherrybank was situated between the end of this row of buildings and the Cherrybank

A TREAT FOR

3d

When the weather is warm, and cooking is more irksome than usual, it is then we appreciate the good things Stirling has prepared to save time and worry. Treat the family occasionally to

STIRLING'S PIES and BRIDIES

They are made with the best possible meat, in the famous Craigie Bakery, and cost only 3d. each. Good for Lunch, Tea or Picnic. Try them now and you'll so relish their goodness that you'll want them again.

STIRLING'S

36 PRIORY PLACE and 98 HIGH STREET, PERTH
'Phone No. 484.   'Phone No. 921

SPECIAL CUT IN TINNED FRUITS

'Easter' and 'Flickenger' Brands
Apricots, -   1/2 and 1/8 per tin
Peaches, 1/3, 1/8 and 1/10 per tin
Greengages, -   -   1/8 per tin
Egg Plums, -   -   1/8 per tin
NOTE.—These are not Dumped Goods

A. L. DARLING,
1 GLOVER STREET.
CRAIGIE, - PERTH.
Phone 265.

Our Motto: SERVICE – SATISFACTION – CLEANLINESS

12 ABBOT STREET, CRAIGIE, PERTH

——— TELEPHONE 658 ———

Craigie advertisements from 1928 and a 1960s advertisement for George Handyside's butchery at the Friar Street/ Abbot Street corner.

Inn with a toilet constructed for the convenience of the drivers and conductors (and possibly some of the passengers!). A steep flight of steps led down to Low Road. This area is now a block of modern apartments but during the 1960s and 1970s it housed a Texaco and later a Burmah filling station.

As in Craigie, another Co-operative store was situated at the corner of Glasgow Road and Oakbank Road around 1900. In later years it became well-known as Bendinger's shop and until its closure was well patronised at lunchtimes by pupils from Perth Academy and Perth High School.

The increasing popularity of private car ownership led to the formation of the Cherrybank Motor Company in 1933. In 1939 the business was acquired by the popular Johnny Welsh who for ten years was St Johnstone FC's regular right back in their successful team of the 1930s and became Cherrybank Garage. For a short time in the early 1970s it was owned by Malcolm Shaw, a former Perth City Dean of Guild who also ran a long established motorcycle business in Perth's city centre. Since then, Cherrybank Garage has flourished under the ownership of the Thomson family.

Before the advent and growth of garden centres in the 1980s, keen gardeners had to use the services provided by local nurserymen and seedsmen. Perth shops such as Alexander & Brown in South Methven Street, Dickson & Turnbull and William Graham's in Hospital Street, Watt's in St John Street along with nurseries such as Rosebank in

Cherrybank Post Office. (photograph from Perth & Kinross Libraries).

Glasgow Road and those in King Street and at Barnhill were the main source of garden seeds, plants and implements. In Cherrybank, on the sloping ground leading from Low Road down towards the Craigie Burn there was Drummond's Nursery which stocked an extensive range of trees, plants and shrubs.

Social Times

The social hours swift-winged un-noticed fleet

(From 'The Cotter's Saturday Night' by Robert Burns)

As Craigie rapidly developed into a separate area of Perth, it was not long before a community spirit emerged. The early social life of the area appears to have been centered at the Craigie Hall which opened around 1870 and was situated at what is now called Priory Court. The hall was used for a variety of purposes before being turned into a contemporary development of apartments in 1996.

Meetings, concerts, dances, parties, whist drives and probably every event that could be associated with a village hall were held within the premises. On school days it was used for serving lunches to the pupils of Craigie School with, for a short time, an additional classroom upstairs. It was the regular meeting place for the Craigie cubs and scouts. In 1950/51 while Moncreiffe

A dance at Craigie Hall in 1921. (Perthshire Advertiser photograph).

Church was being built in Glenbruar Crescent as part of Scotland's new church extension scheme, Craigie Hall was used for the Sunday services.

In the pre-war years of the 1930s and the immediate post-war years of the 1940s and 1950s there was no social media as we know it today. The outside world entered the private home through the daily newspaper and the radio. Office workers put in a half-day on a Saturday morning and shop workers had a half-day on a Wednesday afternoon. Travel outside Scotland was only for a handful of the very affluent and places like St Andrews, Arbroath, Carnoustie and Broughty Ferry were popular destinations for those fortunate enough to get away for a summer holiday. A special summer treat for me was a day trip on the train to Dundee and a sail across the Firth of Tay on one of the 'Fifies' – the ferries which linked Dundee and Newport before the opening of the Tay Road Bridge in 1966. The late 1960s saw the rise of package holidays to the Mediterranean which were cheaper than holidays in Britain, even with air fares factored in.

For an area which during the nineteenth century had been home to both a thriving brewery and a distillery, it is perhaps surprising that it was not until 1971 that a public house became established in Craigie. Indeed, in April 1889 it was reported in the *Perth Courier* that the residents of Newtown and Craigie held a public meeting in Craigie Hall to consider an application by two grocers in the district for a license to sell 'intoxicating liquor'. The meeting voted unanimously against the proposal stating that 'the chief advantage the district offered as a desirable place of residence was the immunity from the unfavourable influences that invariably accompany the near neighbourhood of licensed houses'.

The report also stated that there was a small attendance at the meeting so perhaps the good people of Craigie were really not all that interested! It was, after all, a short walk down the Craigie Steps on St Leonard's Bridge and through the discrete cover of the railway station to the 'near neighbourhood' and the drinking howffs around Leonard Street and the city centre.

The steps from the bridge to the main platform of the station were taken away in 1967 when ticket barriers were introduced in the station thus depriving many Craigie people of a much loved shortcut. This popular route through the station was not officially recognised as a right of way and, in accordance with this, the station authorities

The 'Craigie Steps' leading from St Leonard's Bridge to the main platform of Perth station can be clearly seen in this photograph taken on a cold winter evening.

reserved the right to have the gate on St Leonard's Bridge locked on one day each year.

It was a different story in Cherrybank. An inn has flourished there since the establishment of a drovers' tavern in 1761 and has remained a popular gathering place until the present day. Always independent and family owned, in the 1960s the popular 'Mine Host' of that time, the former World War II air ace Jack Norwell, added a lounge bar. This was later extended by the next owner Jack Horne and, since the 1990s,

The Cherrybank Inn front and rear with the beer garden which was added in 2021. NEXT PAGE: A 1904 stoneware Dublin Stout bottle from the Cherrybank Inn.

by the current father and son proprietors, Jack and Scott Findlay who also upgraded the bedrooms, kitchen and toilets and added an outdoor deck. Further upgrading took place in 2021 with the addition of a beer garden. The Cherrybank Inn was named 'Tayside Pub of the Year' in 2011 and is now one of Perth's most popular social venues serving fine food and a wide selection of spirits and real ales.

By the 1960s a wind of change was apparent throughout society as the restrictions of the post-war years had become largely forgotten. People suddenly became more affluent with car ownership and modern appliances in the home. Gone were the once popular radio programmes such as *Dick Barton, The McFlannels, Hancock's Half Hour* and *The Goon Show*. It was now the age of Elvis, Cliff Richard, The Beatles and James Bond. Most homes now had television sets and people watched *Z Cars, The Black and White Minstrel Show, The White Heather Club* and *Coronation Street*. A new Saturday night satirical programme called *That Was the Week That Was* poked irreverent fun at the leading political and national figures of the day. Men's hair grew longer and ladies' skirts grew shorter.

These 'swinging sixties' continued until the early 1970s and then suddenly ground to a halt as many of the participants discovered family life and the joys of cash flow. The counter-culture became the over-the-counter culture.

From the late 1950s, nights in the pub had ceased to be a male preserve. New licensed premises were opening and the old ones such as the Cherrybank Inn were adjusting to meet with the new female clientele.

In 1966, the MacDonald family, proprietors of the Café Maree in Perth's King Edward Street, opened a new hotel called Lovat House in a stone villa at the eastern corner of Glasgow Road and Pickletullum Road. It soon became popular in the area serving meals and also had a small comfortable lounge bar tucked away in the rear of the premises. Local businessman Gordon Blair later acquired the hotel and, with the addition of a new lounge bar and a large function room, it became widely used for wedding receptions, private functions and supper dances. Over the years, further extensions into neighbouring properties turned it into the thirty-room Lovat Hotel.

By 1971, the old Co-operative building in Craigie at the corner of Abbot Street and Raeburn Place had become vacant and an application by brother and sister Ralph and Norma Giulianotti to turn it into Craigie's

TOP: *The Lovat Hotel.*
BOTTOM: *The Abbotsford Lounge Bar.*

first lounge bar was approved. It was a popular decision as Ralph and Norma were Craigie people whose family had once owned the fish and chip shop on St Leonard's Bridge. The choice of Abbotsford as a name for the new premises was not difficult when Norma spotted that part of one the neighbouring buildings was already named Abbotsford Place.

The Abbotsford quickly became an integral part of Craigie life. Advertised as a place 'to meet friends, take friends and make friends' it became the social hub that had probably been missing in the area since the days of the dances and concerts in Craigie Hall for earlier generations.

Although the Abbotsford became Craigie's first public house, licensed premises had existed in the district for many years. The cattle mart had a licensed restaurant which opened on market days for the farming community and there were also liquor licenses at the West End Bowling Club, Darnhall Bowling Club and in Cherrybank at Craigie Hill Golf Club. In addition, there were the private Railway Athletic and RASC clubs on St Leonard's Bank with the RASC Club being popular for its weekend dances. These two properties are now private homes and apartments. In 1979 the Civil Service Club moved from the old Rob Roy Hotel in Leonard Street (formerly Laidlaw's Temperance Hotel) to custom-built premises in St Leonard's Bank.

During the Christmas period of 2016, businesses based around the Craigie Cross triangle installed lights to give the site a festive atmosphere. Keen to sustain the momentum, the following year saw gravel spread around the memorial benches and the pruning of trees. Volunteers from Beautiful Perth (formerly Perth in Bloom) installed and planted tubs and two-tier planters which now bloom with colour each Spring and Summer. This 2017 photograph shows (Back): Councillor Bob Band and Chic Doogan of the Abbotsford. (Front): Councillor Michael Jamieson with Monica Stronagh, Barbara McDonald and John Summers of Beautiful Perth. (Photograph from The Courier).

AGRICULTURE AND INDUSTRY

Tell me o' Scottish enterprise and canniness and thrift

Hugh MacDiarmid

During the eighteenth and nineteenth centuries most of the higher slopes of Craigie and Cherrybank would have been given over to farmland with sheep, cattle and perhaps oxen being grazed around the aforementioned 'neat leas' and on the burgh muir at Hillend.

The grazing and keeping of sheep and cattle had been in existence since the twelfth century and the *Exchequer Rolls* for 1378 showed nearly forty five thousand hides exported from Scotland.

The main crop grown would probably have been barley which would have found a ready market in the local brewing industry. There was a substantial farm, called the Hill Farm of Pitheavlis situated close to the Necessity Brae where, according to an 1866 Ordnance Survey map, the farm steading incorporated a horse

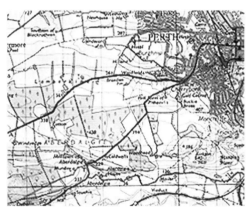

This 1950s map shows some of the prominent farms situated near Cherrybank.

mill powered from the circular horse-engine house. Although the farm steading was later re-modelled, the engine house remained roofed until at least 1901 and may well have survived until the demolition of the steading in the early 1970s to make way for the construction of the General Accident's new headquarters complex.

The productive farms of Woodhead of Mailer near the Aberdalgie road, Broxden, Lamberkine and Cultmalundie were (and some still are) prominent in the area. Indeed almost the entire Earn valley as far as Aberuthven and beyond was studded with farms bearing such

names as Windyedge, Chapelbank, Strathy, Drumtogle and Maidenplain.

The nineteenth-century St Magdalene's farm was once situated on what was to eventually become Glenturret Terrace in the Moncreiffe housing estate.

Cottage industries were a sustainable part of the area's employment in lower Craigie and also in Cherrybank with the only real industry in Craigie centred around Craigie Mill. However, all that was to change when the railway terminus was built in the mid-nineteenth century and Craigie was soon to be seen as an ideal situation for industrial development and commercial enterprises.

Apart from the growth of residential housing, Cherrybank remained largely untouched at this time. It was not until the 1970s and the expansion of Perth towards the western edge of the city that it was seen as a suitable place to establish new businesses or move some existing companies from the city centre to the outskirts.

Market Days

From Victorian times, Perth's major commercial businesses all centred on the railways and most of them aligned their premises accordingly. In 1886, a firm called John Swan and Sons Ltd opened a livestock mart at the lower end of Needless Road called the Northern Mart. The mart remained under the ownership of this company until bought a few years later by Alexander Hay.

Alexander Hay had pioneered the cattle-marketing trade in Scotland. In 1830, he commenced business as Hay, Burnett & Kyd from a stance in Perth's North Port and it was from this small beginning, with a few cattle and sheep, that the enterprise was to develop into one of the largest stock sales in the country. Increased trade necessitated first a move to Dunkeld Road and then to a prominent site adjoining the Logiealmond Tavern – a hostelry by the Ladeside at the corner of Mill Street and Methven Street.

Livestock auctioning was then in its infancy and for a long period only small numbers of stock came forward. In the beginning, sometimes a day's best business was confined to the selling of a couple of cattle and five sheep. It is on record that, about 1850, a good average sale consisted of around thirty sheep and ten cattle weekly. Farmers were then, without any form of licensing, permitted to roup their beasts in their own 'ferm yairds'. Dealers circulated extensively on the farms, purchasing stock individually.

However, the foundation had been laid and with his son as colleague and successor, Alexander Hay's business flourished and expanded. In 1871, the next move was to an area at the corner of Princes Street and Victoria Street where the large and well-equipped Victoria Mart of Hay & Kyd was established. Here throughout the year, at stated times, shows of cattle and horses were introduced, together with the celebrated wool sales under the management of Alexander Hay, Jun., who held his auctioneer's licence for sixty two years. In addition he was joint agent of the Perth branch of the North of Scotland Bank.

TOP: A view of Hay's Mart from the Needless Road entrance. BOTTOM: A view inside Hay's Mart looking towards Abbot Street. (Photographs courtesy of Mr A S Hay).

The progress of the firm was remarkable and in 1905 the more conveniently situated and better appointed Northern Mart premises in Craigie's Needless Road were acquired from Swan and Sons and renamed the Perth Livestock Mart under the ownership of Hay & Co. Ltd.

The young Alexander Hay was also responsible for initiating the special fat stock sales at

the Christmas period and it is in this trade of fat cattle that Hay & Company became widely associated. Following these early beginnings, the firm developed their weekly fat stock sales until they became probably the largest in Scotland prior to the grading control of 1939. The proximity of the mart to the Glover Street rail marshalling yards convenienced the operation of the business and butchers came from all over Scotland, and some from England, to buy quality meat for the nation's larders. Depending on the season, five to six hundred head of cattle and up to six thousand sheep could pass through the mart at these big Monday sales before being railed to their final destinations.

Livestock not sold was moved on foot to the firm's farmland at Hillend in the Burghmuir area of Perth. It was a common sight on market days for the residents of Needless Road to see sheep and cattle being driven up the road – but not always to plan. A regular occurrence was for cattle beasts to enter private gardens when enticed by an open gate. The flatted homes in Castle Terrace and Kinfauns Crescent were a particular target for the beasts and the cattle drovers had their work cut out recovering the trapped and sometimes panic-stricken animals from the communal closes of the flats. They didn't move on without leaving their trade-marks and leaving the occupants to remove the evidence with pails of water and scrubbing brushes!

TOP: *A 1954 view of the extensive livestock pens at Hay's Mart.* MIDDLE: *The sale ring. (Photograph courtesy of Mr A S Hay).* BOTTOM: *A sale of tractors and farm machinery in 1954. (Photograph by The Farming News).*

Further development and expansion took place at the mart over the years. A licensed restaurant and bar was introduced and, in the late 1940s, a loading bay was constructed in Needless Road to facilitate the

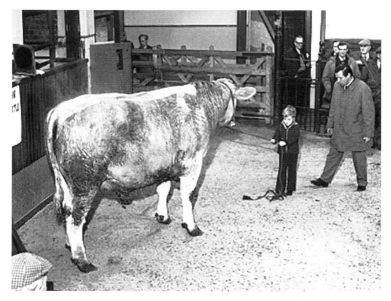

The little boy holding the big bullock in this 1974 photograph at Perth Livestock Mart is four and a half year old Peter John Hay, watched by his father, mart director Alexander S.Hay. (Photograph by A C Cowper & Co., Perth).

moving of livestock by road. The firm's work in commercial livestock was extensive with the big sales of store stock and pedigree ram and pig sales also coming under their year's calendar. In addition to livestock, the company developed farm implement and machinery and motor vehicle sales.

The mart covered a considerable area and the livestock pens stretched all the way to Craigie School in one direction and to Young Street and the school playing field in the other. Many a

TOP: *The attractive frontage to Hay's Mart which has remained.* BOTTOM: *A view of the site of Hay's Mart following demolition for the housing development of Raeburn Park. Glover Street and and the Perth Station clock tower are in the background. (Photograph courtesy of Mrs J MacGregor).*

football had to be retrieved (and cleaned) following an over-exuberant kick over or through the wire fence! Market days virtually took over this part of Craigie and it was common practice for farmers' cars to be parked for half the length of both sides of Needless Road and along Gray Street and Wilson Street.

During the late 1980s, Hay's Mart was taken over by Caledonian Marts (Stirling) Ltd, a consortium of farming interests. The Hay tradition of over a century and a half ending with Alexander S Hay and Stewart A Hay, the great-grandsons of the founder.

The last livestock sale at what will always be referred to in Perthshire parlance as 'Hey's Mert' was held on Monday, 27th July 1992. Fittingly, the last beast to enter the auction ring belonged to Sandy Hay, great-grandson of the company's founder. As a gesture to his wife Kay's special charity, the £1086.50 proceeds from the sale of the animal, an Aberdeen-Angus bullock went to Cancer Research. The bullock made the day's top price and was bought by the Dundee butchers, Scott Brothers.

Mr Hay had a total of eight animals from his farm at Cultmalundie forward for the historic final sale and said that while it was a sad day for him, the break had been made four years previously when the mart was sold. He added 'I think I will feel it worse when the bulldozers move in to clear the site for housing development.'

The mart finally closed on Friday, 31st July 1992 with an equipment auction, one of the items up for sale being the auction ring itself.

One aspect not affected by the new development of Raeburn Park was the mart office with its attractive frontage in Needless Road. The agricultural connection with the site remains to this day, the office premises now being occupied by the Scottish Federation of Meat Traders Association.

The Craigie and Cherrybank Weavers

'If it wasna for the weavers, what would be do?
We wouldna hae claith made oot o' our woo.
We wouldna hae a coat, neither black nor blue,
If it wasna for the wark o' the weavers'.

(Scots song by David Shaw)

The weaving industry in Perth can be traced back to the thirteenth century. It is recorded that in 1210 William the Lion forbid anybody to make or dye cloth who was not a burgess

within the town's Merchant Guild which was effectively the town council of that time. The Guild's duty was to protect the financial interests of merchants and craftsmen and it guarded its monopoly keeping the weavers at arm's length. In 1424 an Act allowed for the freedom of trade corporations in Scotland and, as a result of that Act, the Weavers Incorporation was formed in Perth to provide support and protection for its members. The

TOP: *A handloom weaver at work in his cottage. (Photograph from the Scottish National Archive).* BOTTOM: *The old weavers' cottages at Croft Park in Craigie. (Photograph from Perth Museum and Art Gallery).*

Weavers Incorporation owned several cottages, such as those at Croft Park in Craigie, which were rented to freedom weavers.

By the late 1700s, the weaving trade in both Craigie at Croft Park and in the nearby hamlet of Cherrybank appears to been at its peak. Earlier, the handloom weavers had traditionally woven wool but now the weavers' clients were mainly local families who would supply the weavers with flax to create an item of cloth. Working at home, the weaver's wife would spin the flax into yarn which the children would then wind onto pirns or bobbins. Once the yarn was prepared, the weaver would throw the shuttle backwards and forwards over the loom while working the pedals of the frame. As well as linen, a coarse fabric of linen warp and woollen weft was also woven for use as clothing or blankets by the weaver's family. The weavers would often take their cloth into Perth on Fridays where they could be sure of selling it to the merchants, some of the cloth finding its way to the London market.

By the beginning of the nineteenth century, the war with France, the development of factories and the introduction of power looms saw the home trade diminish. What had once been a well-paid middle class profession collapsed and, by the mid 1800s, many of the handloom weavers ended their days in poverty.

A reminder of the Cherrybank weaving industry remains to this day with the Weavers' Well which is situated in a field on the Glasgow Road in a nearby field to the Woodlands development.

Craigie Mill, Brewery and Distillery

Craigie Mill was situated at what is now the end of Windsor Terrace beside the waterfall which carries the Craigie Burn down from the higher land of Craigie Hill. Long before the arrival of the railway in the mid-nineteenth century, and the development of the present Craigie, it was an area of intense activity and was the scene of an important brewery, a thriving distillery, a flock mill, a flour mill, a steam laundry and, until the 1970s, a dyeing and cleaning business.

When war broke out in 1939 a rifle range was established at Craigie Mill for the training of members of the Home Guard.

During the eighteenth century many of the buildings situated in the closes and vennels of Perth were occupied by brewers who kept public houses and retailed their own ales. By the year 1780 there were over sixty houses involved, the principle ones being The King's Arms at the bottom of High Street which enjoyed the patronage of the Duke of Atholl and many of the county's nobility; The Old Ship in the Skinnergate's Thistle Close (often frequented by the renowned fiddler Neil Gow) and the Salutation, so named because the landlord John Burt shook hands with Prince Charles

1875 map of Craigie Mill with the distillery and mill dam marked. The mill dam was situated where Craigie Knowes Road, part of upper Queen Street and Queen's Avenue would be formed later. Moncreiffe Terrace is shown on the bottom right corner.

in 1745.

Alterations in the excise laws eventually drove those small brewers out of the trade with large scale breweries being given a preference in the duty. The well-established brewery at Craigie Mill was one of three breweries left in Perth (the others being Clocksery and the Perth Brewery) and, until around the mid-nineteenth century, the Craigie Brewery engrossed much of the local brewing industry.

Scotch whisky has a unique quality. It reflects the climate, water, people and the whole environment of Scotland. It is imbued with its history and has achieved an extraordinary place in people`s lives all over the world.

The practice of distillation made its way to Scotland from Ireland between the twelfth and fifteenth centuries and became a common practice among Scottish monasteries. There is mention in the Exchequer rolls of James IV (these rolls were the record of the Scottish kings' household expenses) of a purchase of aqua vitae from the Friar John of Lindores Abbey near Newburgh, Fife in 1494. Interestingly a new distillery has now been founded among the ruins of that ancient monastery.

In the seventeenth and eighteenth centuries, distillation was widespread in Scotland and virtually every farmhouse had a small still. Following the introduction of excise taxes on alcohol in 1660 most of them, particularly in the Highlands, continued to operate illegally until in 1781 all private distillation was banned. Some illicit stills which were being operated by bootleggers became licensed and eventually became major distillers in their own right. The oldest distillery in Scotland, Glenturret near Crieff and officially founded in 1775, began as an illegal facility on a farm and its bootleg production goes back to

It is not clear if the Craigie Distillery which was founded in 1825 by James Ramsay was one of these early stills, perhaps supplying hard liquor to the monks of the area. What is known is that it was a distillery of some note. Like the Craigie Brewery it would have been perfectly situated with a supply of water from the Craigie Burn waterfall and barley from the surrounding fields.

The Parliamentary Papers and the Accounts and Papers of the House of Commons detailing excise collection in Scotland show that, in the year 1828, the Craigie Distillery owned by James Ramsay & Co. produced 25,172 gallons of distilled malt whisky. Between 1824 and 1828, the county of Perthshire had forty seven distilleries listed in the annual excise returns with Craigie showing the third highest. In 1828 the highest was Tullibardine at 60,984 gallons, the lowest being Gillybank at 780 gallons.

Presumably much of the distilled Craigie malt whisky would be supplied to many of the licensed victuallers in Perth for their own blending as it was common practice for some grocers to produce their own varieties of blended whisky. In 1901 an advertisement appeared in *Leslie's Perth Directory* offering Old Highland malt whisky for 17 shillings (85p) per gallon and in 1910 a bottle of McIntosh's No. 2 Special Whisky cost 3/–.

Local whisky blending actually continued until around the 1970s with firms such as P MacArthur & Sons (MacArthur`s Highland Whisky), C C Stuart (Currie's No 10 and Charlie Stuart), R B Smith & Sons (Moorland), Peter Thomson Ltd (Beneagles) and McDiarmid's (Schiehallion) producing some most acceptable blends.

Perth`s whisky giants Dewar's and Bell's commenced whisky blending in 1846 and 1851 respectively. Matthew Gloag & Son (established in an Atholl Street grocery business in the early 1800s) began producing their Grouse brand in 1896 which became so popular that in 1905 it was re-named The Famous Grouse. In 1842, when Queen Victoria and Prince Albert attended a banquet in Perth, it was Matthew Gloag who supplied the wines.

During the latter part of the nineteenth century, whisky distillation at Craigie Mill appears to have ceased production and the premises became part of the already established flock mill and a steam laundry. In 1941, a malt store and loading dock were added to the former complex of malt barns and laundry. Until around the late 1950s a flour mill was operated by the Veda company, the producers

CRAIGIE Steam LAUNDRY

TOP: *An early 1900s view of Craigie from the roof of Craigie Mill showing Wilson Street with Craigie Church in the background.* BOTTOM: *Craigie Steam Laundry advertisement of 1929. (Perthshire Advertiser photograph).*

of malted bread.

The Craigie Steam Laundry operated beside the road leading from Queen Strret to Craigie Mill during the 1920s and 1930s. From the 1940s until the around late 1970s or early 1980s the premises became Mitchell's dyeing and cleaning works and are now a small housing development .

Once the flour mill ceased production, the area for a number of years became a caravan site before being developed into the contemporary retirement apartments of the aptly named Millburn Court in 1992. The old mill is a now private house but the Craigie Burn still tumbles over the waterfall and is a spectacular sight in times of heavy rain or severe frost.

Friarton Brick and Tile Works

Although slightly out of the Craigie area at Friarton, the brickworks of James L. Wood & Son are worthy of mention.

A native of Leeds, James Wood (1819-1909) came to Scotland at the time of the construction of the Scottish Central Railway and also carried out large contracts in the building of bridges in connection with the railway in Morayshire, Inverness and other parts of Scotland.

Joined later by his young son Charles (1844-1909) as James Wood & Son they supervised the installation of Perth's drainage system in 1860 and were also the sole contractors for the building of the Moncreiffe Tunnel.

Map showing the position of the Friarton Brick Works.

In the early 1860s the firm founded the Friarton Brick and Tile Works and the Moncreiffe Pottery on the lands of Friarton Farm using the whole clay found on the farmland. In 1881 a 'dugout' canoe from the Neolithic period was discovered underneath the clay at Friarton Farm.

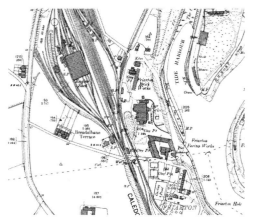

The company never fully recovered from a serious fire at the un-insured premises in 1906 and in 1909 James Wood died at the age of ninety, followed only a few weeks later by his son Charles who tragically drowned in the River Tay. These events led to the closure of the company in 1911.

The Tay Salmon Fishing Company

The salmon fishings of the River Tay have always been a source of income to the proprietors of the surrounding land as well as offering both employment and pleasure to many individuals. Net fishing on the Tay started several hundred years ago and by the mid-eighteenth century the superior quality of Tay salmon was widely recognised and had become a huge business with vast quantities of salmon being exported to several European countries including ports in the Mediterranean.

The red brick building which is situated on St Leonard`s Bridge and extends down part of St Leonard`s Bank was once the headquarters of the Tay Salmon Fishing Company which was established in 1899 by P D Malloch. The company bought up fishing rights along the river and its estuary and by bringing them under one umbrella it became one of the biggest such operations in the country.

Fishing by sweep nets on the lowers reaches of the Tay, particularly around Seggieden and Walnut Grove, was a way of life for generations and at one time provided a popular source of income for local students during their summer vacation. It came to an end in 1996 thus closing a chapter on an industry which once employed hundreds.

The late Mr David Clarke received his first wage packet from the company at age seven helping to repair nets on the banks of the Tay. This passion would see him acquire the company several decades later.

The St Leonard's Bank premises which once oversaw the storing and packing of freshly caught Tay salmon are now utilised by a number of small businesses.

John Dewar & Sons Ltd

On the fringe of Craigie, the Glover Street area between Blair Street and Graybank Road from the late nineteenth century and for much of the twentieth century was a hive of intense industrial activity. Going northwards from the Glover Street/Needless Road corner, the eastern side of Glover Street (the area now occupied by Bookers, the Leisure Pool and Dewar's Centre) was almost entirely given over to railway marshalling yards with factories and warehouses established on the western side.

TOP: *This 1950s photograph shows industrial Glover Street looking towards Craigie from the Dewar's corner. The railway station and marshalling yards are prominently featured top left and the West End bowling green at the corner of Gray Street and Needless Road can be seen in the top right corner. At the bottom left are the sheep pens of Macdonald Fraser's Mart with Rosslyn House (formerly the Perth Poorhouse and later Bertha Home) bottom right.* (Photograph courtesy of Diagio Ltd). BOTTOM: *Dewar's Corner. Once a familiar landmark at the corner of Glover Street and Glasgow Road. (Photograph from Perth & Kinross Libraries).*

When John Dewar, the son of a Perthshire crofter, built a distillery at Aberfeldy on the Pitilie Burn which had previously been the water source for an illicit distillery, little did he realise that he was to become the founder of a great whisky dynasty. In 1846, Dewar set himself up as a wine and spirit merchant in Perth and by 1870 was receiving orders from Inverness in the north to Edinburgh in the south. He was joined in the company by his two sons John Jnr and Thomas ('Tommy') and the company became known as John Dewar & Sons. John Jnr was created the first Lord Forteviot and the charismatic and entrepreneurial Tommy toured the world appointing agents in twenty-six countries and it was Tommy Dewar who later, as

Lord Dewar, gifted Kinnoull Hill to the city of Perth.

In 1887, the first London office was opened and in 1894 Dewars established their bonding, blending and bottling premises on Glasgow Road, conveniently situated for the railway marshalling yards on Glover Street. The towering red brick whisky bond was a prominent Perth landmark for many years and the company's cooperage and box factory was situated on the land bordered by Glover Street, Graybank Road and Gray Street.

Dewars remained in Glasgow Road and Glover Street until moving in 1958 to custom-built premises on a twenty six acre site at Inveralmond. The red brick bond and the distinctive clock on the Glover Street corner remained as a Perth landmark until the building of the new ice rink (appropriately named the Dewars Centre) in the late 1980s.

During the 1960s and early 1970s, the building in Glover Street was used as a cash and carry business by the Perth firm of wine and spirit merchants, D McDiarmid & Sons Ltd, who owned a number of grocery stores in the city and county and were also the producers of an excellent blended whisky called Schiehallion. Part of the premises was also used by Bands of Perth, a game-dealing business run by Tom Band and his sons.

The building later had several occupants such as the electrical company of James Scott and has also been used as a fitness centre. In 1996, when Scottish Hydro Electric re-located, Perth & Kinross Council acquired the lease of the building, by then known as The Atrium, in a £157,000 deal and later used the premises as the main council offices while their High Street premises were undergoing extensive refurbishment. The entire building was demolished in 2019 and re-built as a care home.

Thomson Craik & Co. Ltd

For many years one of the major industrial companies in Craigie was the aerated water firm of Thomson Craik & Co. Ltd, an amalgamation of two earlier companies, W B Thomson Ltd. of Blackford and John Craik & Co. of Perth.

In 1895, a Perth man, William Thomson, had acquired William Eadie's Inn at Blackford where he commissioned the building of a brewery which opened in 1897 and the following year became a limited liability company under the name of W B Thomson Ltd. Maltings were added to the brewery and the company began to manufacture aerated water but by the early 1900s had run into financial difficulties. As a result, the aerated water and bottling sides of the business were separated from the brewery with the former merging with John Craik & Co. of Perth to form Thomson Craik & Co. Ltd.

Two early Thomas Craik advertisements.

THOMSON, CRAIK & Co.
(LIMITED.)

Aerated Water Manufacturers
and Malt Liquor Merchants,.

**GLOVER STREET,
PERTH.**

At its Glover Street premises, the new firm quickly became one of the two major lemonade producers in Perth, the other being John Campbell Ltd. in nearby Fues Road. Many Perth people still have fond memories of popular TC products such as Limeade, Orangeade, Orange Crush and Cream Soda.

As well as manufacturing their own variety of aerated drinks and ginger beer they also acted as malt liquor merchants for many popular ales and stouts of that time which include familiar names such as McEwan's, Tennent's and Calder's. Indeed, it was Calder &

THOMSON CRAIK & CO.
(LIMITED)

Malt Liquor Merchants.
‑:‑

Sole Wholesale Bottling Agents for

Meux's London Stout,
Gaymer's Attleborough Cyder,
Gonilo Carlsberg Lager Beer,
Orangeboom Pilsener Lager,
Prestonpans Beer.

Wholesale Bottling Agents for

Bass in Bottle,
Barclay Perkin's London Stout,
McEwan's Ales,
Calder's Brilliant Ale,
Guinness's Stout,
Tennent's Lager Beer,
Jeffroy's Lager Beer.

Co. of Alloa who, in 1916, had acquired the former Blackford brewery firm of W B Thomson Ltd.

In 1952, Thomson Craik & Co. became a wholly owned subsidiary of the Perth brewery company of John Wright & Co. whose brewing

LEFT: *Thomas Craik lorries outside the factory in Blair Street.* RIGHT: *The Spirax binding premises. (Photograph from Parth & Kinross Libraries).*

roots in Perth dated back to 1786 when William Wright, the uncle of John Wright, formed the Perth Brewing Company. In 1961, Wright's were acquired by the Usher Vaux brewing company and later by Britvic Soft Drinks Ltd. (formerly the British Vitamin Products Company) who had become part of the Allied Breweries Group in 1968.

Manufacturing continued at the Glover Street factory until its closure in 1990 when the premises were demolished and rebuilt as the Glover Court flatted housing complex. A pharmacy and a medical practice are also now part of the once-thriving lemonade works.

Spirax Binding (Scotland) Ltd

In 1943, William Munro of the Munro Press (publishers at that time of the *Perthshire Advertiser*, *Scottish Field* and *Farming News*) founded a company called Spirax Binding to bind their *Scottish Field* calendars. As the company rapidly developed, they moved their premises in the early 1950s from the city's Watergate to a Grade B listed Art Nouveau building in Craigie at the corner of Glover Street and Blair Street. This brick building which was built in 1903 as John McArthur's Bobbin Factory was used as a factory in the 1920s and 1930s by a company of cabinet makers and saw temporary use as a fire station during World War II.

In their new premises and now under the ownership of the Milne family, Spirax established itself as major players in the UK print binding and finishing industry and at one time employed one hundred staff. In 1980, the firm moved to custom built facilities at Inveralmond but unfortunately, due to rising costs and the introduction of cheaper foreign prices, they reluctantly had to cease trading in 2008 with the loss of thirty seven jobs.

After the Spirax move to Inveralmond, the Glover Street site was used as print-works by two long established Perth printing firms – firstly Milne,Tannahill & Methven Limited followed by Woods of Perth (Printers) Limited. Other sections of the factory premises have been used at different times by a joinery firm, an antique warehouse and a carpet company.

By the 1980s, the trend was for local industries to move out of the city and residential areas to industrial parks situated on what had previously been 'green field' sites. By the time the livestock mart left

Craigie in 1992, the only remaining industry in the district was on the southern side of Glenearn Road (on the old grounds of Craigie Haugh) and at Friarton and the harbour area where a number of businesses, warehouses and industrial units had already become firmly established and continue to flourish

It was at Cherrybank, the original quiet weaving hamlet of the nineteenth century, that major change was to develop and which we shall read about in a later chapter.

EDUCATION AND RELIGION

This nation must rank among the most enlightened in the universe.
Education, religion and literature have made Scotland something
beyond compare.

Charles de Remusat, (1797-1875)

Scotland has long enjoyed an international reputation as being one of the best-educated countries. The foundation for this reputation was laid in the seventeenth century and was the result of Calvinist emphasis on reading the bible. Early educational establishments were run by the Church and were open to all boys and girls regardless of social status. The openness of the Scottish system ran all the way from the schoolroom to the university and a talented working class boy through intelligence and hard work and the utilising of a generous bursary system could gain a university education.

Religion in Scotland has been one of the defining characteristics of national identity. The Union of 1707 provided for a separate religious system to that of England and, until recently, Presbyterianism was used to define what it means to be Scottish. This inevitably created divisions within society, the most obvious being that between Catholics and Protestants.

We have already described the area's early religious background but with the coming of the railway and subsequent development, both church and school were soon to become an integral and harmonious part of life in Craigie and Cherrybank.

School Days

Oor schule's the best schule,
It's made o' stanes and plaster;
The only thing that's wrang wi' it,
Is the bauldy heided master.

(old street rhyme)

EDUCATION AND RELIGION

The Craigie Industrial School, properly known as the Perth Ladies' House of Refuge for Destitute Girls, was situated at Craigie House on Craigie Knowes Road on what is believed to have been the site of the old castle of Craigie and original home of the Ross family. The industrial school movement of nineteenth century Britain focused on orphans and neglected or abused children and provided them with residential accommodation, food, education, religious instruction and training for work.

The school appears to have been a sister institution of an industrial school for boys situated at Fechney in Perth's Dovecoteland area. Under the supervision of a matron it aimed to provide an elementary education and religious instruction to neglected young girls aged between ten and fourteen although these ages were later lowered. Typical of the intake was a girl of twelve whose father had died and whose alcoholic mother had forced the girl into thieving.

According to the *Perth Post Office Directory* of 1854, the school was instituted in 1843 with The Most Noble the Marchioness of Breadalbane as the Patroness and The Hon. Mrs Arthur Kinnaird as President. The Vice Presidents were Mrs Stewart Sandeman of Bonskeid; Mrs General Lindsay of Earlybank House, Craigie; Mrs Stuart of Annat; and Mrs Thomson of Balgowan.

The original school was situated in Methven Street before moving to a location at the southern end of Tay Street but when the railway was brought across the river in the early 1850s, it was necessary to relocate the school to Craigie. The new refuge consisted of four bedrooms, classrooms for basic education and workrooms for acquiring maternal skills and those necessary for life as a housemaid.

The following article from *The Perthshire Courier* of 8th June 1854 gives some idea of the girls' lifestyle:

> The girls of this institution, by the benevolence of a few friends, enjoyed a delightful trip to Bridge of Allan on Her Majesty's Birthday. They visited Major Henderson's park where they had a pleasant hour's amusement, then went to the mill-house where they delighted the company by singing some of their best hymns and after rambling on the hill behind the mill, gathering wild flowers, they adjourned to the residence of our respected townsman, Baillie Pullar of Keirfield, who kindly supplied them with an excellent dinner and entertained them by showing them the process of

bleaching the cloth they so often stitch. After spending a happy afternoon at his hospitable mansion, they returned home at seven pm delighted with their trip.

They have lately had a visit at the Refuge of their old friend Mr Maiben, who gave the Misses Lowe a large order for stockings for the boys at his institution at Whitechapel, London. We would take the opportunity of stating, that should anyone be desirous of benefiting the Refuge, they can effectually do so, by order for knitting, crotchet work, or plain sewing.

In 1924 it was reported in the *Perthshire Advertiser* that: the property in High Craigie forming the Perth Ladies' House of Refuge for Destitute Girls, comprising the buildings and garden ground extending to one and a quarter acres, were offered for sale at a price of £2500 but no offers were forthcoming.

Following the school's closure in 1924, the remaining girls were transferred to Wellshill Industrial School which had been built next to the Fechney School for Boys which also closed in 1924. Despite the closures, the original trusts continued and in 1936 were amalgamated into the Perth Homes Trust. In 1950, the trust purchased Balnacraig in Barnhill's Fairmount Road and the Wellshill girls took up residence there.

During World War II, and for a number of years afterwards, the premises saw military use as the headquarters of the Highland Division followed by civilian use by the Civil Defence. During the 1960s and early 1970s it was used as offices for the Meat and Livestock Commission. It is now the Craigieknowes Care Home.

Craigie School

Craigie School opened in August 1884 and prior to that date the need for a school in that area of the city had been most evident. Since the opening of Perth Railway Terminus in 1846 there had been a formation of streets with tenements and terraced houses west of the Terminus. Many of these houses accommodated railway workers and their families and the children of these families required schooling.

In these days, the school was simply known as Western District Public School with other city schools called Central District,

Southern District and Northern District. When Western District School opened it was merely continuing an educational tradition which had already spanned half a century. By the decision of the Perth School Board, the staff of the National School in Watergate, Perth, transferred to the newly built school in Craigie to receive and instruct scholars from five to fourteen years of age.

Craigie School (then Western District School) in the early 1900s looking down Abbot Street towards Craigie Cross and St Leonard's Bridge. The Co-operative Buildings are in the centre of the photograph. (Photograph from Perth & Kinross Libraries).

The building was constructed with Huntingtower sandstone with an interesting octagonal cookery and laundry room of Errol brick added in 1929. The first instalment of central heating was also completed in 1929 but surprisingly electric lighting was only installed in 1949 after the World War II. In 1942, the railings in Young Street were sacrificed for the war effort but those that remain now in Abbot Street are the original. New toilets and cloakrooms were added in 1965 and a major structural alteration was made in 1972 with a new classroom block of three rooms which allowed three older classrooms on the east wing of the school to be formed into a general purpose room and kitchen area. Further alterations took place in 1994/95 when the school was totally refurbished.

The first headmaster of the school was Mr William Barclay who, along with his staff, had transferred from the Watergate School. He held this position until 1911 when he was succeeded by Mr John Henderson (1911-1922). Like Mr Barclay and Mr Henderson, headmasters of the school at that time tended to be fairly long serving, notably Mr Charles A Lunan (1930-1950) and Mr Daniel Cameron (1950-1963).

The Craigie School playing field.

When the school opened in 1884 an attendance of one hundred pupils is

—93—

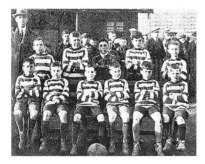

TOP: *The Craigie football team who were league and cup champions in 1920. The teacher on the left is Mr J Fairweather who later became headmaster of Cherrybank School. (Perthshire Advertiser photograph).*

MIDDLE: *As part of the war effort in 1940, the girls of Western District (Craigie) School were active in the knitting of blankets for minesweepers. Left to right: May MacDonald (140 squares); Margaret Drummond (100 squares); Sheena MacDonald (100 squares). One hundred squares made a complete blanket. (Perthshire Advertiser photograph).*

BOTTOM: *First day at school! Mabel Dochard, Gordon Duncan, Jean Anderson, Gordon Mathewson and Mhoira Calder leaving their Evelyn Terrace homes in 1947 for their first day at Western District (Craigie) School). (Perthshire Advertiser photograph, courtesy of Mhoira White).*

recorded but by November of that year the school roll had increased to one hundred and fifty eight boys and one hundred and thirty nine girls under the supervision of six members of staff. By 1885 the number of pupils had increased to three hundred and eighty seven and an extra teacher was employed at a salary of £70 per annum. The now established school was in a developing area with houses and tenements being erected and the nearby cattle mart opening in 1886. In that year too, the School Board approved an increase in salary to £200 per annum for the headmaster. By 1922 the school roll was four hundred and forty one and in 1932 it was recorded as five hundred and forty eight with the octagonal cookery room being utilised as a classroom. In that year also, a frequent visitor to the school and generous benefactor, Sir Francis Norie Miller the chairman of the General Accident Assurance Corporation and chairman of the Perth School Board, made a gift of the ground north of the school for use as a playing field and, for thirty athletes, a drinking fountain was installed at the Young Street end.

The school survived the dark and tragic days of two World Wars. Little is mentioned in the school log book of World War I until March 1915 when the school closed for an afternoon to collect funds for the Perthshire Motor Ambulance Car. In December of that year there was a request by the military authorities for the occupation of the school buildings by a garrison

'Over the top' in the obstacle race at the Craigie School sports day in 1950. The author is the boy on the left with Ian McGlashan on the right. The interested spectator is headmaster Mr C A Lunan. (Perthshire Advertiser photograph).

Chaired with the Norie Miller Cup is Eric Fair, captain of the Craigie School football team which defeated St Ninian's 3-0 in Perth Schoolboys' final at Muirton Park in 1953. Also on show is another Craigie trophy, the league championship shield which is being held by Robert Hall. (Perthshire Advertiser photograph).

of artillery who were stabling their horses in the nearby mart. As a result, arrangements were made for the pupils of Western District and Southern District schools to meet mornings and afternoons alternately

LEFT: *A Craigie School football team of 1957. Back row (left to right): David Stewart, Randy Watt, Ian Watson, Brian Wilson, Sandy Leslie, Stewart Bousie. Front row (left to right): Tom Reddie, Tom Marshall, Kenny Marshall, Drew White, Russell Soppil. (Perthshire Advertiser photograph).* RIGHT: *The 1964 Craigie School cricket team that defeated Kinnoull School in the final of the Perth Schools Cricket Competition for the P.A Cup. The captain, James Muir, is holding the trophy. (Perthshire Advertiser photograph).*

every fortnight using Southern District School. The roll was then five hundred and twenty three and the younger infants went to St Stephens Church Hall in Paradise Place. The pupils returned to their own school the following April.

With the outbreak of the World War II, the school enrolled sixty five evacuees from Glasgow who were billeted in Viewlands House. School routines changed, gas mask drill became a regular feature and three air raid shelters were installed in the school playground, each capable of accommodating fifty pupils and the wide

TOP: *Craigie School class 1948.* BOTTOM: *Craigie School class 1953.*

pend of the Co-operative Buildings at the corner of Abbot Street and Raeburn Place was fitted out as a fourth shelter. Despite the outbreak of war, the telephone was installed in the school in 1940 and that same year 'the boys' gate' with its dangerous steps and pit was put out of commission. There was also consideration of the girls' gate and a new gate on the corner of Young Street and Abbot Street was introduced.

TOP: *Craigie School class 1965*. BOTTOM: *Craigie School class 1978*.

When war ceased, educational progress and change continued. The Glover Street Social Committee gave £10 as the first instalment towards a wireless set and speakers for radio lessons in the school. These partially offset the withdrawal of specialist teachers from primary schools in 1947 when the school leaving age was raised and these teachers were required in secondary schools.

In these post-war years many new houses were built in the Craigie area causing a large increase in the school roll. As a result, Craigie Church Hall was rented to accommodate the needlework class. School lunches continued to be served in Craigie Hall in Priory Place and it is recorded that during the war, in September 1942, the price of school dinners was raised from 2d. to 4d. resulting in feelings of exasperation and despair!

A Parent-Teacher Association was formed in 1951 which, as well as forging a closer link between school and parents, aided school activities and projects to the greater benefit of the children.

In the Coronation Year of 1953, thirty two trees and shrubs were planted in the ground facing Raeburn Place to commemorate the occasion. It was in that year also that the name of the school was changed from Western District to Craigie School and a school badge was designed by the headmaster, Mr Daniel Cameron, to incorporate the historical associations of the area.

Western District was the primary school for Jessie Jordan who lived in Friar Street and was convicted of running a German spy ring from her Dundee hairdressing salon during World War II. Fortunately, many other former pupils have gone on to more successful and distinguished careers in life including the popular Scottish entertainer, the late Andy Stewart, who was a pupil during the 1940s when his family lived in Rose Crescent before moving to Arbroath.

Cherrybank School

The original Cherrybank School dates back to before 1862 and was founded by a pioneer educational body in the city, The Cherrybank, Burghmuir, Pitheavlis and Upper and Lower Craigie School Society. The School Board minutes of 30th October 1863 recorded the school being in a most ruinous condition and such was the condition of the building that the headmaster told a school board meeting that unless a new school and schoolhouse were ready by Whitsunday Term, he could no longer remain teacher at the school.

The cost of re-building the school was £686 and the society received a government grant of £207.17/6d. Even allowing for monies raised by the society, a considerable deficit remained and the scheme was in danger of being abandoned until a Miss Jane Ross made up the difference of around £300. The school and schoolhouse

LEFT: *Cherrybank Scholl in 1928. (Perthshire Advertiser photograph).* RIGHT: *Pupils from Cherrybank School who represented their alma mater in the Borders Challenge Cup for Scots Folk Song in 1924. (Perthshire Advertiser photograph).*

were completed by 1865 and the school board assumed responsibility in 1873.

The generous benefactor, Miss Jane Ross, lived at Oakbank House (later Cleeve) with her sister and three servants. They were descended from the Ross family of Craigie mentioned in an earlier chapter and according to the 1871 census would have been sixty three years old and her sister sixty five. Additional land for the new school was gifted by the ninth Lord Elibank of Pitheavlis Castle.

Sir Francis Norie-Miller of the General Accident Insurance Company who was the chairman of the Perth School Board during and after World War I took a special interest in the affairs of the school. The school roll of honour listed sixty five former boy pupils serving during that war and to each Sir Francis donated a silver commemorative medallion.

The school, which was built by James Ritchie, consisted of three separate buildings linked by steep paths. It discontinued as a primary school in 1937 with the juniors and seniors transferred to Western District School (now Craigie) and Caledonian Road School. The infant class continued at Cherrybank under their teacher Miss Smith.

Cherrybank School pupils at their 1957 Christmas party. (Perthshire Advertiser photograph).

Cherrybank School class from around 1925. (Perthshire Advertiser photograph).

In 1930, under headmaster Mr James Mackie (right) and Miss Margaret Thomson (left) the Cherrybank School choir secured second place in Scots Folk Songs (A Class). (Perthshire Advertiser photograph).

In 1959, the school closed as such and was annexed by the Junior Academy before operating as a local authority school catering for children with special educational needs. Cherrybank finally amalgamated with the Glebe School, Scone and in 2007 work commenced in the grounds of Perth Academy on the construction of a new campus, Fairview School.

Over the years St Leonard`s Bank in Craigie has been the home of two schools – The Misses Hindmarch`s Academy during the nineteenth century and later, from 1927, The Bernard Holt School.

The Bernard Holt School at Nos. 5 and 6 St Leonard`s Bank was a private preparatory school which catered for boys from the ages of four until around fourteen, most of them as day pupils although there were some boarders. In their distinctive red blazers the boys of the Holt School were a familiar sight in Perth until the late 1940s.

In 1948 the school moved from Perth to Jardine Hall at Lockerbie before moving again in 1963 to Whittingehame House in East Lothian – the former home of A J Balfour, Prime Minister from 1902 to 1905.

During the 1940s the headmaster was a Mr Witheroe who retained

Boys of the Bernard Holt School pictured before a cricket match on the South Inch in 1940 against Newstead School, Doune. (Perthshire Advertiser photograph).

this post at both Jardine Hall and Whittingehame House before retiring in 1964. He was succeeded by Lawrence Read, a former Craigie boy from Northbank House, who had attended the school in St Leonard's Bank as a day pupil during the mid-1940s and held the position of headmaster at Whittingehame House until the closure of the Holt School in 1980.

Perth Academy and Perth High School

Close to Cherrybank in the Viewlands and Oakbank areas are the six-year comprehensive secondary schools of Perth Academy and Perth High School.

The name of Perth Academy first appears in 1542 when it was founded by the town council making it one of the oldest schools in Scotland and up until the 1800s was one of a variety of small institutions in Perth specalising in particular fields of education. From 1807 these institutions were housed in a new building in Rose Terrace and known as public seminaries. In 1892, under the terms of the 1878 Education Act, control of the schools was transferred from the town council to a newly created school board and the institution was officially named Perth Academy.

In 1915 the

RIGHT: *Perth Academy and Perth Junior Academy shortly after the opening in 1932. (Perthshire Advertiser photograph).* BELOW: *Inch View Primary and Nursery School.*

Academy amalgamated with Sharp's Institution in the city`s North Methven Street. Perth Academy moved to the site at Viewlands in 1932 when a fee-paying Junior Academy was established for primary school pupils but later became the present Viewlands Primary School. Prior to 1968, Perth Academy was a selective senior secondary school but, along with Perth High School, became fully comprehensive in 1971.

Perth High School was established at Gowans Terrace in the Muirton district in 1950 in a post-war prefabricated building – a type of structure which had not been previously used for a large school in Scotland. The school re-located to its present situation on Oakbank Road in 1969 two years after the opening of the adjacent Oakbank Primary School.

Situated on Glenearn Road, Inch View Primary and Nursery School opened in 2009 and with the closure of the long established Caledonian Road School caters for the primary school children of the city centre along with some from the Craigie area.

This non-denominational school is part of the Glenearn Community Campus and its modern classrooms and the state-of-the-art facilities which include a fully equipped PE room, a library and a dining room ensure a happy, safe and stimulating environment which encourages motivation for learning and growth both intellectually and emotionally. There are fifteen classes for Primary 1 to Primary 7 pupils along with a large nursery and two special provision classes.

The school continues to grow and in November 2020 had a roll of three hundred and sixty pupils.

Craigie and Moncreiffe Church

> When I gang tae the kirk on Sunday,
> Mony's the bonnie lass I see;
> Sittin' by her faither's side
> And winkin' o'er the pews at me.

(From the bothy ballad: 'The Barnyards o'Delgaty')

The origins of Craigie Church go as far back as 1787 when a small chapel called the Chapel of Ease was erected by the Church of

Scotland as a Gaelic chapel in Perth's Canal Street. In 1834 it became known as St Stephen's Parish Church and in 1885 amalgamated with St Andrew's Parish Church in Atholl Street. In 1887 the Canal Street chapel was sold ending one hundred years of worship in the premises and the Perth Presbytery decided to use the money realised from

Craigie Church from Abbot Street.

the sale of the building to build a new St Stephen's in the growing suburb of Craigie.

The memorial stone of the new church was laid on 13th October 1894 by William Whitelaw the Member of Parliament for Perth and the first service was held on 12th December 1895, the officiating clergyman being the Rev Donald McLeod DD. The new Victorian Gothic-style church was built of red sandstone quarried in Dumfriesshire at a total cost of £3,883.19.1d. The architects were Messrs J & G Young and the builders were Fraser & Morton. Mr Fraser's home was in what was later to become the church manse at 46 Abbot Street and Mr Morton's home was in the other half of the villa.

The first minister of the church, the Reverend Robert Oswald BD was appointed in July 1896 at a salary of £80 per annum and the congregation at that time numbered sixty nine. By the end of 1897 the congregation had increased to around one hundred and fifty.

In 1908, a Vestry and Session House were added to the church and a piano was gifted by the children of the Sunday School. The new Session House was soon regularly used by the Work Party,

TOP: *Craigie Church Kirk Session in 1994. The minister (front centre) is the Reverend John Rankin BD.* BOTTOM: *The laying of the memorial stone in 1894. (Photographs courtesy of Craigie Church).*

LEFT: *The Reverend J Roy H Paterson who was minister of Craigie Church from 1955 to 1964. (Perthshire Advertiser photograph).* RIGHT: *The Reverend J Alan C Mathers, the first minister of Moncreiffe Church. (Perthshire Advertiser photograph).*

the Young Men's Guild, the Band of Hope, the Sunday School and the Choir. The church magazine of December 1908, in relating these events, stated that 'room left to add a hall which will run at right angles the present building' but another sixty years were to pass before the hall, which blends in well with the original building, was added in 1970.

In 1903 an anonymous donor gifted a bell which was housed in a special belfry. The bell and belfry were moved when the vestry and session house were added in 1908 and a new belfry built in 1925. In 1970 the belfry was demolished to make way for the new church hall and the bell mounted on a plinth in the church grounds. The bell is inscribed: 'St Stephen's Parish Church – To the glory of God and in memory of a dear sister Frances Crombie this bell is given – O come let us worship – 1903.'

In June 1929, at the time of the Union of the Churches, the name of the church was changed from St Stephen's to Craigie and the first meeting of the Kirk Session of Craigie Parish Church was held on 20th October 1929.

The longest serving minister of Craigie Church was the Reverend John Strathern MA who held that position from September 1920 until his death in August 1954. The present communion table was installed in his memory. At the time of Mr Strathern's death, the church membership numbered four hundred and twenty but by the time Mr Strathern's successor, the Reverend J Roy H Paterson left in 1964 to become minister of Cairns Church, Milngavie, this number had risen to around seven hundred and fifty. Another long serving minister, the Reverend Malcolm N Henry, BD, succeeded Mr Paterson and was minister for twenty two years from 1965 to 1987.

EDUCATION AND RELIGION

By the end of the twentieth century, church congregations were in decline nationally and in order to stay afloat linked congregations had become commonplace. Craigie was not to escape amalgamation and on 22ⁿᵈ July 2009 a Service of Union was held in Moncreiffe Church to finalise the Union of Craigie and Moncreiffe Churches. Although both Craigie Church and Moncreiffe Church continued to have their separate Sunday morning services, the union meant that all business relating to both churches now became the responsibility of the Kirk Session of the united churches.

At the end of the World War II, Scotland witnessed a massive housing construction drive resulting in large-scale population migration with almost one and a half million people re-located from crowded inner city areas to new towns and housing estates. The Church of Scotland viewed this as a challenge to its role as a national church and as an opportunity for church renewal. Known as the Church Extension Movement, the project displayed an energy and imagination during these post-war years in launching a programme of church building in these new towns and housing estates. By the late 1940s, Perth had become very much a part of this scheme due to the growing areas of Moncreiffe, Letham, Tulloch and Muirton.

The first of these new churches in Perth was designated for the Moncreiffe housing estate and the foundation stone for this new £13,000 hall/church in Glenbruar Crescent was laid on 26ᵗʰ July 1950 by Lord Provost Sir John Ure Primrose. That same year, Perth Presbytery gave their formal approval for the appointment of the Reverend J A C Mathers, assistant at the church extension charge of St. James' (Pollok) Parish Church in Glasgow to become minister of the new church and he was ordained and inducted to the charge in St Leonard's-in-the-Fields

TOP: *The original Moncreiffe Church in 1962. (Photograph courtesy of Neal Mathers).* BOTTOM: *In this 1958 photograph, the Reverend R Murray Leishman (right) is welcomed as minister of Moncreiffe Church by the Reverend T B Stewart Thomson the Moderator of Perth Presbytery. Centre is the Reverend Hector Houston, Rhynd. (Perthshire Advertiser photograph).*

Church on December 12th, 1950.

One month earlier, on 14th November, 1950, a Kirk Session was appointed to Moncreiffe consisting of seven elders, four drawn from the supervising congregation (St. Leonard's-in-the-Fields), and three nominated by the Presbytery. The four from St. Leonard's were Messrs William Auld, Kenneth MacAlpine, Angus Fairweather, and Samuel Gibson. The Presbytery appointed Major D C Heron Watson, governor of Perth prison; Mr James A Gibb, whose home faced the new hall-church, and Mr David Drummond. As the new minister was due to be married on 3rd April 1950, a church manse was purchased at 77 Needless Road.

A daunting task faced the about to be married thirty-year-old minister who had seen war service in Palestine with the Royal Air Force as he prepared to establish a church which still had no congregation. The new church was still under construction but Reverend Mathers quickly made plans to gather a congregation using Craigie Hall in Priory Place and did what he always did well, visited within the community. He placed an advertisement in the local paper that advertised the new hall church and, as there was no existing congregation, the new minister placed the following advertisement in the *Perthshire Advertiser*:

Congregation Wanted! Moncreiffe Hall Church. Tomorrow (Sunday). Wanted – 'An Active Congregation'. Service in Craigie Hall, 11am. Sunday School at 2pm. Please make every effort to be present and meet your minister Reverend J A C Mathers. Women's Guild meets on Thursday at 7.30pm.

Two weeks later the same newspaper reported:

Two Sundays have been sufficient to show that there is a bright future for Perth's new church at Moncreiffe. Until his church is ready, the new 'minister of the glens', Rev J A C Mathers, is conducting his forenoon service and Sunday school in the afternoon at Craigie Hall. On Sunday the attendance at the service increased from thirty two to thirty five and the Sunday School figure took a leap forward from forty to sixty.

A later article reported:

The energetic young minister of Perth's newest parish of Moncreiffe and Friarton is already reaping the benefits of his door to door canvassing. Last Sunday, in his temporary church at Craigie Hall, he had ninety seven adults for the morning service and one hundred and fifty kiddies for afternoon Sunday School. The kirk session of Trinity Church, Perth has decided to present the new church with a minister's chair formerly used by the East Church which is part of the amalgamated Trinity and some communion plate which was used in the East Church. The Reverend J A C Mathers has been favourably impressed by the welcome accorded to him by the residents of 'the Glens'. He has now visited over fifty households in this new church extension parish, and has been well received everywhere. Already there are signs that a vital congregation is being built up. The Sunday School has made a successful start and three parishioners have volunteered to be Sunday School teachers. Eight ladies attended the inaugural meeting of the Moncreiffe Women's Guild and other parish organisations will get under way between now and the opening date of the hall church.

The new hall/church in Glenbruar Crescent was dedicated on 8th December 1951 and was an immediate success with its design enabling it to be used both for church services and for the week-night meetings of the various organisations which included newly-formed Boys' Brigade and Girl Guide Companies.

In 1957, the Reverend Mathers accepted a call to become minister of St George's and Trinity Church in Montrose and was replaced by another young and energetic minister, the Reverend R Murray Leishman. Shortly after the Reverend Leishman's marriage in 1962 to the Hon Marista Reith (daughter of Lord Reith, the former Governor General of the BBC) the church manse was moved from Needless Road to Sannox in Craigie Road.

Moncreiffe Church has seen several changes during its relatively short existence, first being linked with Craigend Church following the demolition of that church due to the construction of the M90 motorway. The Reverend Hector Houston who was the minister of nearby Rhynd Church since the late 1950s also ministered at Moncreiffe from 1974 until 1990 making him Moncreiffe's longest serving minister. In 2001 the congregation of Rhynd Church joined with Moncreiffe when their building finally closed.

The present day church building was built in 1977 and is described as 'a beautiful, bright, modern sanctuary capable of seating over two hundred worshippers.'

July 2009 saw Moncreiffe becoming united with Craigie Parish Church to form Craigie and Moncreiffe Church of Scotland. The Reverend Carolann Erskine was ordained and inducted as minister of the united charge on 9th December 2009, almost fifty nine years to the day that the Reverend J A C Mathers was first ordained and inducted to Moncreiffe.

St Magdalene's Church

For many years the Catholic community of Perth was well served by St. John the Baptist's Church in Melville Street and by St. Mary's on the slopes of Kinnoull which opened as a Redemptorist Monastery in 1869. However, after World War II, it became apparent to Monsignor Coogan, the parish priest at St. John's, that the growing number of parishioners could not all be accommodated at the city church. The building of housing estates at Moncreiffe, Letham and Tulloch had taken many Catholics away from the proximity of their parish church in the centre of Perth.

TOP: *St Mary Magdalene's Church.* BOTTOM: *A service at St Mary Magdalene's Church. (Photograph courtesy of St Mary Magdalene's Church).*

To cater for them, it was decided that two new churches would be built in Perth with the Edinburgh architect Peter Whitson, who had designed the Cistercian Monastery at Nunraw in East Lothian, the first monastery built in Scotland since the Reformation, engaged to design them both. Our Lady of Lourdes was to become an independent parish serving the western area of Perth including Letham and Tulloch while St Mary Magdalene's was built at Glenearn Road in Craigie. Both churches were built simultaneously and opened within a few weeks of each other in 1959.

Initially built as a chapel of ease, St Mary Magdalene's soon became a parish in its own right serving an area to the south of Perth which extends to Aberdalgie, Abernethy, Bridge of Earn, Dron, Dunbarney, Forgandenny, Forteviot, Glenfarg and Kintillo.

Interesting features of the church are a crucifix by Benno Schotz and a window by the Perthshire artist William Wilson who, from 1937, became the leading exponent of contemporary stained glass in the United Kingdom. Among Wilson's other notable works is the Black Watch Memorial Window in St John's Kirk in Perth which was unveiled by the late Queen Mother in 1955.

For twelve years from 1992, the parish priest at St Mary Magdalene's was Monsignor Charles Hendry (1933-2020) who was the assistant priest at St John the Baptist's in Perth when the new church in Craigie was built. An extremely popular figure in the city, Monsignor Hendry served as a priest in Perth for forty-five years until his death in 2021.

St Mary Magdalene's is part of the Roman Catholic Diocese of Dunkeld which is believed to have been constituted in the mid ninth century. Dunkeld is a suffragan see of the Archdiocese of St Andrews and Edinburgh and includes the counties of Perth, Angus, Clackmannan, Kinross and North Fife – an area served by thirty five priests and four deacons. The diocese cathedral is dedicated to St Andrew and is now situated in Dundee, rather than Dunkeld, as Dundee is the residence of the majority of Catholics in the diocese.

The Craigie Reformed Baptist Church

For a few years the Craigie Reformed Baptist church, a community of bible-believing Christians held their worship services in a converted house at 34 Glover Street.

Part of a Baptist organisation which has been serving the city of Perth for over fifty years, they now hold their Sunday services in the nearby Moncreiffe area at the Gleneagles Day Opportunities Centre in Gleneagles Road.

The Craigie Reformed Baptist Church when it was located at 34 Glover Street.

The Reformed Baptist Church receives a light-hearted mention in the book *An Innocent in Scotland* by the Canadian author David W. McFadden. Describing a Sunday morning in Perth's city centre, he writes:

> A small yellow bus goes by, taking people to the Reformed Baptist Church, a miserable face in each window. They look as if they're suffering from too much moral superiority. Right in front of a bakery shop on High Street there's a man cheekily putting his hand all the way up his girlfriend's skirt, and on a Sunday morning too. He also seems to be probing her ear with the tip of his twitching tongue. Maybe the Reformed Baptists looked so miserable because their eyes had offended them as they passed by these horny devils.

TRANSPORT, TRAFFIC AND FLYING CIRCUSES

Noo I've got a situation, and it suits me up to date;
I'm wi' the Corporation - Jings aye, but they are great!
I'm drivin' yin o' thae electric trams that noo days rin –
Frae morn tae nicht, when a'thing's richt, I'm as happy as a King!
Oh I used tae like a smoke o' the pipe, but noo I'm on big cigars
Since I became a driver on the electric cars.

(Old Glasgow street song)

Tramcars and Buses

Whilst one does not readily associate Craigie and Cherrybank with tramcars, they once had a proud history in Perth. On 17th September 1895, the Perth and District Tramways Company officially opened a line from the rapidly expanding village of Scone to Glasgow Road in Perth. The trams were drawn by pairs of horses, the service ran at half-hour intervals and the fare for the complete journey from Rose Crescent to Scone was threepence. The frequency of the service was soon increased to once every twenty minutes and in 1898 new tracks were constructed which extended the service to Priory Place in Craigie (via King Street and St Leonard's Bank) and to Cherrybank from Rose Crescent. In 1910 the Craigie terminus was

TOP: *Horse-drawn trams at Cherrybank.*
BOTTOM: *Priory Place. c1898. (Photographs from Perth and Kinross Libraries).*

Perth Tramways: from Glasgow Road to Scone and from Priory Place to Dunkeld Road.

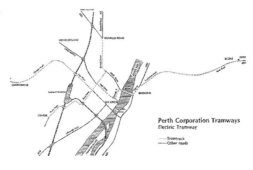

Perth Corporation Tramways
Electric Tramway

moved a few yards to Windsor Terrace to avoid congestion at the junction of Priory Place and Queen Street.

Although the horse-drawn trams gave a satisfactory service, there was soon talk of electrifying the network. The Town Council had already bought out the original company and steps were taken in 1904 to purchase twelve new electric tram cars, to build a power station at the Shore and to proceed with new track and overhead cables.

On 31st October 1905, the first of the new electric trams ran from the High Street to the Scone depot carrying members of the Town Council and their guests. In the evening, one of the trams ran with the corporation band giving selections from the upper deck. The Perth trams were the smallest in the country and ran on single tracks with passing loops at intervals. However, despite the high hopes of the Council, the new service never ran at a profit and although various measures were taken to increase profitability, none had the desired

Low car number 11 turning into Priory Place at Craigie Cross having successfully negotiated the climb up St Leonard's Bank and the crossing of St Leonard's Bridge. (Photograph from Perth & Kinross Libraries).

TOP: *Priory Place, the terminus for the Crsaigie tram in 1906. Tramcars ran from the High Street to Craigie every twelve minutes.* BOTTOM: *In 1910 the terminus for the Craigie tram was moved one hundred yards to the end of Windsor Terrace. (Photographs from Perth & Kinross Libraries).*

effect.

During World War I, the maintenance of the track was largely neglected and by 1919 the Council was faced with the decision to spend a considerable amount of money on new equipment or to phase out the trams in favour of buses. To some extent the Corporation's hands were tied by an order passed in Parliament in 1908 which gave the Corporation 'power to run omnibuses within the Burgh and also in connection with the tramways beyond the Burgh for a distance not exceeding three miles from any part of the tramway'.

In 1927, a private company, the Perth General Omnibus Company was formed and, with no prior warning, commenced operating with four vehicles in direct competition with the Corporation-owned trams on the Scone to Cherrybank route on Monday, 7th November – the same day that at a Council meeting to decide the future of the trams it was resolved to effect a gradual changeover to buses. By the end of the month the Perth Corporation had purchased six Thorneycroft buses and this was to see the start of a 'bus war' with both the Corporation and then the rival firm introducing new routes such as from the Cross to Darnhall Drive.

Faced with this bewildering choice of vehicles the public deserted the trams and after two weeks the tram takings had dropped by over £90 per week. However, to enable the Council to keep within the aforementioned 1908 Act, a skeleton tram service was provided until a new order was promoted to allow the Corporation to run buses in all locations. By the end of 1928 only two tramcars were still in service.

They made one or two daily trips over the system rarely carrying any passengers and finally, on 19th January 1929, with no fanfares and very little interest, the last car made its last journey in Perth bringing to an end the era of the Perth tramcars.

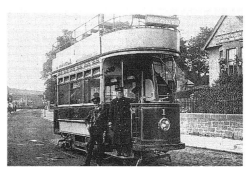

By the summer of 1928, the Perth Corporation were running buses from Scone to Cherrybank every ten minutes; the Cross to Craigie and to Darnhall Drive at a twenty minute frequency which gave a ten minute service to Craigie Post Office. The predatory tactics of the Perth General Omnibus Company had continued with the rival firm duplicating routes and offering penny fares but this came to an end with a Corporation takeover in

TOP: *Number 1 tramcar at Charrybank.* BOTTOM: *The number 9 tramcar at Cherrybank. The Scone to Cherrybank tram ran every ten minutes.*

1929. In 1933 four double-decker buses (two Thorneycrofts and two Crossleys) were introduced on the Scone to Cherrybank route.

In April 1934, the Corporation was approached by Walter Alexander & Company of Camelon near Falkirk with a view to taking over the running of the Perth bus services and the offer was accepted.

Amongst the Perth area bus services transferred to Alexander`s were: Cherrybank (Oakbank Road) and Scone (Mansfield Road or Highfield Road); High Street (The Cross) and Craigie; Darnhall Drive and Hillyland or Tulloch Terrace; Darnhall Drive and Claremont Place; Fitzroy Terrace and High Craigie. In February 1938, despite a five hundred signature petition, the Craigie route was altered from following the old tram route to operate from King Edward Street, South Street, Scott Street and Kings Place.

The author's father with the last tram from Charrybank to Scone.

In the post-World War II years, with

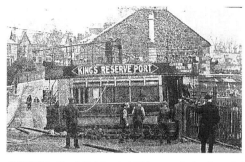

ABOVE: *On 31ˢᵗ March 1929, one of the discarded trams ws moved from the rails at the Craigie terminus to the Corporation Works Yard at Craigie Haugh. The burgh surveyor, Mr T McLaren, is seen supervising the opeation.* RIGHT: *One of the last of the old Perth tramcars was used as a shelter for bus passengers waiting at St Leonard's Bridge. This tramcar was gifted to the town by ex-Bailie J K Taylor, who owned the Craigie Post Office. (Perthshire Advertiser photographs).*

the growth of the Moncreiffe housing estate, Craigie was served by two routes, one being from Hunter Crescent at Tulloch to Darnhall with a terminus at Glenlochay Road and the other from Muirton to Moncreiffe at

TOP: *A 32-seat Thorncroft UB.* BOTTOM: *a Thornycroft BC with a 26 seat Perth-built body.*

LEFT: *This double-decker is pictured at the foot of Oakbank Road in Cherrybank between 1936 and 1938. Four 48-seat double-decker buses were purchased in 1932 for the Scone to Cherrybank route and became part of the Alexander's fleet in 1934.* RIGHT: *A Darnhall bus at the Riggs Road bus garage in 1964. The bus is an AEC Regal with Burlingham body and was painted in two shades of blue.*

Glengarry Road via Priory Place. Both routes sharing the bus stop at Craigie Cross. Cherrybank was still served by the Scone to Cherrybank service.

During the 1980s the Perth firm of Stagecoach became the bus operators throughout the city and continues to serve the people of Craigie and Cherrybank.

Traffic Problems

There were no by-passes around Perth in the early 1970s and the entire closure for several months of Glasgow Road between the Glover Street and Murray Crescent junctions led to major traffic issues in the area.

This was a particular problem for the Glover Street, Priory Place and Needless Road residents as all transport heading westwards from the city or coming from the Edinburgh Road direction was forced to travel along these streets. As more transport companies were now using road travel instead of rail, the worst problems were created by heavy goods vehicles or juggernauts sometimes travelling in convoy along these narrow thoroughfares which at that time were free from load restrictions. Agricultural traffic going to and from the livestock mart added to the problem and, in Needless Road, the residents were

The one-way system that was installed in Glover Street in 1995 did not help this unfortunate motorist. (Photograph from The Courier).

concerned by the effect the vibration from these vehicles was having on the structure of their properties.

Even after the Glasgow Road was re-opened again, many of the lorry drivers still decided to use Needless Road as a shortcut towards Cherrybank adding to the fury of the local people. Eventually the council erected load restriction signs with a seven and a half ton weight limit in Glover Street and Needless Road and the problem was somewhat eliminated. Although the restrictions were still occasionally flouted, heavy vehicles stopped using these routes but the use of Needless Road as a 'rat run' between Cherrybank and Craigie for private cars continued.

Prior to the increase in private car ownership which began around the late 1950s the area had been relatively free from traffic problems. The main problem usually arose on the twice weekly market days when the limited parking at the livestock mart led to farmers having to park their vehicles in the surrounding streets. It was, however, the imminent closure of the Mart in the early 1990s which was to cause further concerns.

Once planning approval had been granted to develop the livestock mart into the Raeburn Park housing development, there was immediate concern about the traffic volume which would be created by one hundred and nineteen new homes. A Young Street resident, Louis Flood, stated that 'the proposal will almost double the number of houses in Young Street and at the same time halve the amount of parking space available'. He pointed out that the Victorian villas had no room for off-street parking and said 'it is dangerous enough here at the moment when parents are dropping and picking up children – what will it be like with many more cars in the immediate area?'

In November 1992, at a public meeting held in Craigie School attended by local councilors and planning officials, issues regarding the traffic and safety issues were aired. Needless Road was described as 'being like a race track' and a Glover Street resident said 'Glover Street was not built for speed yet motorists tear along it at fifty miles per hour'.

The development of Raeburn Park went ahead as planned and speed calming was introduced in the area. Mini roundabouts, road humps and pavement extensions appeared in strategic positions throughout Craigie with a section of Glover Street between Needless Road and Craigie Cross having a special give-way system installed.

Although these measures may have helped to alleviate some of the issues expressed, they have by no means cured them and the still increasing volume of car ownership and limited number of parking spaces remains a problem. This problem was again raised in 2017 when plans were approved, despite local protests, to demolish the lock-up garages in the lane between Needless Road and Cavendish Avenue and replace them with a private dwelling.

Cherrybank's Flying Circuses

In the early 1930s the farmland fields of Woodhead of Mailer at the top of the Necessity Brae hosted impressive Air Circuses held by competing air display companies.

The first of these is believed to have been Captain C D Bernard's Air Tours which performed at Woodhead of Mailer on 26th and 27th September 1931. Bernard himself was an aviation celebrity having broken several world records which included England to India in seven and a half days, Cape Town in twenty and a half days and the first non-stop flight from England to Africa (Tangier) in twenty one and a half hours. His air tours offered trial flying lessons under the tutelage of Glasgow-born James Mollinson. In 1932, Mollinson married one of the most eminent female pilots of her day, Amy Johnson, famous for her solo fight to Darwin Australia in a De Havilland DH60 Gipsy Moth. James Mollinson was also an aviation record breaker

Sir Alan Cobham's Airspeed AS.4-ABSI three engine, ten seat aircraft pictured at Woodhead of Mailer in 1934. This photograph was taken by the author's mother who was a passenger on one of the flights.

and often flew with Johnson. At this Woodhead of Mailer display, Captain Bernard provided the leading edge of the eight-plane display in his record-breaking Fokker that he dubbed 'The Spider'.

These Woodhead of Mailer aviation displays attracted and thrilled large crowds but having such large crowds in this part of Perth created transport difficulties. On Sunday, 27th September 1931 with large numbers of vehicles amassing on the air circus, a Perth Corporation omnibus taking locals out to the air show collided with a motor car in Needless Road but, fortunately, no one was injured in the accident.

One month later, the world-famous Berkshire Aviation Tours Ltd came to Woodhead of Mailer. Their advertisements for the display pronounced the air circus as providing 'the most exciting display of flying ever given and a roar from beginning to end'. They also promised 'selections of music and announcements by loudspeaker' and also offered a novel attraction 'Bombing the Bridal Pair'. To coincide with this air circus, the Alhambra Cinema in Kinnoull Street showed 'Hell`s Angels', the Howard Hughes air epic which starred Jean Harlow. Hughes himself having made early forays into the early aviation world.

Another aviation circus took place on Tuesday, 22nd August 1933 held by the Scottish Motor Traction Co. Ltd, who ran a garage (SMT) in Dunkeld Road. Advertised as 'Scotland`s Own Air Circus –the most comprehensive, spectacular and daring display of Scotland`s progressing aviation', the event offered flights to the public at five shillings each. Flying performances with Dragons, Fox Moths and Avro Cadets included 'stunting', 'crazy flying', 'bombing', a race around nearby landmarks and exhilarating parachute plunges by parachutist A C Fairley.

A few weeks after the Scottish Motor Traction event, the British Air Hospitals Pageant came to Perth on 12th September 1933 and again attracted large crowds. Their displays included 'bottle shooting', 'crazy flying', and 'wing walking'.

The following year, 1934, saw another air display company at the Woodhead of Mailer site. This time it was one run by the ground-breaking aviator Sir Alan Cobham. Cobham`s flying air circus toured Britain during the summer months and between 1932 and 1935 his aerial displays attracted upwards of four million spectators and almost a million passengers were treated to aerial experiences which became known as 'Five Bob Flips'. My late mother was one of those who, along with her twelve year old nephew, flew in one of these 'flips' at the 1934 air display. I remember her telling me that afterwards it took her about a week to get the knots out of her long blonde hair!

THE SPORTING LIFE

There's a breathless hush in the close tonight
Ten to make and the match to win.
A bumping pitch and a blinding light,
An hour to play, and the last man in.
And it's not for the sake of a ribboned coat,
Or the selfish hope of a season's fame,
But his captain's hand on his shoulder smote
'Play up! Play up! And play the game!

(Sir Henry Newbold, 1862-1938)

Sport has always played a significant part in the lives of the people of Craigie and Cherrybank. The golf course at Craigie Hill (one of three golf courses established within the city limits of Perth), the tennis courts at Darnhall and the bowling greens at Darnhall and the West End were to become and, in most cases still are, major sporting facilities in the area. The more recent attractions of the ice rink and indoor bowling at Dewars Rinks and the Leisure Pool on the site of the old railway yards in Glover Street can today be said to be on the border line of Craigie in the same way as once were the Recreation Grounds at Craigie Haugh the original home of St Johnstone FC.

When St Johnstone played at Craigie Haugh

In 1884, with the Scottish Football Association having been formed in 1873, football was increasing in popularity and Perth had several teams playing the sport such as Fair City Athletic, Erin Rovers and Caledonian (based at Perth Station). By the autumn of that year they were to be joined by

The Recreation Grounds at Craigie Haugh, St Johnstone FC's first football ground, is clearly marked in the centre of this map next to the Rope Works. (Courtesy of the National Library of Scotland).

—121—

another team, St Johnstone, formed by members of a local cricket team seeking to occupy their time once the cricket season had ended. Once the club had been formed as a separate entity from the cricket team, they played their early football matches on the South Inch and were soon to become the team most associated with the town from which it took its name – Saint John's Toun.

The club's first president (a prominent local curler named George Valentine) and the original twenty members of the club were instrumental in securing the lease of a vacant piece of land at Craigie Haugh, close to the South Inch, which became St Johnstone's first ground and re-named Recreation Grounds. The grounds were officially opened in August 1885 with a match between the leading team of the time, Queens Park, who defeated Dundee's Our Boys 6-0.

For almost forty years the Recreation Grounds were St Johnstone's home and some outstanding games were played there with the small ground sometimes packed to capacity. The highest recorded attendance was on 14th April 1923 when twelve thousand were crammed into the park for a Division Two match against Clydebank, the Perth club having finally been admitted to the Scottish League in 1911. The final match at the Recreation Grounds, which resulted in a 4-2 victory over Kilmarnock, attracted an attendance of between 7000 and 8000.

TOP: *A section of the crowd at a match against Raith Rovers in 1921. Nearly every man in a bunnet! (Perthshire Advertiser photograph)*. BOTTOM: *An exciting moment during St Johnstone's home match against Broxburn in 1924. McKinlay the visiting goalkeeper has just fisted out and the Saints' players pictured are Fleming, Rollo [in the air], Hart and McRoberts. (Perthshire Advertiser photograph).*

In 1924, having suffered regular problems with flooding, St Johnstone moved to Muirton Park on the northern edge of Perth which would become their home for the next sixty five years.

Perth Craigie FC and Other Clubs

Perth Craigie FC was formed, mainly by railway workers, after the First World War and soon made their presence felt in the old Perth Junior League.

Craigie FC pictured at Jeanfield Park in 1920. Back row: Cameron, Dow, Duff, Peddie, Wilson. Front row: Rae, Spence, Anderson, McCowan, Christie, Roberts. (Perthshire Advertiser photograph).

Playing in their familiar Queens Park-style strip of black and white striped jerseys and white shorts, their home ground was on the South Inch on a pitch running parallel to the Craigie Burn.

The changing rooms were in the Old Mill in Windsor Terrace which meant a trot before and after matches along the length of Windsor Terrace then through the tunnel below the railway line before reaching the playing pitch. Jim Galloway, a former Craigie player from the late 1950s and early 1960s still recalls these changing rooms and the teams washing after matches from buckets of cold water.

For many years, a stalwart of Perth Craigie Football Club was Andy Lumsden who worked at Craigie Mill and was the club coach, trainer and general mentor to many of the players. Andy was widely known

TOP: *A victorious Perth Craigie team and club officials pictured at Muirton Park in April 1930 when Craigie defeated Dunblane Ashfield in the final of the Lindsay Cup. Back row: Moyes, C Panton, Cowper, J Panton, McDonald, Thain. Front row: Stobie, Allan, Henderson, Guild, McNeil. (Perthshire Advertiser photograph).* BOTTOM: *Perth Craigie FC 1958/59. The photograph includes (Back row) Jim Galloway (far left) Jim Ewing (third left), Alistair McGregor (fourth left), Dave Baird is on the right beside club secretary Jim Imrie. Bob Halley and Hamish Watt are seated first and second left in the front row. (Photograph courtesy of Jim Galloway).*

as 'Mr Craigie FC'

During the 1930s and up until the mid-1950s there was ample scope for the younger footballers of Craigie and Cherrybank to enhance their skills. Some eventually moving into the Junior and Senior ranks.

These were the 'fitba-crazy' years. In addition to Schools, Boys Brigade, Scouts and Wednesday Half-Holiday leagues, there were two very successful and highly competitive boys' football leagues – the Perth Minor League for teenage boys and the Perth City Boys' League for a slightly older age group. Over the years there were teams such as Scone, Earnvale, Stanley, Bridgend Hamlet, Burghmuir Rovers, Bridge of Earn, Perth Boys Club, Kinnoull, and Muirton Youth Club.

Craigie had two teams in the City Boys' League – Knowelea during the 1930s and Craigie City Boys from the 1930s to the mid-1940s. Playing throughout the war years, Craigie had a particularly successful season in 1941-42 when, in addition to being league champions, they also won the 'PA' and Norie-Miller Cups.

Cherrybank started with a team in the Perth Minor League in the late 1940s then moved into the City Boys' League in the early 1950s. In season 1952-53, like the Craigie team a decade earlier, they were winners of the 'PA' Cup and the Norie-Miller Cup. The Cherrybank teams consisted mainly of boys from nearby Perth Academy who preferred the round ball to the oval one of their rugby-orientated school!

Following the disappearance of Perth Craigie from Junior football in the 1960s, mainly because of the reconstruction of the new Tayside leagues, the area had no recognised football team. However, in 2009, a

TOP: *The Craigie City Boys' team of 1941 which defeated Scone City Boys in the final of the PA Cup. (Perthshire Advertiser photograph).* BOTTOM: *The PA Cup of 1943 being presented by Sgt William Russell, former Hearts and Chelsea footballer to D Small, the Craigie captain.*

The Cherrybank football team of 1950-51 that played in the Perth Minor League. Back row (left to right): Alec Forsyth, Jimmy Fraser, Jimmy Winton, Jimmy Buchan, Bob Kettles, Bill Walker, Chick McGregor, Ian Calderwood. Front row (left to right): Hamish McLeod, Alistair Smith, Allan Whyte, Bill Hendry, Scott Gardiner. In later years, Allan Whyte played left back for St Johnstone and Scott Gardiner was a prominent member of the invincible Perthshire County Cricket team of the 1950s and 1960s. (Perthshire Advertiser photograph).

TOP: *The Cherrybank City Boys football team of 1953: winners of the 'P.A' Cup and the Norie-Miller Cup. (Perthshire Advertiser photograph).* RIGHT: *During the 1930s Craigie had another football team named Knowelea which played in the Perth City Boys' League.* BOTTOM: *2019 photograph of Craigie Amateurs FC. (Photograph courtesy of Craigie Amateurs FC).*

new Craigie FC emerged to play in the Perthshire Amateur League with their home matches played at Huntingtower.

Craigie Hill Golf Club

> Mysterious game! Thou can enthrall
> The young, the old, the low, the tall;
> Priest, savage, soldier, hoary sage
> Have each confessed the noble rage.
> Play well, play ill, 'tis all the same,
> The passion glows with equal flame.

(From 'Golf' by Neil Ferguson Blair, 1840)

Craigie Hill golf course opened in 1911 on the former Craigie Wood and came about mainly because of congestion on the North Inch course where many of Perth's working classes had taken up the sport. Although judged by some at the time as being an unnecessary addition to the existing courses on the Inch and on Moncreiffe Island, Craigie Hill quickly proved itself to be a huge success and by 1913 had a membership of six hundred. Early practical advice offered by noted architects Willie Fernie and Joe Anderson resulted in Craigie Hill becoming one of the best engineered courses in the Perth area.

Craigie Hill's first annual report recorded that the club had funds of £321 but stated that this money would be required 'to meet the costs of providing lavatory accommodation for the clubhouse'.

Craigie Hill's founders and its early management committee sought to keep the club within the means of the local community and, in doing so, built and maintained a loyal base of members throughout not only the Cherrybank and Craigie area but the larger community of Perth.

In 1913, the course was described as offering 'rare attractions to the man or woman who revels in fresh air combined with bracing exercise and exciting sport'. A later anecdote spoke of a dyspeptic individual not knowing the relish of mustard until he had eaten lunch after a vigorous round at Craigie Hill

The opening ceremony on 10th June 1911. (Photograph courtesy of Craigie Hill Golf Club).

TOP: *Craigie Hill golf course. (Photograph courtesy of Craigie Hill Golf Club).* LEFT: *The 12th hole at Craigie Hill in 1950. (Photograph by Davidson of Perth).* BELOW: *Gene Sarazen playing in an exhibition match at Craigie Hill c1930. (Perthshire Advertiser photograph).*

on a crisp and clear morning in October!

The original clubhouse, situated close to the path which runs from Cherrybank to Upper Craigie and built of corrugated iron, was in use until about 1965 when the present clubhouse was opened slightly further up the hill. This necessitated a slight change to the opening holes of the course. The opening of the new clubhouse, along with improved catering facilities, greatly extended the

Dai Rees drives off from the first tee during a 1947 exhibition match at Craigie Hill. He is watched by Norman Von Nida, Jimmy Adams and Bill Shankland (behind him). Rees was runner-up in The Open in 1953, 1954 and 1961 and was captain of the British Ryder Cup team on five occasions. (Perthshire Advertiser photograph).

social membership of the club with events such as quiz nights, winter bowling competitions and Burns Suppers. Saturday night dances were extremely popular during the 1970s.

Over the years Craigie Hill has produced some of Perthshire's outstanding golfers, many who have distinguished themselves at local, national and international level. Some are mentioned in more detail in a later chapter of this book but Craigie Hill will always be synonymous with the names of Jessie Valentine who won both the Scottish and British Ladies' Championships; Fiona Anderson, a Scottish Ladies' champion; Garry Harvey, a British Boys' champion and later a golf professional. Bill Laidlaw who became assistant professional to the great Henry Cotton was tipped as a future winner of The Open had he not been tragically killed during war service with the RAF.

Exhibition matches featuring some of the world's leading golfers were once a regular feature at Craigie Hill. I recall being taken by my father in 1947 to watch one of these matches which featured the top Australian golfers Norman von Nida and Bill Shankland along with the great Welsh golfer Dai Rees. Although, a few years later, my early golf was to be played over the city's North Inch course (using my Dad's old hickory-shafted clubs!) then later at the King James VI club on Moncreiffe Island, it was really that Sunday afternoon at Craigie Hill which introduced me to the wonderful world of golf.

Another exhibition match which I also attended was in 1959 and featured the former Open champion Max Faulkner along with the great Scottish golfing duo of Eric Brown and John Panton.

At the end of the twentieth century, many Scottish golf courses were facing a struggle to survive and a lot of golfers were now unwilling to commit to the time required to play a round of eighteen holes. As a result, nine-hole golf courses were becoming increasingly popular.

By 2005, Craigie Hill was in a precarious financial situation. But, as they were about to announce another substantial annual loss, they were offered a possible lifeline by the local building firm of G S Brown Construction.

A 1959 exhibition match at Craigie Hill. Mr William Miller, club captain and County Association president, is seen third left with Eric Brown, Max Faulkner, Pitlochry-born John Panton and Dick Smith, the Scottish amateur champion. (Perthshire Advertiser photograph).

At a packed meeting held in the Dewar's Centre in November of that year, club members voted overwhelmingly in favour of striking an agreement with the St Madoes based company which would see the lands of the Craigie Hill course becoming used for a new housing development with the golf course being relocated at a new complex at Tibbermore which would have one eighteen hole golf course and one nine hole course. Despite the enthusiasm of the members to this proposal, the scheme failed to materialise.

However, in December 2019, an ambitious blueprint to redevelop the eighteen-hole set-up of the course into a nine-hole layout complete with a new clubhouse and practice facilities was wholeheartedly approved by the Craigie Hill members. In a newspaper article, club captain Crawford Conochie is quoted as saying 'the resounding vote provides much needed security as the board seeks to ensure the long-term viability of a golf course in the heart of the city'. It was hoped that the transition of the golf course from eighteen to nine holes would be completed by around 2025.

Craigie Hill Curling Club

> Frae northern mountains clad with snaw,
> Where whistling winds incessant blaw;
> In time now when the curling stane
> Slides murm'ring o'er the icy plain.
>
> (From 'To Robert Yarde of Devonshire'
> by Allan Ramsay, 1724)

Curling, a game which has been taken to the other colder parts of the world, has a long history in Scotland as can be seen from the above quotation from Allan Ramsay, and there are recorded accounts of a challenge match about throwing stones across ice at Paisley Abbey in February 1541. Almost certainly, the game as we know it today is Scottish in orgin as the only other part of the world that has claimed it, namely the Low Countries of Europe, are deficient in the hard igneous rock from which the main implement of the game, the curling stone, is made.

When the Grand Caledonian Curling Club was instituted in 1838 for the purpose of 'regulating the ancient game of curling by general laws', the four by two form of the game was chosen. By 1842 the new

national club had obtained royal patronage and has been known since as The Royal Caledonian Curling Club – the RCCC.

From 1838 onwards, the game exploded in popularity until by the end of the nineteenth century almost every county had at least one club affiliated with the RCCC. Originally, curlers played on natural lochs and specially constructed ponds and almost every parish in Scotland had its custom-made curling pond.

TOP: *The original members of Craigie Hill Curling Club photographed in 1912 at the opening of the club's rink which was situated in an old quarry at Craigie Hill. (Perthshire Advertiser photograph).*

LEFT: *Members of Craigie Hill Curling Club in 1928. Left to right: W Rodger, W Leiper, J Hair, W Miller, J Guild, W K Anderson. (Perthshire Advertiser photograph).*

RIGHT: *A match in progress at the Craigie Hill curling rink in 1930. (Perthshire Advertiser photograph).*

Craigie Hill Curling Club was instituted in 1911 and their first curling match was played on 8th January 1912 at their specially constructed rink which was situated in an old quarry at Craigie Hill golf course.

The outdoor rink at Craigie Hill was the club's home until 1936 when the club, which had originally been a limited company, went into liquidation – a fate which was probably linked to the opening of Perth's original ice rink in Dunkeld Road in 1935. Fortunately records show the club, which had been admitted to the RCCC in 1924, quickly reformed with twenty four regular members and thirteen occasional members with an annual membership subcription of five shillings. The patron of the club at that time was Lord Forteviot.

Although matches were now being played indoors, as opposed to the original outdoor rink at Craigie Hill, when the Grand Match was played outdoors at Carsebreck Loch near Blackford two rinks from Craigie Hill Curling Club took part.

Today the club has an active membership and now play in the Forteviot, Club and Carse Leagues as well as in various knockout competitions. They still play their matches in Craigie, at Dewars Rinks in Glover Street, and have teams in Divisions 2 and 3 of the Super Leagues. Their own internal league has led to a pro-active approach in encouraging new members from the beginners' ranks.

In 2012 the Craigie Hill Curling Club celebrated their centenary year with several special activities including a bonspiel with three other curling clubs who were also celebrating their centenary – Monifieth, Wengen and Bearsden.

Bowling and Tennis Clubs

Over one hundred years ago, when there were stirrings throughout Perthshire to provide bowling greens and club facilities, Perth's West End Bowling Club was one of the first names that sprouted in that first flush of enthusiasm. A meeting in Perth's County Hotel in February 1887 brought agreement that a club should be formed and the first president was Councillor David Nairn Shaw.

A piece of ground to the west of Swan's Mart was acquired from Mr Stewart Gray of Kinfauns at a rental of £18.13/1d per year and today the club still flourishes on that original site.

Work then got underway in laying out the green with best Ayrshire turf and a groundsman was employed full-time at twelve shillings a week. A mower was naturally an essential item and one was

LEFT: *A 1930s bowling match. (Star Photos, Perth.* BELOW: a painting by C A *Wallace of the opening of the bowling green in 1888 and a 2005 photo from the same angle. The station tower and Kinnoull Hill visible behind the trees.*

purchased for £6.2/6d and it is also believed by some members that the roller secured for £8.7/6d is the same one in use today. The club mus have been an exclusive one because membership of the club, which was all male at that stage, cost one guinea annually. Sets of bowls were available at twenty-five shillings and suitably inscribed with members' initials.

The first game was played on 21ˢᵗ July 1888. Local dignitaries who attended the opening ceremony, which was carried out by the Sheriff Clerk, included ex-Lord Provost Martin, Beveridge the builder, Thomas Chalmers the solicitor, Nicoll the bookseller, Peddie the ironmonger and Wallace the coal merchant. Pullar's Silver Band (later to become the Perth Silver Band) played. When the club celebrated its

The West End Bowling Club's centenary celebrations in 1987. (Photograph courtesy of the West End Bowling Club). Right: The West End were the Scottish and British Isles Fours Winners in season 1984/85. Left to right: Jim Bright, Bill Gorham, Jim McGregor and Derek Bright.

centenary in April 1987 the band of that year was invited to return.

The first competitive game was against Crieff followed by matches against Kinnoull, Balhousie and Bridge of Earn.

West End were quick to branch into the wider spheres of the sport. They joined the Scottish Bowling Association in 1893 and, in 1901, entertained touring teams from Australia and New Zealand. A Canadian team played at the West End green in 1904 and, that same year, the club was granted its first liquor licence.

A clubhouse was built on the Glover Street side of the ground and in 1907 it was insured for £200 at an annual premium of five shillings. This building served the club well until 1974 when it was replaced by a new structure on the Gray Street side of the ground at a cost of £7,500. In 1978, an extension was added to give complete facilities and car parking was included on the Needless Road side.

The club continued through the period of the World War I and when the World War II started in 1939, the first mention was the cancellation of the whist drive on 26th September that year. By 1940, war charity days were being observed although all away games that year were cancelled because of the gravity of the situation.

During the 1920s, family days were very much the vogue with everyone from the very young to the elderly much in evidence. By the 1930s, Ladies' Day had become established and women were now playing an active role in the club although it was not until 1974 that a Ladies' Section was formed with Mrs M. Anderson as president.

With the development in the 1920s of new housing around Darnhall Drive and Murray Crescent and the influx of new residents to the area, the Perth Town council were quick to realise the need for recreational facilities in the area. A bowling green and tennis

LEFT: *A group of tennis enthusiasts who took part in a tournament at the Darnhall tennis courts in 1924. The group includes Mr R G Henderson, the secretary of the Darnhall Club and the treasurer Mr J W Pearson. (Perthshire Advertiser photograph).*
RIGHT: *Members of Darnhall Tennis Club in 1981. Left to right: Gwen Kyle, Gordon Rattray, Gillian Nairn, Bill MacDonald, Beryl Christie, Alan Nairn, Charlotte Nairn. (Perthshire Advertiser photograph).*

courts were established with Lady Forteviot officiating at the opening of the tennis courts in May, 1923.

Darnhall Tennis Club continues to thrive with considerable investment put into its facilities in recent years. Tennis is no longer just a summer sport at Darnhall and the club is now open all year round with three floodlit all-weather bitumen surfaced courts and one additional court for mini tennis. This inclusive club is run by the members for the benefit of the community and vigorously promotes the sport of tennis to all ages and levels of play. Bill MacDonald was the club president for fifty years!

TOP: *The Darnhall bowling green pictured after its closure. Pitheavlis Castle and the houses of Orchard Place are in the background.* BOTTOM: *The tennis and beach volleyball complex at Darnhall. (Photograph from Darnhall Tennis Club).*

The Darnhall Bowling Club had its first full season in 1954. The club was founded by a local police officer (later Chief Superintendent) Alistair Harrower who knocked on doors around Craigie and recruited one hundred and forty members. For almost the next sixty years it became a popular club socially but also producing some high quality lawn bowlers who distinguished themselves in local and national competitions.

Darnhall was one of five bowling greens in Perth which were maintained by Perth & Kinross Council. Sadly, due to cost-cutting measures introduced by the Council in 2012 and with membership down to only twenty five, the club was unable to finance the maintenance of the facility on their own and had to close down.

In 2019, four hundred tonnes of sand were poured onto the old Darnhall bowling green to create a beach volleyball court for the Small Countries Association Volleyball Finals which attracted competitors from across the UK and from Greenland, Cyprus, Liechtenstein and the Faroe Islands. It's hardly Copacabana! But, although over twenty five miles from the nearest sea beach, the old bowling green at Darnhall has now become a beach volleyball centre run under the auspices of

The opening of the Pitch and Putt course on St Magdalene's Hill in 1960. Lord Provost John T Young is seen putting out and the others in the foursome are ex-Bailie George Valentine (right), Mrs Jessie Valentine and Denis Christie, the North Inch golf professional. (Perthshire Advertiser photograph)

the Perth Volleyball Club.

For a number of years a popular Craigie attraction was the Council-owned Pitch and Putt golf course situated at the top of Glenlochay Road on the lower slopes of St Magdalene's Hill with a panoramic view over the city and the Tay valley. The course was popular with both novice golfers and also with more experienced golfers who would use the facility to improve their short game.

PARKS AND GARDENS:
WALKS, WOODLAND AND WATER

Craigie Knowes

> Frae Buckie Braes to Craigie Knowes
> And round by Callerfountain Hill,
> There's woods and walks and haughs and howes
> Abune the falls at Craigie Mill.
>
> Craigie Knowes
> Gin morning daw
> I'll hear the craw
> On Craigie Knowes
> Wauk up the sin…

(William Soutar)

Craigie Knowes is described by the Royal Commission on the Ancient and Historical Monuments of Scotland as: 'a craggy plug of igneous rock and bearing evidence of both large and small-scale quarrying around its edges. The largest workings to the East are now covered by houses and gardens whilst most of the workings are heavily overgrown.'

The area was once a popular Perth picnic spot and trysting place with stone tables, neat pathways and a flagpole situated at its highest point. Over the past few decades it has been largely ignored and become a small wilderness of birds, whin and brambles situated amongst suburban housing but still affording panoramic views over Perth.

Two views from Craigie Knowes around 1904 (John E Craven, Perth).

LEFT: *Bramble picking at Verena Terrace near Craigie Knowes in the 1920s. The copper beech tree in the photograph still stands in the garden of Mount Craigie (Photograph from Perth and Kinross Libraries).* RIGHT: *Modern Craigie from Craigie Knowes.*

'The Bonnie Knowes o' Craigie' was written in the 1920s and for many years was popular at concerts and soirees in and around Perth. There were different versions of the song, one being recorded in the 1970s by local folk singer Mary McCann. This version is by David McCormack:

Along the pleasant banks of Tay,
In many a livelong summer's day;
I've sung the ever tuneful lay
Of the bonnie knowes o' Craigie.

By Springland's ivy mantled tower
I've rowed to Annaty's fair bower,
As the gleam of twilight's peaceful hour
Crept o'er the knowes of Craigie.

I've climbed the hill of Murrayshall,
As evening heard the blackbird's call,
And watched the moonlight softly fall
On the bonnie knowes o' Craigie.

Ere the blithe skylark stirred the corn,
I've trod Kinnoull at early morn,
To see the rising sun adorn
The bonnie knowes o' Craigie.

I've gaed through lonely Quarrymill,
Fair Lignwood's fields and Dowie's rill,

Quiet Gannochy and Lochy Hill,
To the bonnie knowes o' Craigie.

Let us again the toast declare,
Here's to Perth, the city fair,
The lads and a' the lassies there,
And the bonnie knowes o' Craigie.

A few years earlier, around 1899, another song, 'Auld Craigie Knowes', written by Alexander McLeish, a Perth poet of that time. It also extolls its scenic virtues:

There's a dear weel kent spot no far frae oor toon,
An' dear has it aye been to me,
For there in the sweet sunny springtime o' life
I hae wander'd and played fu' o' glee;
An' altho' I should roam far across the braid faem,
Far awa' frae its haughs an' its howes,
O fondly I'll cherish, while life still remains,
The mem'ry o' auld Craigie Knowes.

The laverock ascends wi' the dew on its breast,
To welcome the dawn o' the morn,
An' the sang o' the thrush frae yon blackthorn tree
Awa' on the saft wind is born.
An' the dew glitters bricht 'neath the sun's gowden beam
Where the kye an' the sheep calmly browse,
Sweet thoughts o' my childhood endear ilka scene
That lies roon my auld Craigie Knowes.

I've watched the red sun as it sank in the west,
Far ahint yon wild mountains sae grey;
I've watched it be-gilding Kinnoull's sombre crest
An' kissin' the breist o' the Tay.
An' I've pu'd the wild rose frae yon love haunted side,
Whaur in richest profusion it grows;
It was there someone whispered her promise to me,
On the green slopes o' auld Craigie Knowes.

The Craigie Knowes Tank

At the end of World War I, a rhomboid shaped tank was gifted to the city in recognition of Perth's efforts in connection with the war savings effort. For years the gift of the tank became a subject of dispute and discussion. It first lay at the Corporation Depot at Craigie Haugh before being moved to Tay Street and the machinery removed from its interior. It lay there derelict but as the site was considered unsatisfactory, the Town Council considered the question of transferring it to another location. A site on the North Inch was selected but residents objected to the tank being placed near their homes. It was then suggested that the tank be broken up and sold for what it was worth but more sentimental arguments were put forward towards its preservation and ultimately it was decided to place the tank on Craigie Knowes.

The tank's journey from Tay Street to Craigie Knowes was described in the *Perthshire Advertiser* of 20th July 1921:

TOP: *The Craigie Knowes tank pictured after its arrival in July 1921 with the houses of Queen's Avenue in the background (Perthshire Advertiser photograph).* BOTTOM: *Craigie Knowe in the present day.*

The necessary machinery being forthcoming, the tank was moved from Tay Street to its final destination yesterday. Early in the morning the echoes in Tay Street were aroused by its start on its last journey and by mid-day it had been taken to the Princes Street end of the South Inch. In the afternoon it resumed its journey, accompanied by an admiring and curious band, and by way of the Edinburgh Road and Moredun

Terrace, under the supervision of Mr Gordon Clark, the son of the Reverend P A Gordon Clark, and an ex-tank officer, by fits and starts it, about six o'clock, arrived at the final resting place.

As the tank passed along Edinburgh Road on its way to Craigie Knowes, a local wag was overheard saying 'Whaur's the war noo?'

The tank lay on Craigie Knowes for several years where it was a source of attraction to the youth of Craigie. Ultimately it fell into total decay and in 1931 was converted into scrap iron. The only part of the tank which was retained was the inscription plate (much battered having served for years as a target for stones) which became an exhibit in the city's museum.

The Buckie Braes

> Monie a bairn frae our toun
> In the canty simmer-days,
> Monie a bairn frae our toun
> Haiks up to the Buckie Braes

(William Soutar)

The Buckie Braes is a small woodland glen at Cherrybank adjacent to Craigie Hill golf course. It is formed from an old quarry where two streams, the Buckie and Craigie Burns, converge between the volcanic rocks of Craigie Hill and the sandstone formation to the west and cascading over waterfalls to become the main Craigie Burn which eventually joins the River Tay at the South Inch.

The Buckie Braes were developed by Perth Corporation in the years before World War I. From the 1920s they became a popular haunt for generations of Perth families who spent many hours exploring the nooks and crannies or strolling through the paths and glades of this idyllic setting.

Although some dismay was expressed at the loss of some natural and arboreal species prior to the development of the area, these fears were soon forgotten as the area grew in popularity, particularly with its close proximity to the Cherrybank tram and bus terminus.

According to a 1920s local advertisement for recreative attractions: 'This popular resort known as 'the children's paradise' contains refreshment rooms, swings, see-saws, maypole, pond and excellent facilities for picnic parties.'

For many years this little woodland glen was Perth's favourite picnic spot with its swings, stone picnic table, open fire-grates for tea making, an ice cream hut and the ever-present fascination of waterfall and stream. Brambling was often carried out in the upper banks and many a fine pot of bramble jelly found its way to Perth tea tables after a happy afternoon at the 'Buckies'. Thirsts were quenched from the crystal clear water of Cock Robin's Well and, at one time, an added attraction was a captured German cannon from World War I which eventually found its way to the scrap drive of World War II.

The iron bridge at the entrance to the Buckie Braes.

In *Hame Links,* a book of Scottish poetry published in 1930, William Paton of Luncarty wrote of the beauties of the Buckie Braes in the poem 'Buckie Braes':

If ye wad spend a blithsome 'oor
Amang the bonnie bowers sae green,
Let's gang to whaur the air is pure
An' there enjoy the sylvan scene.
The mavis cheers the wood wi' sang,
Love is the measure o' its lays;
Oh, what a joy to be amang
The beauties o' the Buckie Braes.

There at the blush o' early morn
When bud and blossom glint wi' dew,
Ye bless the day that ye were born
An' life tak's on a brichter hue.
When Sol shines doon wi' genial ray
An' sets the yellow whin ablaze,
A poet couldna feel but gay
When musin' on the Buckie Braes.

'Tis peacefu' at the gloamin' fa',
The ripple o' the burnie's sang;
Ye're laith to rise an' gang awa',
The nicht it never seems ower lang.
Here in the shelter o' the shade
The happy lover fondly strays,
An' mony a lovin' vow's been made
That's sacred to the Buckie Braes.

The slopes o' famed Kinnoull are grand,
That guard auld Perth, the city fair;
There's no' a toun in a' the land
That wi' St. Johnstoun can compare.
Whaur beauty lies on ilka side,

TOP: Children on 'the joy *wheel'*, *a photograph taken at the inauguration of the Buckie Braes (Perthshire Advertiser photograph).* BOTTOM: *The swings with one of the stone picnic tables in the foreground (Photograph from Perth and Kinross Libraries).*

TOP: *The see-saw.* BOTTOM: *Cock Robin's Well.*

Here lichtsome I could spend
  my days,
An' blithely sing wi' joy and
  pride
The beauties o' the Buckie
  Braes.

TOP: *Fun on the see-saw and on the May Pole, an innocent game derived from a pagan tradition. (Photographs from Perth and Kinross Libraries).* MIDDLE: *Cock Robin's Well where many generations of youngsters enjoyed drinking from the crystal clear water. (Photograph from Perth and Kinross Libraries). A recent photograph of Cock Robin's Well (photograph by Ian Macpherson).* BOTTOM: *In the 1930s a winter mantle of white adds beauty to the Buckie Braes. (Perthshire Advertiser photograph).*

PARKS AND GARDENS

The Cherrybank Gardens

In 1928, and through the generosity of Lord Forteviot, a children's playground was laid out on the area of ground to the west of the Low Road tenements and swings and other children's amusements were provided. The playground came about because of the danger created by passing traffic to the children of Cherrybank while playing on the street and by the inadequacy of the Cherrybank School playground.

Created in 1984 by the Scotch whisky company of Arthur Bell & Sons Ltd in the grounds of their Cherrybank complex and opened to the public in 1988, the imaginatively designed eighteen acres of Cherrybank Gardens were for several years one of the top tourist attractions in the area. They were home to Europe's largest collections of heathers and, in 1992, forty six thousand visitors took in the sights of the gardens during its season from May to October.

The Bell's National Heather Collection, under the expert supervision of head gardener Norrie Robertson, contained the flowers and foliage of some fifty thousand plants representing over nine hundred varieties of heathers in a stunning setting on a hillside overlooking the city of Perth. In 1989, the gardens had a royal visit from Prince Charles and Bell's produced a special whisky decanter to celebrate the occasion.

In addition to the amazing display of heathers, the gardens consisted of woodland walks with an abundance of wildlife, garden seats and even a challenging putting green with putters and balls supplied.

They were influenced by a water theme and had six large ponds containing goldfish and trout, fountains and an acoustic pool. A miniature Crystal Palace contained an aviary for a mixed flock of budgerigars and cockatiels and in one of the trellis gardens there was a set of tubular bells. Public art had pride of place in the shape of sculptures by Ian Hamilton Findlay, Laurence Broderick, Sadie McLellan and Iain

Workmen taking a break during the construction of the children's playground at Cherrybank. (Perthshire Advertiser photograph).

Various views of Cherrybank Gardens.

Mackintosh. There was also a coffee shop and gift shop and a 'Pride of Perth' exhibition which illustrated the story of Perth from mediaeval times.

In 2002, the gardens were gifted to Scotland's Garden Trust and in March 2004 the Trust announced their intention to develop the Gardens and the adjacent land out to Broxden into a £30 million National Garden for Scotland to be named 'The Calyx'. Sadly, disappointment followed in 2007 when the project failed to gain the required funding from the National Lottery and the gardens closed soon afterwards. The area earmarked for what could have become one of Scotland's major tourist attractions then lay derelict for several years before being bought for a new housing development.

I am not sure if, although the Cherrybank Gardens were a popular attraction to visitors from all over the world, they were ever fully appreciated by the local people. Perhaps it was just a case of when something is on your doorstep you take it for granted!

Needless Road floral display, c1990. The 'hands' supporting the floral globe of the world were designed by the late Perth artist, Jean Harkess. (Photograph by Ron Harkess).

However, the name of the gardens has not died and today Scottish country dancers worldwide regularly perform the popular 'Cherrybank Gardens', a three-couple Strathspey devised by the late John Drewry.

In 1990 a dedicated team of gifted volunteers began the Perth in Bloom campaign which soon grew to such an extent that within a short time became recognised both nationally and internationally with great success. Fortunately, some samples of heathers from The Cherrybank Gardens had been retained and have since been re-planted by the campaign. The transformation of many of Perth's dead spaces into garden areas of floral magnificence became a major feature and attraction. .

The garden area at the corner of Needless Road and Glasgow Road became one of these award winning displays.

Callerfountain Hill and Spinkie Den

> Up by the caller fountain,
> A'through a simmer's day,
> I heard the gowk gang cryin
> Abune the ferny brae.

(William Soutar)

Although the hill is officially known as St Magdalene's Hill, the name used by the Perth Council who manage this nearly half

TOP: *Trees on Callerfountain Hill with Perth in the distance.* BOTTOM: *Part of the walk behind Craigie Hill golf course leading from Buckie Braes to Callerfountain.*

a square kilometre of public space, Callerfountain is still the popular name used by many generations. A communications mast is now situated on the nearest part of the hill with another two masts situated on one of the other summits, Mailer Hill, which overlooks Kirkton of Mailer and Craigend.

Callerfountain, is named after a spring of fresh water which was once a popular picnic spot in a shaded glen on the hill. Although the M90 motorway now cuts through part of the hill, the planners had the foresight to install a footbridge over the motorway thus ensuring the continuation of what for decades has been a popular and beautiful area of open walks, woodland and spectacular views.

Coming from the Craigie direction the hill goes upwards from the top of Glenlochay Road and for a number of years a challenging pitch-and-put golf course was laid out on the lower slopes. The hill, in places, offers panoramic views over Perth, the Tay Valley and northwards towards the Grampians.

The park was gifted to Perth in 1954 by the James Duncan Trust to commemorate the coronation of Queen Elizabeth.

Although not officially given to the citizens of Perth until the 1950s, Callerfountain had been a popular walking and play area for several generations, However, in October 1907 it was reported that Joseph Allison appeared at Perth Sheriff Court charged with having trespassed on the land of Callerfountain without permission of the owner Sir Lindsay Wood. He was fined £1 or ten days imprisonment.

Perth's original city gunpowder store was built in 1838 at Tullylumb to supply city merchants and traders with gunpowder for shooting and quarrymasters for blasting. By 1873 Perth had expanded so far to the west that the building was considered to be too close to habitation. A new site was found at St Magdalene's Hill in 1877 and the new magazine which was licensed to store 20,000lbs of gunpowder opened in 1878. By the 1960s as the local demand for gunpowder had diminished, the store was sold to the Perth Quarry Company for a price of £500 who then operated the adjacent quarry with a licensed capacity of 4,000lbs of explosives. At one time the daily twelve noon blast from the quarry was as familiar to the residents of Craigie as the One o'Clock Gun is to those of Edinburgh!

A popular walk from Craigie was to take the path over the top of Callerfountain Hill then cut off to the right and climb over a wooden stile into Spinkie Den, so named for its profusion of primroses in springtime. Spinkie Den led through another woodland walk which came out at Woodhead of Mailer farm. From there it was an easy walk along a country road and down Necessity Brae. As an option, the walk could be extended from the Woodhead of Mailer road by cutting through the Cuddie's Strip and back to Craigie by the path behind Craigie Hill golf course or into Cherrybank by going through the Buckie Braes.

The Woodside Walk which leads from Cherrybank to the top of Craigie Knowes Road is still a popular stroll and at one time the 'wee woods' on the land now occupied by the modern homes of Craigie View were a popular children's play area.

The Weavers' Well

As the name implies, the Weavers' Well at Cherrybank (sometimes referred to as Jenny's Well) was once a popular spot with the weaving community in the area. The well can still be found on the left hand side of the old road into the Woodlands estate – now an access road into the modern homes and flats of Cleeve Park..

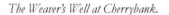

The Weaver's Well at Cherrybank.

The well would have been a gathering place for the people of Cherrybank where the young people would laugh and dream of their tomorrows while the old folks would sit and remember their yesterdays.

In 1899, the Perth poet Alexander McLeish wrote the following poem, 'The Auld Weavers' Well':

It's no in sculptured granite, nor in marble quaint and braw,
But oh, its waters gurglin' clear are free to ane an' a';
Baith man an' beast when wearit sair, there linger for a spell,
For the best o' life's elixirs leaves the auld weavers' well.

The merle there fu' aften sits and shak's the simmer air,
The flow'rs that blossom by its side are ever fresh and fair;
An' the gowden-breastit robin that gaes jinkin' thro' the dell,
Aye leaves his sweetest notes beside the auld weavers' well.

A wee bit burn wi' noisy mirth gaes gaily bickerin' by,
Upon its sweet and limped breast the simmer sunbeams lie;
An' ae aik tree, a' boo'd wi' age and winter's blast sae snell,
Flings twa-three broken shadows roon' the auld weavers' well.

The weavers there in by-gone days were afttimes wont to meet,
An' dream o'er vanished pleasures by its waters pure and sweet:
Oh! Could thae modest stanes but speak, what secrets they could tell,
O' the plots an' plans unfolded by the auld weavers' well.

But noo, alas! thae days hae fled, ilk weel-kent face is gane,
For death, the hoary-headed loon, has ta'en them ane by ane;

And in the quiet green kirkyard in silence noo they dwell,
Nae mair we'll hear their voices by the auld weavers' well.

But aften I can see them yet in fancy sittin' there,
The saft wind wavin' to an' fro their scanty byart hair;
I hear them hum their auld, auld sangs, hoo sweet, ah! nane can tell,
For happy was ilk heart beside the auld weavers' well.

O, there I love to wander when the day has gane to rest,
When the gowden glow of sunset throws its glamour o'er the west;
For ilka howe and haugh aroon' is deck'd by nature's sel' –
That's hoo I love to linger by the auld weavers' well.

According to a 1906 plan of Perth's sites of antiquities by Thomas McLaren, Perth's assistant burgh surveyor of that time, there was another well called the Watercress Well which was situated on the Craigie Burn close to what is now Orchard Place.

The Craigie Burn and Flash Flooding

From its source above the Buckie Braes to Cherrybank where it is joined by the Scouring Burn, the Craigie Burn winds its way in a

The Craigie Burn waterfall in full flow and on a calmer day.

downward course past Orchard Place and Balmoral Place and alongside Queen's Avenue before dropping down over the sometimes spectacular Craigie waterfall. It then follows a course alongside Windsor Terrace and the path that leads from Glenearn Road and Priory Place past the houses of Croft Bank before turning along the side of the South Inch to join the River Tay.

Decades of youngsters have built dams on its upper stretches, fished for 'baggie minnows' on the lower stretch near the South Inch railway tunnels or found it a popular place for just general 'mucking about'.

However, there is an old saying that water, like fire, can be a good friend but can also be a bad master and this has been the case with the waters of the Craigie Burn on several occasions, particularly in 2002 and again in 2020.

In eastern Scotland, the summer of 2002 had been much wetter than average. June and July had seen intense convective thunderstorms with the result that rainfall totals were about 150% above average and river flows were above 400% on some catchments. All of this had created a severe impact on river levels throughout Perthshire.

On 6th August, Perth and the surrounding area had been enjoying fine weather with blue skies and warm sunshine persisting for most of the day. However, as the afternoon progressed, the area around Pitlochry became dominated by strong thunderstorms which produced intense localised rainfall over steep mountain catchments. I recall my wife and I being in Pitlochry that afternoon and can honestly say that neither of us had experienced such fierce rainfall. Indeed we had to turn the car around to commence our journey back to Perth by another route when the bridge we were approaching was suddenly washed away. The damage from this rainfall and rapid runoff was spectacular within the Tay and lower Tummel valleys and while driving home the following words from 'The Deluge' by the Scottish poet W D Cocker came to mind:

An' the burns a' cam' doun in a spate,
An' the rivers ran clean ower the haughs,
An' the brigs were a' soopit awa',
An' what had been dubs becam' lochs.

As the extent of these intense thunderstorms increased, Perth

Craigie floods 2002: The Craigie Burn in flood at Balmoral Place; The car park at the Cheerrybank Inn under water; Flood water at the corner of Queen Street and Darnhall Drive.

was not to escape the ferocious downpours. Just before 5pm a classic 'hammer-head' thundercloud had positioned itself immediately above the Craigie Burn catchment area and for one hour the rainfall was relentless in its intensity.

The storm led to spectacular overland 'sheet wash' down public roads in the Oakbank area with surface runoff finding its way into the Scouring Burn at Cherrybank. Further downstream, in Craigie, the surface runoff was also very significant. Overland flow washed out large cobbles and stones from surrounding fields and much of this debris became piled up against parked cars. Drains (locally known as 'condies') soon reached their capacity and rapidly began to issue flood water back out onto main roads, pavements and residents' gardens. In some locations even manhole covers were lifted off.

Most significantly was the out-of-bank flow from the Craigie Burn itself. A combination of very intense rainfall on a predominantly urbanised catchment produced a spectacular 'flash flood' which took less than an hour to peak. Flooding occurred in the upper reaches around Cherrybank Gardens where a partially blocked culvert forced waters to pond up to a depth of several feet within the Gardens before flowing across part of Necessity Brae and down a steep grass verge into the car park of the Cherrybank Inn where some vehicles were submerged. Where the Craigie Burn meets another of its tributaries, the Buckie Burn, parts of Low Road in Cherrybank were ripped up due to the high flow velocities.

Arguably, the most spectacular out-of-bank flow took place in Craigie along Queen's Avenue, Queen Street and Windsor Terrace. Instead of following the normal course to Windsor Terrace via the waterfall at Craigie Mill, the flood waters poured along Queen's Avenue, Queen Street and down a steep hill into Windsor Terrace where they rejoined the main watercourse. Several cars were partially flooded on these streets. Despite this temporary 'flood bypass' route, enough water was still following the normal course of Craigie Burn to ensure that the Craigie Mill waterfall was a spectacular sight.

There was also a third route taken by some of the flood water to rejoin the main Craigie Burn channel. This involved flowing along the full length of Queen Street and out onto the very busy Glenearn Road to find its way back to the main channel. Unfortunately, much of the flood water flowed along the walled walkway on the north bank of the Craigie Burn and through the tunnel into the South Inch causing severe flood damage to the Inch itself. Understandably, the annual Perth Agricultural Show due to take place on the South Inch later in the week was cancelled!

In August 2020 a similar event occurred. In Craigie there was damage in Queen Street and Windsor Terrace. In Cherrybank the houses in Low Road were severely affected with the Cherrybank Inn suffering around £30,000 worth of damage.

MYSTERIES, MYTHS AND MURDER

> The mysterious myths and legends,
> A true fact or a fake fact,
> No one really knows for sure.
> All these stories passed down
> from generation to generation,
> Makes a person wonder why?

(Derek James, 2013)

The Cuddies Strip Murder

When one considers the turbulent and violent history of Perth in bygone days (including the assassination of King James I) it is perhaps surprising that violent crime has played little part in the city's more recent past. Like any other town of comparable size, it has had serious assaults some of which have resulted in deaths, but in the main they have been crimes of passion where the victim has been known to the perpetrator. However, in 1935, the community was rocked by a vicious deed still referred to locally as 'The Buckie Braes Murder' or, more accurately, 'The Cuddies Strip Murder'.

By continuing uphill through the Buckie Braes at Cherrybank, a wooden swing gate leads out onto open grazing fields and a path runs alongside the golf course towards Callerfountain Hill. Near the start of this path, beside a wooden gate, another narrower path with a stile once broke off at right angles and continued for about a half mile through a narrow strip of trees, gorse and broom before joining the Aberdalgie road at the top of the Necessity Brae. Known locally as the 'Cuddies Strip' or 'Cuddies Track', it was once a favourite walk with courting couples and although most of the eastern half nearest to the Buckie Braes was sacrificed during the 1970s for the building of the M90 motorway, the western half of the Strip remains much as it was in the 1930s.

It was to the Cuddies Strip that a young Perth couple, eighteen-year-old Daniel Kerrigan and his seventeen-year-old girlfriend, Marjory Fenwick, made their way on the evening of Wednesday, 14th August 1935. Danny was well-known in the city. An apprentice glazier

Cuddie's Strip

with P & T McLeod, St. John's Place, he lived at 18 Union Lane in the city centre. A talented footballer, Danny had joined the junior side Scone Thistle the previous season from Craigie City Boys and had attracted the attention of local Scottish First Division side, St. Johnstone. On the Monday evening he had played in Scone's first match of the new season and had played well at outside left in their 4-1 victory over Perth Celtic. He was described as 'a perfect gentleman, on and off the field' and had also been an enthusiastic member of the 11th (Middle Church) Company of the Boys Brigade. Marjory Fenwick was a small, attractive brunette who lived with her parents at 8 Longcauseway, in the Dovecoteland area of the city, and had three older sisters and a brother. She was a frequent attender at dances in the city and worked in the confectionery factory of John Campbell Ltd in Fues Road.

Danny and Marjory had known each other for about three years and had been going out on Wednesdays and Sundays since the beginning of the year. That August evening, Danny called at Marjory's home at around 7pm and suggested going to see the Shirley Temple film *Bright Eyes* at the Kings Cinema but Marjory said that she was not too keen about Shirley Temple and the young couple decided, as it was a pleasant evening, to go for a walk. Wandering aimlessly through the Craigie area of the city with no particular place to go in mind, their route took them to Cherrybank and into the Buckie Braes and eventually the Cuddies Strip.

They remained in the middle section of the Cuddies Strip until darkness started to fall then, hearing the distant ten o'clock chimes of the Perth Academy clock, decided that it was time to head back to Perth. They had just started walking back along the narrow wooded track, chatting and joking and paying little heed to the surroundings, when they were startled by the sound of a gun apparently fired at very short range from behind them and Marjory felt something whistle past her ears. The startled couple spun round in sheer fright and

Danny had just exclaimed 'You're not going to faint, are you, Madge?' when a second shot rang out and he fell to the ground with blood streaming from his face.

As Marjory knelt over her unconscious boyfriend crying 'Danny, Danny, speak to me – it's Madge', she became aware of the presence of a man standing beside her. A man whom she later described as having 'glaring eyes' and with a handkerchief covering the lower half of his face. When she asked him what he was doing the man didn't answer and, thinking only of Danny, asked the man to watch over him while she ran to fetch assistance. She had only gone a few yards when she realised that she was being pursued. Although running as fast as she could, considering she was wearing fashionable court shoes, Marjory was unable to escape from the man running alongside her. The terrified girl reached the stile at the end of the Cuddies Strip and had one foot on it when she felt the man's hands gripping her and pulling her back. Despite her struggles, Marjory was hauled back into the bushes and her clothes were ripped from her body. She was gagged with her own undergarments, her hands tied behind her back with a handkerchief and sexually assaulted. The man then bound Marjory's feet and leaving her lying in the bushes headed back in the direction of Danny Kerrigan. A few minutes later she heard a shot and it was later surmised that the man had returned to where Danny lay and fired another shot at his chest.

Left alone in the darkness, the frenzied girl struggled to free herself but it was nearly an hour before she was able to slacken her bonds and struggle to her feet. Picking up her swagger coat which was lying nearby and securing it around her, Marjory left the remainder of her scattered torn clothing and footwear and fled barefoot towards the Buckie Braes, still not fully aware of Danny's condition.

Also in the Buckie Braes that Wednesday evening were another young Perth couple, John Spence and Dorothy Ewan. They had walked along the path through the Braes and then followed the path through the swing gate into the field where they sat for some time before leaving with the intention of catching the last bus into town from Cherrybank. Returning into the Braes through the gate, they had gone about twenty yards down the path when they heard the sound of someone running in the field on the other side of the fence. Mr Spence later told how a girl came to the side of the fence crying 'Can you help me, Mister?'. It was Marjory Fenwick. Mr Spence and

Miss Ewan then assisted her over the fence thinking at first that it was someone who had lost their way. They then noticed that she had some underwear round her neck, a handkerchief tied round her right wrist and was wearing neither shoes nor stockings. In a distressed and hysterical state, Marjory explained how she had been with a boy who had been shot and that a man had stripped her and carried her into the bushes. They assisted her down the path towards Cherrybank but on the rough ground their progress was painfully slow and it was nearly midnight before they reached Pickembere Cottages at the entrance to Buckie Braes.

John Spence quickly phoned the police from the call box at Cherrybank and also on the scene by this time was James Drummond, assistant janitor at Perth Academy. The first police officer to arrive was the local constable stationed at Cherrybank, James Ptolmey. Bravely accompanied by Marjory, who was given a pair of shoes by a Mrs Angus who lived in one of the cottages, he immediately set out with Spence and Drummond back through the Buckie Braes to the scene of the tragedy.

They found Danny Kerrigan in the same spot where Marjory had left him, about two hundred and fifty yards from the stile she had been attempting to climb when caught by her assailant. He was lying on his back with a green handkerchief, later disclosed as having been taken from Danny's top jacket pocket, covering his face and tucked in carefully below his chin. Although this was not mentioned at the later trial, apparently it was a custom among tinkers to cover the face of a dead person. There were gunshot wounds to Danny's face and chest.

With the arrival of other police officers a full scale murder investigation was launched but the culprit had by this time gained several hours advantage in making his getaway.

Marjory Fenwick was taken to the Drummond's home in Oakbank Terrace where Mrs Drummond kindly provided her with clothing and at 4am she was taken home to her mother who had by this time been informed by the police of the night's events. Later that morning, the distraught Kerrigan family were told the devastating news and Danny's body was formally identified by his mother and grandfather.

Although the first report of the murder was dealt with by the Perth City Police, as the murder had actually happened a few hundred yards outside the burgh boundary, the investigation was carried out by the Perthshire County Constabulary. Acting Chief Constable MacPherson,

Inspector Davidson, Detective Sergeant Campbell and other officers

This composite picture, which appeared in The Courier & Advertiser on August 24th 1935, shows the location of the murder. Taken from Craigie Hill golf course, it gives an idea of the countryside into which the culprit escaped.

were all at the scene of the tragedy before 2am on Thursday morning. The police scoured the hills and woods around the Cuddies Strip by torchlight for any clue or sign of the murderer. Cars coming in and out of Perth were stopped for any possible helpful information and details were circulated to the police of the neighbouring counties and to Dundee, Edinburgh and Glasgow. At this stage of the enquiry, the only description the police had of Danny Kerrigan's killer was from the meagre information supplied by Marjory Fenwick: 'About 30 years of age, 5ft 3 or 4 inches in height, reddish complexion, flattish nose, staring eyes, dressed in a dark jacket and dirty cap'. It was this description of a man with 'staring or glaring eyes' which was to capture the public's imagination.

The search continued throughout the day. The Cuddies Strip was sealed off as the undergrowth and the route followed by Marjory and her attacker were thoroughly combed. In the evening two aeroplanes flew for several hours over a wide circuit of the surrounding area. Two witnesses came forward who had heard shots the previous evening. The Cuddies Strip was not far from Hill of Pitheavlis Farm occupied by William McDougall. Although Mr McDougall had heard nothing unusual, his son William and a friend, Joe Wilkie of King Street, Perth, had been working on a motorcycle in the farmyard at around 10pm when they heard two shots coming from the direction of the Cuddies Strip. Under the belief that it was a poacher shooting rabbits, they thought no more about it.

After examination by a doctor and despite the shock of her traumatic experience less than twenty four hours earlier, Marjory and her mother accompanied the police to the Cuddies Strip on the Thursday afternoon. After Marjory assisted the police with a reconstruction of the movements of herself and her assailant, she and her mother were then driven to the County Police headquarters in South Street for a further one hour interrogation.

As the investigation continued, it was proved that the wounds on Kerrigan's body had been caused by the charge from a shotgun. The licenses granted for permission to use such firearms were closely scrutinised by the authorities and, in particular, those of persons who had recently obtained such a license. A strange feature of the case was that none of the clothing torn from Marjory Fenwick's body had been recovered and it was thought that the murderer must have taken them with him when making his escape. The shotgun had also not been traced.

All over Britain 'the man with the glaring eyes' was reported as having being spotted and the false alarms were many. Perth was now full of rumours of suspects and imminent arrests. Several people came forward claiming to have seen suspicious characters afoot that night.

William Pickard of 16 Queen Street in the Craigie district told how at 11.30pm he opened his gate to take his dog for a short walk when a man coming down the street saw him and turned and fled. He reached the junction at the top of the street and made to go up the hill but changed his mind, turned back into Queen Street then ran up Wilson Street as fast as he could go. If the murderer had come into Perth from the Cuddies Strip by way of Upper Craigie then that is the route *On Saturday, 17ᵗʰ August 1935, thousands of people lined the streets of Perth when the remains of Daniel Kerrigan were interred at Wellshill Cemetery. This Perthshire Advertiser photograph shows the cortege passing along South Methven Street.*

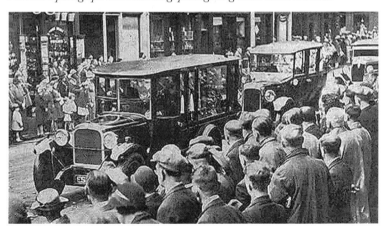

he would probably have taken. Two waitresses in the refreshment bar at Perth General Station told of a mysterious stranger they had seen in the room at around midnight. They were suspicious of his appearance and general demeanour, had failed to draw him into conversation and after finishing his tea he had quickly disappeared. Was that the same man spotted by Mr Pickard? The St Leonard's Bridge which crosses the railway lines at Perth station is just down the hill from Wilson Street and in the 1930s a flight of wooden steps led from the bridge onto the main platform. The question arose whether he had escaped into the Highlands on the Inverness train which left Perth at ten minutes to one.

False rumours circulated around the city when a man from Marjory Fenwick's neighbourhood and then two men from the city's Meal Vennel were interrogated by police. A gun spotted at Friarton by train passengers, who thought they had spotted the murder weapon, turned out to be an ordinary air rifle and two bundles of clothing discovered at Broughty Ferry were found to be totally unconnected to the crime. However, one vital find was the discovery by John Sharp of County Place, Perth of a second cartridge believed to have been fired by the murderer, the police having already found the other cartridge.

Two significant facts quickly emerged. It was now certain that Danny Kerrigan had been robbed of his pocket book which contained some letters and photographs, including one of Marjory Fenwick, and a sum of money believed to be between ten and twelve shillings. This was the first indication that robbery may have been a motive for the crime. In addition, the police had now been successful in tracing the laundry mark, M12, on the handkerchief which had been tied round Marjory's wrist during the assault.

On the evening of Sunday, 18th August the occupants of a house in Kinnaird Bank, Craigie were startled to hear a crash downstairs and, shortly afterwards, a man was seen running across Moredun Square in the direction of Craigie Knowes. Two police officers were summoned but after searching the house, garden and the Knowes were unable to trace anyone. However, the district's proximity to the scene of the murder lent colour to the theory that the intruder may have been hiding under cover in the neighbourhood and had been attracted to that particular house because of its unoccupied appearance – it was being redecorated and the curtains had been taken down. The intruder had overturned and broken a glass screen but nothing was found to be missing.

The police were also considering the possibility that two men may have been involved. Could one man concealed in the bushes have fired the shot which hit Danny Kerrigan, with the assault on Marjory Fenwick being committed by the man who stood beside her and then chased her along the path to the stile? With the investigation into its ninth day and the public demanding an early arrest, the officers of the County Constabulary were reinforced by two Glasgow detectives, Detective Lieut. Leith and Detective Sergeant MacDougall, recognised as being among the top criminal investigators in the West of Scotland.

In a further development, a former Perth man was held for questioning in Paisley. John Keir Cross, later to become a well-known writer, broadcaster and producer with the BBC, had left Perth a few days after the murder having given up his job with the General Accident insurance company on a sudden impulse. He was travelling southwards by bicycle as a wandering busker (he performed a ventriloquist act) and had mentioned to several people during his journey that he had known Kerrigan at school and had been in the Buckie Braes a few days before the murder. Cross was camping as he travelled and one night, acting on information received, three policemen arrived at his tent and he was arrested on suspicion of murder. Fortunately, a friend in Perth was able to prove that he had been with him in a Perth café at the time of the murder and, after a great deal of telephone communication between Paisley and Perth, it was agreed that Cross could not have committed the crime and he was released after spending a night in the cells.

Although the information relating to the laundry mark found on the handkerchief which had been tied round Marjory Fenwick's wrist had been withheld from the press and public, the police were now able to establish that as a vital clue. The handkerchief belonged to David Douglas of Aberdalgie House, Perthshire. He had got it from an Indian tradesman in South Africa and it had been stolen from Aberdalgie House in July along with a telescope and an alarm clock. The police now knew that whoever had broken into Aberdalgie House was their prime suspect for Danny Kerrigan's murder and the brutal assault on Marjory Fenwick. There was also a distinctive smell of wood smoke on the handkerchief which made the police reasonably sure that they were looking for someone who had been, or was still, living rough in the area.

About a mile away from the Cuddies Strip, on the south west side of Callerfountain Hill and close to Aberdalgie House, lies the farm of Kirkton of Mailer. On the evening of Wednesday, 28th August exactly three weeks after Danny Kerrigan's murder, Detective Lieutenant Leith and Sergeant Macdougall visited a tent on the farmland and took possession of various articles including a telescope. The occupant of the tent was arrested. Shortly before 11pm the same evening and, following an identification parade attended by Marjory Fenwick, Acting Chief Constable MacPherson made the official announcement that a man was in custody. The following morning, John McGuigan, alias John Milligan, a twenty-four-year-old farm labourer, Kirkton of Mailer, Parish of Forgandenny appeared before Honorary Sheriff Substitute Duncan McNab on two charges, one of murder and one of rape. Following the court proceedings, the prisoner was taken out of the building by a side entrance to avoid the crowd of several hundreds who had been gathered since early morning and escorted to Perth Prison. The following Tuesday, McGuigan made a second appearance in Perth Sheriff Court – this time on a charge of theft by housebreaking.

He was described as a squat, sallow, swarthy Irishman of tinker extraction. Most weekends he visited his parents at 'the berries' in Blairgowrie and worked occasionally at Kirkton of Mailer Farm where he enjoyed an acquaintance with some of the younger workers.

Neatly dressed in a dark grey suit and well groomed, John McGuigan gave the appearance of being unmoved as he sat in the dock when his trial opened at the High Court in Edinburgh on Monday, 25th November. Pleading not guilty, he faced three charges:

That between May 14th and August 14th, 1935 he did break into premises known as Aberdalgie House and did there steal a handkerchief, telescope, alarm clock, purse, razor and a football. That on August 14th, 1935 at the Cuddies Strip, he discharged a loaded shotgun at Marjory Watson Fenwick and Daniel Kerrigan and that he did shoot the said Daniel Kerrigan in the chest, neck and face and did murder him. The third charge was that at on the said August 14th, at a stile on the south side of the field, he did assault the said Marjory Watson Fenwick, seize hold of her, carry or drag her along the ground, throw her down, compress her throat, tie her hands, and did ravish her.

Marjory Fenwick entered the witness box shortly after mid-day and a crowded court, which included a number of Perth people in the public galleries, heard her tell the story of her ordeal in a composed, but occasionally almost inaudible voice. There was a particularly tense moment when, reminded by the presiding judge Lord Aitchison that John McGuigan was on trial for his life, she pointed to the accused as the man who had assaulted her on that fateful August night. Marjory Fenwick was in the witness box for two hours and forty minutes recounting the story of her ordeal.

Of the seventy-one witnesses cited by the Crown, several spoke of having been in the vicinity of the Cuddies Strip that evening. One witness, twenty-five-year-old Arthur Hill, told of hearing two shots coming from the direction of the Strip while walking towards the Buckie Braes with his girlfriend and said that he later heard a third shot from the same direction just before they reached Cherrybank about half a mile further on. Robert Barrie, Robert Stewart, Alexander Stewart and Will Speedie all spoke of being in the Cuddies Strip during the course of the evening and had spotted a man on his own, wearing a cap and a heather–grey jacket, coming down from the wood on Callerfountain Hill from the direction of Kirkton of Mailer. Presuming him at first to be a gamekeeper and none of these men having any love of gamekeepers, they had hidden behind a dyke until he had passed. Another witness, William Gow, identified McGuigan as a man he had seen in the Cuddies Strip during the afternoon of 14th August watching courting couples through a telescope and he had spotted him again in the area with his telescope at 8.30pm. It was also mentioned that there was a large bush ten yards from where Danny Kerrigan's body was found which would have offered a place of concealment for the murderer.

Eighteen year old John Peddie, a ploughman at Kirkton of Mailer Farm, told the court how the McGuigan family lived in a tent half a mile west of the farm steading on the way towards Aberdalgie. He said that some days John McGuigan worked on the farm but other days he did not. Peddie told how he was aware that McGuigan possessed an unlicensed double-barrelled shotgun and on the night of the murder had been out with a friend and passed McGuigan's tent but he was not there. He saw McGuigan next day and asked him if he had been out shooting 'and accidentally shot the man'. McGuigan made rather a strange reply, 'I thought you would be thinking that.' He said he had hidden the gun because he had no licence and 'was frightened for the police getting it.' However another witness, John Arnott, spoke of the accused as having a single barrel rifle which he used for duck shooting on the River Earn and kept hidden in a ditch about a quarter of a mile from the tent.

The same day, Ronald Mackenzie was working with McGuigan in a cornfield when they saw a policeman cycling along the road. 'They need not bother going up now', said McGuigan, 'I have my gun away'. Evidence was also given by the grieve at the farm 'What's this you've been up to, John?' McGuigan had looked disconcerted at the question but said that he had been out with his glasses but back in his tent by half past nine. Expert evidence was given that the wounds that killed Danny Kerrigan came from a double-barrelled shotgun fired from eight yards (gun expert) or ten yards (police doctor). This would tie in with the gun being fired from the bushes close to where Danny and Marjory had been sitting.

It seems strange that no sustained attempt was made to find the double-barrelled shotgun which, from McGuigan's remarks, must have been hidden on the night of the murder or the next day and would not be very far from his tent.

As the trial reached its conclusion, Mr Albert Russell KC, on behalf of the Crown, said that the Court had heard the case of a gun discharged by a lurking ruffian and as the victim's life was ebbing away, a man who, he was afraid, was the lurking murderer, committed a revolting outrage upon the young girl who was walking with her lover when the gun was fired. Mr Russell said that Marjory Fenwick had been subjected to a very searching cross examination. It was undoubtedly a story of an extraordinary and most unusual occurrence but it was her account of what took place on the night in question. Mr Russell further stated that fingerprint evidence had proved that it was the accused who had broken into Aberdalgie House and among the articles stolen was a telescope and the handkerchief which had been used to tie Marjory's hands together. Although the gun used in the shooting had not been found, evidence had been given that the accused had a gun and evidence had also been given that the accused had been seen in the Cuddies Strip at during the afternoon and again during the evening. Was there any reasonable doubt, he asked, that the man who assaulted Miss Fenwick was also the man who fired the fatal shot at Kerrigan?

Before calling upon Mr Wardlaw Burnett to make his speech for the defence, Lord Aitchison referred to an interesting point of law in regard to the relationship of charges in the indictment. It was open to the jury, he said, to find a verdict of guilty of murder and to acquit on the charge of rape, although, no doubt, the evidence upon the third charge must be taken into account in considering the second because it was quite impossible to split the case into apartments in considering the charge of murder.

The counsel for the defence, Mr Wardlaw Burnett KC, said that the charge of murder depended entirely on the evidence given by Marjory Fenwick, the sole witness to the actual shooting. Mr Burnett told the Court:

> I don't say the girl was manufacturing evidence or making up a story, the shooting of Kerrigan is true, the whole of her story as presented by her is not one that you can accept implicitly at her hand. You must remember that although she has told the same general story from the beginning, she was, when first seen, a girl in a distressed and hysterical condition and a man's life is not to be sworn away by the evidence of a hysterical girl. Miss Fenwick's story is so astounding and improbable, whether you regard the circumstances connected with the shooting and the remarkable fact that she herself was not injured, or of the assault upon her, that it is not one which you, in this grave case, will accept as a full and truthful account of what happened, even if you make all proper allowances for the state of mind of the girl.

Mr Burnett pointed out that no gun had been traced that linked the shooting to John McGuigan and without this vital evidence it was impossible to convict the accused of murder on the unsubstantiated evidence of one or two witnesses.

On the sixth day of the trial, Saturday, 30th November, the two hours and twenty minutes summing-up of the judge, Lord Aitchison, reflected that the evidence against McGuigan was quite considerable. He told the jury:

> Don't forget, when you are in the region of crime of this gravity you are definitely in the region of the abnormal. People who commit crimes of this sort are not to be measured by ordinary

standards. Also remember the man who was capable of shooting Kerrigan dead in the presence of that young girl when they were sweet hearting together was a man capable of any crime. There is no doubt that whoever committed this crime was a man of low and degraded mentality... the first three or four witnesses who saw her had not the least doubt the girl's story was true... if the accused was the man who stole the handkerchief from Aberdalgie and tied it on her wrists, then the inference that he was the man who fired the shot became inevitable. It was circumstantial evidence; but they had the clearest evidence of Marjory Fenwick that though she did not see him pull the trigger, the accused was there at the time.

The jury of eight women and seven men retired to consider their verdict and returned two hours and ten minutes later. In the tense silence of the crowded courtroom, the foreman announced that they found McGuigan guilty of housebreaking and theft, guilty of rape, but by a majority of nine to six they found the murder charge Not Proven.

In passing sentence upon the prisoner, Lord Aitchison said:

John McGuigan, you have been acquitted of the charge of murder that was brought against you, but you have been found guilty by a unanimous verdict of the jury of a grave charge of housebreaking and theft, and of the very grave crime of rape. In order that you might have an absolutely fair trial and in accordance with our Scottish practice, your criminal record was not disclosed to the jury. It is before me now. I find that in 1929 you were convicted of assault; in July 1929, you were convicted of theft by housebreaking; in September 1929, you were convicted of theft; in May 1932 you were convicted of theft by housebreaking; and in February 1934 you were convicted of theft, the indictment containing four charges. I am satisfied from your criminal record and from the convictions that are now recorded against you that you are a dangerous criminal, and that it is necessary in the public interest and in your own interest that you be detained for a very considerable time. In considering what sentence I ought to impose, I leave completely out of account the grave suspicion that has attached to you in connection with the murder of Kerrigan. You have been acquitted of that and I leave any suspicion that might attach to you completely out of account:

but, having regard to the gravity of the offences of which you now stand convicted, and of your record, the sentence is that you be detained in penal servitude for ten years.

It was generally felt that John McGuigan was a very fortunate young man, as a murder verdict would almost certainly have meant the death penalty.

Marjory Fenwick endured a very considerable ordeal in seeing her sweetheart brutally murdered beside her, almost immediately afterwards being raped and later having to suffer in court from the hostile questioning and occasional innuendoes of the defence council. Though only seventeen, she stood up to the pressures exceedingly well.

In an interview in *The People's Journal* of 7th December 1935 she is quoted as follows: 'I spoke nothing but the truth. There was, however, much more I could have said but somehow or other I never got the chance to say it. Indeed when Mr Burnett (Defence Council) was addressing the jury I felt like jumping up and requesting to be allowed to go into the witness box again. With another half hour there, I believe I could have cleared up a number of hazy points.'

The Preacher's Well and The Devil's Pulpit

On the Craigie Knowes Road side of Craigie Knowes, just before Squire's Cottages, there is an old drinking fountain known as the Preacher's Well. The fountain was installed in Edwardian times by those involved in the temperance movement to keep men from the pubs while on long Sunday walks.

In more recent times when members of the South Perth Green Spaces Group noticed that tree root growth was causing the fountain to collapse, they raised funds to allow for its restoration by David Wilson, a local artist and stonemason.

The fountain has inscriptions on three separate panels. The left hand inscription

The Preacher's Well

reads 'The Bosk above the Well' (bosk being an old Scots word for small wood); the centre one reads 'The Preacher's Well. Rest in Thee'; and on the right side 'Known as the Devils's Pulpit'.

Legend has it that the preacher was none other than the Devil himself who is reputed to have stood on the top of the Craigie Knowes cliff above the well and preached a sermon to the people of Perth encouraging them to dishonour the Sabbath and lead a life of debauchery.

The tale is related in the following poem by 'Cantor' which was published in the *Perthshire Courier* on 7th January 1868:

The sun long down o'er the caller fountain,
Leaving the knowes in mirk;
By Cherry Bank road was seen dismountin,
A blacksmith – or a stirk.
Whether the eyes which saw were blinded,
And it was one, or both,
Or half and half they had designed it,
I know not, by my troth!

From a chariot we'll say he alighted,
And carefully scraped his shoon.
Till with the sparks of the furze was lighted,
Serving in place of the moon.
From a fiery chariot he descended,
Then sprung on a ledge of rock,
Which 'neath his feet first swayed and bended,
Then moulded with the shock.

I really hope you may gulp it,
It seems so very queer –
Into the form of a splendid pulpit
That stood for many a year.
The holes he kicked for his feet to stand on
Seemed as if chiselled out
And from the scale that they were planned on,
He must have had the gout.
His knuckles on the trap then sounding,
Just like Revival Bell,

NAE PLACE MAIR BRAW

The half dressed Pop came wildly bounding,
For something new to tell.
They gathered round in a circle, quaking;
Wild eyes and drooping jaws;
As from his pouch he is seen taking
A ponderous book of Laws.

He lighted his nails on the trap before him,
By which to see the print,
And grinned as the sulphorous smell rose o'er him
Seeming to pleasure in't.
Then opening the book at a well-thumbed quarter,
'Twas marked with a Roman cross –
Displayed a mouth like an Armstrong mortar,
Or rather an ancient fosse.

His teeth were fangs of choicest metal,
With grooves for them to lie in,
And they seemed to be in splendid fettle,
From crunching the bones of the dying.
'And first' he cried – in accents clear,
That seemed to come from a distance,
Even to those whom stood quite near –
'I claim your bold assistance.

'In keeping up with the gallant times,
When all the land was frisky,
And lads – could scarce lisp Scottish rhymes –
Could swill at Scottish whisky.
'There's no delight' again he cried,
'In hearing old men prosing,
Like boys and women stupified –
 Half cursing and half dosing.

'Then here's unto the good old days,
With licks and liquor plenty:
Gudemen wi' not too gentle ways,
Gudewives not over dainty.
'When everyone could take their glass,

Mid jovial songs and laughter,
And thought but of the time that was,
Ne'er gloomed of what came after.'

He raised a rummer up on high
And drained it to the dregs,
Then in rushed Tam to hae a dram,
That shook him off his legs.
And manners that are bad they say,
Communicate like lightning;
So all the rest would ha'e ane tae,
Till each cheek was like whitening.

He then turned o'er another leaf,
And pointed with his finger:
'So now! My good friends! To be brief,
'Tis rather cold to linger.
Keep in on Sabbath afternoon,
And do not spare the 'drink';
The gay hedgerows of emerald June
Might help to make you think.

Don't have too many active games,
Not stupid mental training;
The one makes cowards like King James,
The other's always straining.
In spending at the race or fair,
Be ye there with the inmost.
But – sanitory matters – there
Do ye aye 'druttle hinmost'.

And, take my word, 'fore very long,
I'll love your city dearly!
Alas! that demon prophet's tongue
Should speak the truth – or nearly.
Now you're my followers every one'
He cried, 'both soul and body;
I'll hold well tethered as you run,
And keep you to the toddy'.

He leaped into his glowing van,
And cuffed the charioteer –
A little imp all black and tan,
With a smell of bitter beer.
The furze around burnt to the ground,
With this smell of atrocious twist;
And his chariot wheel, as he crossed the hill,
Cut a pathway through the schist.

Which, to this day, by the Earn way,
Is a terror to wayfarers –
Big or little, grave or gay,
Pedestrians or airers.
The words he spoke, from the point of rock,
Sank deep into each bosom;
And ever since, his bearers wince
At thought of the preacher gruesome.

The Broxden Curse

Just west of Cherrybank is the Broxden Roundabout where routes to Dundee, Edinburgh, Glasgow, Inverness and Perth all converge. It is one of the most dangerous and notorious road circles in Scotland. In one year alone, according to Police Scotland, there were over seventy accidents reported on that stretch of road and mainly as the result of lorries and heavy goods vehicles overturning as they negotiated the bends of the circle. I had a personal experience of this in 1988 when I watched an articulated lorry turn on its side and come to rest just a few feet away from my car. A lucky escape!

Many theories have been put forward as to why this happens – such as bad road alignment or the fact that, because of too many routes being close together, the junction should have been designed with fly-overs and slip roads instead of a roundabout. No expert has yet provided a reason or solution to the problem. However, perhaps if the road engineers had consulted some of Perthshire's travelling people they would have learned that the area nurses a curse.

In her excellent book, *Way of the Wanderers,* about the travelling people of Perthshire, the writer Jess Smith tells the tale of old Annie's stone and I am grateful to her for giving me permission to reproduce the story here:

Over two hundred years ago, in a strip of woodland between the Lamberkin path and Tinkers Loan, a worried and desperate father-to-be, a pedlar Bobby Naismith, was holding his young wife Alison's hand as she urged him to send for the herb wife. In these days, poor women unable to afford a midwife would get the herb wife to help with the delivery of their babies. This was only thought necessary in the birth of a first child or in dire need and in this case it was Alison's first child and she was in severe distress.

Leaving Alison as comfortable as possible in their bow-tent home of hazel sticks and animal skins, Bobby set off to fetch old Annie Milady, the nearest herb wife, who lived over three miles away in a tiny cottar house near Craigend on the outskirts of Perth.

He had only gone a mile when a band of men, uncouth and foul-mouthed with drink, barred his way. From their appearance, Bobby recognised them as army deserters and that their purpose was robbery. 'Let me go unhindered, lads,' he said 'for I have a wife who needs help to bear her baby, and I am in haste to fetch the herb-wife' and he spread his hands to show that he carried nothing, neither a purse nor weapon.

One of the band of ruffians stepped forward and without a word turned Bobby around and whipped of his leather belt making his shirt loosen and his plaid fall to the ground. The reality of fear crept through his body and he prayed and pleaded with the men for compassion. 'O God almighty, whatever you men have done and whoever hounds you for it, my eyes will not witness your presence on this path and my words will never tell of it. Let me pass. My sixteen-year-old wife is in fear this very minute. Allow me to go in peace for the herb-woman.'

The ruffians then set upon Bobby. One almost knocked him over while another prodded his ribs with a sharp stick and mocking him, 'Oh yer wee wife's haein a bairn. Yer wee wife canna dae it herself. Oh shame.' Bobby tried not to provoke them with an angry answer. Alison's situation helped him to remain strong and he didn't want to show his anguish. He felt like a trapped mouse being tormented by a cat and he was way out of his depth.

One of the gang, bushy-bearded with massive forearms, who

appeared to be the leader as he seemed to hold more authority than the rest, issued an order. 'Shut up! I'll see if this intruder has the guts to put me back.' He turned to his cohorts and said, 'What have ye men? Shall we let him pass or will we charge him a mighty penny for toll, or will I teach him not to come running past our hollow without permission?' 'Charge the fool' was the men's reply. 'Did ye hear them, lad', said the bushy-bearded leader, 'We want a florin from you'.

Bobby winced. The last thing his pride wanted to do was to pay money to these villains but the vital thing was to get away. In this desperate state he would have given anything he had just to get away. 'I don't have a farthing, let alone two shillings' he told the man, 'But if you let me pass I'll borrow the money from the herb-wife'.

The leader lowered his menacing gaze and handed Bobby back his belt saying 'Here laddie, stop fretting, put on your plaid. We don't want your pennies. We got lucky in a cock fight yesterday and don't want your money. But I'm dreeling for a smoke, are you sure there's no baccy hidden in that bonnie white sark?'

Bobby, thinking that the whole thing had been a jest, shook his head at the question then heard the rascal whisper to him through clenched teeth. 'You must know laddie, we canna let you go free. There's a troop searching for us. We deserted Fort Geordy and have been on the run for six months now. We keep clear of the law by silencing witnesses. So, laddie, it's now time to finish you off. Want to go clean with a stroke of the knife or take on me and my boys one by one?'

Bobby wasn't sure if the man was still playing mind games with him or whether he would really relish cutting his throat. But Alison's predicament and not his own safety was all that mattered. As he bent down to pull on his plaid he glanced around looking for an opening through which he could escape. It would probably mean death to make a run for it but he was desperate.

Reading his mind, the bearded red-faced leader kicked out, knocking Bobby flat. 'You're going nowhere laddie!' He pulled out a short broken-bladed sword from a leather scabbard and began to hack wildly at Bobby's clothing. Bobby had no choice. He knew that Alison left alone and without help would certainly die so he lunged at the brigand who was about to end his life and put all his strength behind a heavy tackle. Down and over a rocky outcrop they tumbled, rolling further away from the other outlaws who were laughing and drinking. Bobby fought with the desperation of a cornered rat and with a fierce swing of his arm caught his opponent with a jagging uppercut which sent him down like a sack full of stones. In blind panic Bobby made off in a homeward direction but still had courage to shout out to the other outlaws, 'The barrack at Fort George will hear about you lot. I'd scatter if I were you. This miserable excuse for a man is dead in the grass if you want to check'.

Alison had had her own battle while he was gone but as he entered their tent he heard the sound of a baby's cries. Inside he embraced his wife but they decided it was no longer safe to stay in the quiet corner of Lamberkin Wood. As Alison was too weak to walk, Bobby harnessed up his old horse and made a comfortable bed for his wife and baby son in the cart.

Half a mile from the path barred by the deserters there was a lesser-known drovers' route which would take the around their camp to a cottage owned by a candle maker. Bobby knew the candle maker and his wife who were a decent couple who bought his long lasting washing pegs and other pedlar wares.

But the moor's unwelcome band of remaining deserters were not finished with young Bobby and were waiting for them on either side of the winding track. Surrounded on all sides, Bobby stood aghast with his wife and new-born child. 'They'll kill us Alison' he cried. 'Take the baby and get into the bushes. I love you Alison. Kiss my son for me, lassie'.

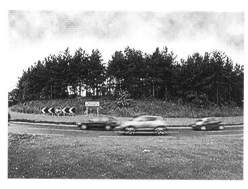

The Broxden Roundabout

Bobby fought that day with a passion that none of the outlaws had seen before and before the club was raised that delivered the fatal blow he had taken three of his enemies with him. Alison was left lying in her own blood but the brigands did spare the life of the baby.

When the candle makers chanced upon the horrific scene they found Alison clinging onto life. With her dying breath she was able to tell what happened and they reassured her that they would look after the tiny boy.

When the news of the terrible tragedy reached old Annie Milady, the herb-wife, she covered her head in a black shawl and went to the grisly scene. Carefully, she and other local folks cleared a plot in the gorse bushes and buried the young couple there. The old horse was sent for butchering and the upturned cart with its improvised bed was burned.

After the mourners left, old Annie unearthed a large stone and rolled it to the spot where the young couple had been killed. She knelt down and uttered a few ancient incantations over the stone and the place of death.

> On this stone I put a curse:
> Wheel rolls and rim over,
> Watch now ye wild rover,
> Earth ripple and rumble,
> Cart coup and load tumble.

Today's Broxden Roundabout is believed to be situated on the exact spot of Annie's stone where the curse was made by the old herb-wife. Next time that you drive on that bit of road be extra careful and remember the curse and the pedlar's fate with respect.

The Craigie Stores Bairn

At the end of Windsor Terrace in Craigie a steep flight of stone steps leads up to Moncreiffe Terrace. For many generations of Craigie residents these have been known as the Witch's Steps or Witch's Stairs. Various suggestions have been made as to the reason for this name.

One popular idea is that many years ago a young girl going off to a fancy dress party dressed as a witch lost her footing at the top the steps and fell all the way down to Windsor Terrace and was killed.

It is also said that the steps are haunted by a cruel witch and an

The Witch's Steps and the witch's claw!

interesting feature is the shape of a hand or claw set into the stone wall at the top of the steps.

In 1992, the people of Craigie were shocked by reports in the local press of the body of a newly born child being discovered in a garbage bin at the rear of the shop in Craigie Place known as Craigie Stores, close to St Mary Magdalene's Church.

Mr Jimmy Forbes, the owner of the shop, was deeply distressed and started a fund to raise money for a gravestone for the child. The kind-hearted community of Craigie were quick to rally to the cause and named the child Mary Magdalene Glover. A gravestone was erected at her burial place in Wellshill Cemetery but, despite, strenuous efforts by the police, the mother of the child was never traced.

The following poem by a Craigie resident, John W Spiers, was published in the *Perthshire Advertiser* in remembrance of the baby:

My first home was in a rubbish bin
And clothed in a plastic wrap;
With some shame, I had no name,
No love or no mother's lap.
It wasn't to be, this world to see,
To be happy with sisters and brothers,

To have lots of friends on which life depends,
Like them that had Fathers and Mothers.
A new life has shone, from my friend John,
With a stone and nice flowers to cover,
In a happy place with God's grace,
And my name is now Miss Mary Glover.
My ordeal will cease, I am now at peace,
You have helped me to go on my way,
But don't be upset, to you I'm in debt,
I'm being loved in heaven every day.
There is a treat in store, I've not had before,
And I know that this day will come,
I'll be first at the gate and happy to wait,
With my own dear Mum.

Ghosts and Hauntings

As previously mentioned, Rosslyn House on the Graybank Road/Glover Street/Glasgow Road corner was formerly the Perth Poorhouse and built in the mid-nineteenth century on the site of the former Playfield of Perth.

It is recorded that executions and the burning of bodies took place in the Playfield lands during the seventeenth century and over the years some strange happenings, or perhaps hauntings, have happened within the present building – now luxury apartments. Footsteps have been heard in corridors during the night, electrical appliances and lights have switched on or off and the sound of weeping has been heard.

In the 1960s, when the building was called Bertha Home, a resident found a bathroom door locked and heard the noise of splashing and running water through the closed door. A few minutes later they returned to find the bathroom empty, completely dry and very cold. It would appear that ghosts don't need to use towels!

It is said that Pitheavlis Castle in Needless Road once had a ghost – a lady spirit known as the Grey Lady. Some people maintained that she was the mother of Patrick Oliphant searching for her son who was killed while attempting to reach the safety of the castle after the Battle of Tippermuir in 1636. It has also been said that the spirit would sometimes make an appearance around early September on the anniversary of the battle.

I do know of an occasion, back in the 1970s, when a young child in a Needless Road house spoke of seeing a lady dressed in old fashioned clothes standing in her bedroom and looking out a window. On another occasion, in September 2014, a Perth plumber working alone on the central heating in another Needless Road house told the occupants on their return that he had seen an elderly lady, again dressed in old fashioned clothes, sitting on a chair at the top of the stairs.

Another tale is that the Grey Lady would sometimes make herself known following the death of a resident in the area near the castle. A clock might suddenly stop, a picture fall from a wall, a water tap might be turned on or perhaps a closed door or window would be found open.

Obviously there are logical and plausible reasons for any of these events occurring but there was an occasion in November 1983 when I had a personal experience which, to me anyway, still defies any logic or explanation.

It happened on the day my mother died. I went into the front room of our Needless Road home to find a photograph of my parents, which had always stood on the mantelpiece over the fire, lying in the middle of the room. It was out of its frame with the glass undamaged. If it had simply fallen off the mantelpiece the glass would have been smashed on the fireplace tiles.

Perhaps Shakespeare was right when he wrote in *Hamlet* that 'there are more things in heaven and earth, Horatio, than are dreamt of in your philosophy!'

EATIN' TATTIES, CHIPS AND PEAS

Hello, hello. We are the Craigie boys;
Hello, hello. The boys who make a noise;
Up to our knees in candle grease,
Eatin' tatties. chips and peas,
We are the Craigie boys.

(Old street song with local variations)

Youthful Years

Throughout Britain, the 1940s had been a decade of challenge for everyone. The hardships and fear created by a world war were immense with the bombing of cities and towns and evacuated children facing the hardships of being parted from their parents. The rationing of food, clothing and petrol was a way of life.

For the first five years of my life my father had been a virtual stranger and I had begun my schooling at Craigie School (then Western District) by the time he returned home after doing war service with the RAF. I was one of the lucky ones as there were children in my class whose fathers had not returned. My Primary 7 teacher, Mrs Morrison, lost her husband in World War I and then her only son in World War II.

Perth had been fortunate in escaping the German bombers during World War II although there had been no room for complacency amongst the residents of Craigie. The close proximity of Perth Railway Station and the prolific number of crowded troop trains using it meant that it was seriously regarded as a prime target. Indeed an attempt was made at bombing the station when a train spotted disappearing into the darkness of the Moncreiffe tunnel at Craigend was mistaken for a train entering the blacked out station. Interestingly, in 1999 two unexploded World War II bombs were unearthed in the garden of a house in nearby Fairies Road in the Oakbank area and close to Cherrybank.

My mother used to speak of hearing the distinctive sound of waves of the Luftwaffe's bombers passing overhead from Stavanger in Norway on their way to the destructive bombing of Clydebank. She maintained that the safest place for us to be on such occasions was in the cupboard under the stairs of our Needless Road home rather than in one of the two air raid shelters situated at each end of the lane between Needless Road and Cavendish Avenue.

Despite the restrictions of food and clothes rationing, growing up in Craigie and Cherrybank in the postwar years was a lot of fun. It has probably been so to every generation but there was a lot to be said for life in the 1940s and 1950s which is probably missing in today's electronic and more affluent age.

For many of us brought up around Craigie and Cherrybank, life was idyllic in many ways. We had perfect freedom to wander wherever the mood took us as long as we were home in time for meals. We were expected to get around on our own, on foot or by bike or bus, even to the extent of going downtown alone. It was a rare mother who picked up her child from school even during torrential downpours or heavy snowfalls. We knew the postman, the milkman, the lamplighter, the local policeman and all the delivery men by name. The way the society of that time worked – mothers at home, sometimes a grandparent living with the family – there were fewer opportunities for people to get into trouble. Discipline for children included a sharp glance or word from *any* adult. The neighbourhood looked after its own – or so it seemed.

Perhaps it was a golden age. There were fewer disaffected adults than there are now, likely because they had gone through two decades of war and economic depression – the 'been down so long this looks like up' syndrome. Looking back, it seems that the world was a much safer place then. Our world was full of simple although sometimes risky pleasures. There was the building of dams and fishing for 'baggie minnows' in the Craigie Burn; wandering the nooks and crannies of Buckie Braes and Craigie Knowes; boating and putting on the South Inch; sneaking in to the Cleeve House estate to play on a rope swing; playing amongst the muck of the sheep pens in the cattle mart; gathering chestnuts in autumn and then stringing them for the games of 'chessies' in the school playground where we also cast our first glances into the female world of gym slip, skipping rope and peevers! Sweets were still rationed until 1953 but there were threepenny bags of chips available from the fish and chip shops at St Leonard's Bridge and Glover Street at the foot of Needless Road or from a converted bus, complete with chimney, which served the area as a mobile chip van. A wee bag of sherbet from the Craigie Co-op was a delicacy!

For those of us who lived around Needless Road, Cavendish Avenue, Gray Street or Pitheavlis there was the attraction of the 'big field' – a vast area bounded by Cavendish Avenue, Pickletullum Road and Pitheavlis Terrace. This was our sledging run in winter; it was where the 'Guy Fawkes' bonfire was built each November; it was where gang huts were built in summer; it was where we played 'Cowboys and Indians' or emulated whatever action film we had recently watched at the Saturday morning GB Club films at the Cinerama in Victoria Street. It was where on at least a couple of occasions we set the entire field on fire! Suddenly, one day in the early 1950s, the bulldozers moved in to start the building of Stuart Avenue and Pitheavlis Crescent, the lower northern side of Cavendish Avenue and the western side of Pickletullum Road, thus ending years of daring and sometimes dangerous youthful pleasures.

Those who grew up in the Darnhall area and in the post-war houses of Woodside Crescent, Glamis Place and Balmoral Place had the attraction of the swing park at Darnhall Crescent (it also held a 'Guy Fawkes Night' bonfire); the 'wee woods' alongside the path between Craigie Knowes Road and Cherrybank which eventually were to become part of the Craigie View development; the 'half mile' sledging run from Craigie Hill to Craigie Knowes Road; and 'Logie's Field' between Craigie Knowes Road and Queen's Avenue – named after the horse which for many years was a popular attraction for the children of Craigie and Moncreiffe. In the 1970s the field gave way to the modern houses of the Craigie Knowes Avenue cul-de-sac.

But there was always football in the Craigie School playing field between Young Street and Needless Road and, for a few short weeks in summer, there was also cricket (sometimes using a telegraph pole as a wicket). The Saturday morning football matches of the early 1950s between Needless Road and

The 13th Perthshire Craigie Cub pack photographed during a rally at Muirton Park (c1951). (Perthshire Advertiser photograph)

Some members of the Craigie Cubs preparing for one of the popular cub Gang Shows which were held annually in Craigie Hall during the late 1940s and early 1950s and were one of the highlights of the social year in Craigie. There are a lot of 'weel kent' lads in this photograph including Donald Mackay (back row, extreme right) who was Dundee United's goalkeeper in the 1960s and later became manager of Dundee.

A fancy dress party in Craigie Hall around 1952 held by the Craigie Cubs and Craigie Brownies. (Perthshire Advertiser photograph).

Cavendish Avenue were played with all the enthusiasm and intensity of any Old Firm match or Tayside Derby! The unwritten rules allowed Needless Road to recruit players from around Darnhall, Wilson Street and Glover Street while the 'Cavvy Avvy' team could enlist players from

Two groups of Brownies and one of Girl Guides (all c1960s)

Gray Street, Pickletullum and Pitheavlis. There was also a hockey pitch in the playing field alongside Needless Road and the

A 1960s photograph of Craigie Church Girl Guides who lent a helping hand at a church bazaar held in the City Hall which raised over £1000 towards the church hall building fund. (Perthshire Advertiser photograph).

Children of Craigie Road at a Coronation party, 1953).

smaller hockey goals were ideal for impromptu football matches played well into the evenings using the street lamps of Needless Road as floodlights. Many the 'telling off' we received for arriving home late with our school trousers covered in mud – no washing machines at home in these days!

Very much a part of life in those days was the Craigie Cubs. It was almost obligatory for every boy in the Craigie area to join the Cubs. Not only were the Friday night meetings in the Craigie Hall in Priory Place a welcome release from the school week, they also offered an opportunity for boys to mix with others who were slightly older or younger than themselves and many lasting friendships were formed as a result of joining the 13th Perthshire. Much of the success of the Cub pack was due to the endless devotion and enthusiasm of the cub

Twin brothers Neal (right) and Douglas Mathers clearing their father's Morris Minor in Needless Road after a snow storm in 1957. Their father, the Reverend J A C Mathers was the first minister of Moncreiffe Church. (Photograph courtesy of Neal Mathers)

TOP: *Craigie Scouts football team, 1963.* BOTTOM: *Raspberry picking at Bridgeton Farm, 1983).*

master ('Akela') Bert James and a dedicated team of assistants.

On reaching the age of twelve some of the boys joined the equally successful 13th Perthshire (Craigie) Scout troop although many of the others who were now of secondary school age chose to join some of the larger city troops such as the 53rd Perthshire (Congregational Church); the 74th Perthshire (St John's Kirk); the 22nd Perthshire (Wilson Church); or the troop attached to Perth Academy – the 10th Perthshire.

The girls of the area were not forgotten and Craigie Church became home to the

4th Company of Girl Guides and Brownies. With the opening of the new Moncreiffe Church in the 1950s another company of Guides and Brownies was formed there, along with an active Boys Brigade and Life Boy company.

Memories

When you see the morning sunlight
Tint the trees upon Kinnoull,
Or watch the Craigie Burn
As it flows by rocks and pool;
When you pass Pitheavlis Castle
Or climb Callerfountain Hill,
Will you think of the old, old days once more,
Will you? I think you will.

In 2005 a Vancouver businessman, David McDonald, recalled holiday visits during the 1940s to the home of his grandparents, Fred and Ella Impett, who lived in Kinfauns Crescent in Needless Road for over thirty years. David's detailed description of these visits makes interesting social reading:

My grandparents lived in Kinfauns Crescent in Needless Road and I would stay with them during holidays from my English boarding school. At that time the homes were all rented and their front window looked almost straight up Darnhall Drive. The flats were arranged with a plain bedroom window alongside the arched common entrance way and then the bay window of the parlour next to that. Standing on the path and facing the entranceway, you would have to point upwards at about 45 degrees to indicate the bay window of Granny's parlour. Lighting in the house was by gas and the WCs were located on the half landing – I was the talk of the building when I installed a battery-operated electric light in our WC!

Granny's parlour was only used to entertain people you did not really like! It had very formal and highly prized furniture on which one was encouraged not to sit. It also had a piano where my first musical attempts were made. The same room had a curtained-off alcove in which my grandfather slept. The only bedroom was my granny's and was the first door on the left after coming through the front door. The only door to the right, after coming into the front hallway, led into the kitchen and attached to the kitchen was a small scullery in which there was a stove and sink. The cold water tap for the sink was the only water source in the place. There was also a curtained-off alcove in the kitchen in which slept my aunt. The only heating in the whole flat was a fireplace in the kitchen and the fire burned only in the evening and at night. The fireplace in the parlour I cannot ever remember seeing lit. As mentioned before, there was no electricity and they had a battery-powered radio. The radio had a high voltage non-rechargeable battery of dry cells plus a low voltage 'accumulator' which had to be carried down to the Craigie radio shop every month to be re-charged. This accumulator was, in effect, a lead acid battery having a glass case – not to be dropped!

Baths were taken in a galvanised bathtub once a week and this was filled with kettles of hot water. Laundry was done in the washhouse at the rear of the building in a big copper cauldron heated by a coal fire. There was a mangle and a drying green at the back. On rainy days, the damp laundry would be brought into the kitchen, hung on the 'pulley' and hoisted to the ceiling to dry with the heat from the coal fire.

The backyard also had a small area divided into four equal patches for the growing of vegetables – part of the wartime 'dig for victory campaign' I suppose. Next to the washhouse there was a line of small wooden sheds, one for each flat and these served to store coal and garden tools. The coal was delivered from the coal merchant on a flat cart drawn by a Clydesdale horse. The coal was contained in a number of coarsely woven jute sacks and these would be hoisted onto the driver's shoulder and carried into the close and emptied into the respective coal shed[s]. As an interesting aside, the coalman came about every two months but the milkman came daily with a similar horse and cart. My grandfather would wait for these deliveries eagerly, holding a dustpan and broom. His purpose was to collect any horse droppings which could be used to fertilise his vegetable patch. He would range up and down the road for this purpose unless beaten to the punch by another neighbour intent on gathering treasure for his own patch!

EATIN' TATTIES, CHIPS AND PEAS

I have several funny stories of the family, including the night Grandpa's hot brick bed warmer set fire to the bed and, on another occasion, of his battle with a rat in the coal shed. My grandpa would house all sorts of useful stuff in the coal shed including bits of string, pea sticks, spades and a small sack of bone meal. It was the bone meal that attracted the rat and grandpa was determined to catch the robber and despatch it to wherever thieving rodents go in the afterlife. One day, he opened the shed door and spotted the rat eating the bone meal. With lightening reflexes he jumped into the shed closing the door behind him and in the dim light coming through chinks in the wooden door proceeded to flail at the animal with a handy hammer but with more enthusiasm than accuracy. The rat ran up the walls and into recesses in the coal until it finally saw an excellent escape route provided by my grandpa's trouser leg. It climbed up his leg with great speed but, unfortunately for Grandpa, the exact escape route chosen was *inside* the trouser leg! Startled, Grandpa managed to grip the rat through the cloth of his trousers but the animal had reached his crotch and was digging in with claws and teeth. Bursting through the shed door, clutching his crotch, my grandfather tripped and fell onto the drying green where, to the astonishment of neighbours attracted by his cries for help, he lay on his back while holding the angry rat with one hand and with the other hand struggled to unbuckle his belt. After what must have seemed to him an uncomfortably long time, he was able to get out of his trousers and, while standing with bare legs to the breeze, was able to strangle the animal and eventually dump it. To say that Granny was mortified by this spectacle was the understatement of the year!

Alan Cowan, my footballing, golfing, scouting and one of my general 'mucking about' chums of the 1950s sent me the following memories from Philadelphia in the United States:

How could I possibly forget our comings and goings along Cavvy Ave, Wilson and Abbot Streets. And now two thoughts spring to mind – jumping from a brick wall onto the rusted, corrugated iron roof of an old air-raid shelter next to the playing field at Craigie School. Very daring stuff for such young lads!

And how about this – picking up empty Craven A and Woodbine

Alan Cowan (right) and his younger brother John paid a return visit to Needless Road in 2014. They are seen here having an imaginary game of cricket in the Craigie School playing field beside the (now tree covered) telegraph pole which we once used for a wicket. Alan died in 2020.

packets from the muck at the cattle market for my prized collection!

There may still be a wizened old apple tree at the back of 'my old house' at 45 Needless Road which provided apples by the ton year in and year out through the early 50s.

In 1956 when my father announced that he was accepting the position of bank manager in a place called Biggar I thought that it was the end of the world. I had completed a couple of enjoyable years at the Academy up the hill and Needless Road was the centre of my universe. I have travelled from Needless Road to Broad Street – one of the longest and straightest city streets in America – in a wee nutshell of forty nine years.

Ah, memories – they seem at the same time so vivid and remote.

Elizabeth Gray, who as Betty Ogg was one of my classmates at Craigie School (then called Western District) and now lives in Ontario, Canada, sent me this delightful and nostalgic article which she has titled 'Transitions':

April 1949. The day had finally arrived. We were moving house, or 'flitting' as it was more commonly called. I can never understand that term being used for something that couldn't be further from a light and airy movement from place to place. Upheaval, disruption, short tempers and tears seemed to be more the order of the day as we said goodbye to the only home I had known, a two-roomed ground floor flat in a tenement in Inchaffray Street in the city's north end. Perth's building boom after the second world war had resulted in a large estate of council houses being built at High Craigie and it was in this new development that we were allocated a new home.

So off we went.

I had heard of Craigie but had never been there. At eight years old my world had been limited to where I could walk comfortably, such as along the Dunkeld Road to downtown, to school and to visit aunts and uncles who lived fairly close by. So the prospect of going to live in a place I had never seen was a little exciting despite having to leave my friends.

My first memories of moving to Craigie are a little unclear but I do recall what seemed to be a very long trip in the bus – my Dad having gone ahead in a lorry, driven by a workmate, with all our worldly goods on board. After crossing the railway bridge at St Leonard's Bank we entered into what was for me totally unchartered territory. Used to the flat terrain of the north end of town, the steeper streets and much finer houses were an eye-opener for me. As the bus travelled up one particularly steep incline and rounded a bend, there was vista of open fields and rising woodlands on one side and craggy rock faces on the other and I immediately thought that we had moved to the countryside. However, one more bend in the road and that dream became the reality of a very long road again very steep curving up and away, lined with cream coloured identical two storey houses with fences, gates and their own gardens front and back. We had arrived at 'The Glens'! The roads in this particular housing estate had all been named after Perthshire glens and our 'glen' was Glenturret Terrace which was the last street to be completed in that phase of construction. It was a fairly short street and we were in the first block at number 4.

What I remember very clearly about that first visit was the smell of drying plaster, the echoing sounds of our footsteps on the bare floorboards and the size of the living room which seemed enormous to me. Also, as it was April, the house was very cold, the only source of heat being from the fire in the living room which was not yet in use. Downstairs was a kitchen, the living room and a bedroom and upstairs two more bedrooms and, wonder of wonders, a bathroom. To a child being used to running outside to a toilet in the back green, this bathroom was a luxury with its space, washbasin, a big bathtub and the prospect of hot water once we were able to light the fire which also heated the water.

I was shuttled off to the backyard while the furniture was being moved in and immediately was struck by the amazing view of Perth laid out before me. As Glenturret sat high on the side of Moncreiffe Hill, the view was spectacular stretching down the Carse of Gowrie, over to Kinnoull Hill and across town to the mountains in the distance. In all the years that I lived there, I never tired of that view.

There were many adjustments, to be made by living in the Glens, not the least of which was changing schools. I had previously gone to Northern District School, a large imposing red sandstone building situated just across the Dunkeld Road from my home, a mere two minute walk. My new school was Western District, more commonly known as Craigie School and a lot more than a two minute walk away! It was, in fact, a fair walk just to get to the nearest bus stop at the foot of Glenlochay Road and then quite a bus ride to Wilson Street, the closest stop to the school. I loved that trip. Back along Craigie Knowes Road with its crags and open fields, down the brae to Queen Street then up along Darnhall Drive which I thought was very posh wiith its lovely established gardens – very different from our raw and, as yet, uncultivated properties.

Needless Road and Wilson Street with their elegant stone villas and bungalows were also my favourites especially when one of the villas sported the first television antenna I had ever seen and we would all crowd to the bus window to view it as we went past.

Craigie School was a small single storey grey stone building with a small playground and a playing field just a little further up the street. The population was a lot smaller than Northern District but growing fast due to the influx of families to the Glens. As we had moved in April, I changed schools in the middle of term and entered an already established class. It was a daunting experience for a shy child who wore glasses and I was immediately targeted for bullying! At lunchtime that first day in Mrs Brown's class I was the recipient of the ritual haie pulling and chants of 'Four Eyes' and 'Specky Jean'. Fighting back didn't work so I took refuge in the girls' bathroom where I was rescued by a classmate who was obviously the 'alpha female' and escorted to safety. From that moment on, my acceptance was complete and I went on to enjoy happy years at Craigie School and made many friends that I still have today.

Another major adjustment to 'Glen living' was the lack of adjacent shops and services. We had been used to the 'sweetie shop' on the street corner and to the Co-op and a row of shops just up the road. But in the late forties and early fifties there were no such luxuries available yet in our streets. Shops on Glengarry Road would be built in the next phase but that was a year or two away. However, we soon got used to the various vans and carts that supplied us with milk, baked goods, groceries and even a library van where you could borrow and return books.

One outstanding memory is of the milkman's cart pulled by a magnificent Clydesdale who was the delight of all the children in the neighbourhood. I often wondered how the milkman got his round completed in a day such was the adoration that horse received. So there was mass panic on the icy day the horse slipped on the steep corner of Glenturret and went down. All the available men in the area quickly gathered to help the horse regain his feet but, not long after that, the milkman's cart was replaced by a van – much to the disgust of the young folk and the disappointment of the keen gardeners who missed collecting the spoils of the horse's visit.

Any lingering misgivings I had about living in Glenturret were swept away that first summer by the utter joy of the freedom of playing up Callerfountain Hill, to which access was literally steps away from my front door. It was reached by a short path between the two houses across the street and a closed farm gate which was much more fun to climb over than use the turnstile at the side! In Inchaffray Street we had streets, wynds, closes and pends to play in – here we had miles of fields, trees, streams and the springiest turf grassland I have ever known where the 'Glens' kids could spend endless summer hours adventuring freely and only coming home in time for tea. Winter time was no different, there being an impressive sledge run, called 'Huttons' for some reason, that claimed a few broken glasses, front teeth and the odd broken arm!

At weekends my Dad and I would take our labrador, Star, and walk the hill for hours, sometimes accompanied by a bag of ferrets borrowed from a neighbour, and maybe bring a rabbit home for dinner – not my favourite meal!

There was also the quarry. Perth Quarry Company was still functioning in the fifties and blasting was carried out almost daily. There would be a warning sound and then we would hold our breath waiting for the bang! The quarry was strictly off limits but my Dad knew some of the quarrymen so I did get a visit to their 'tea shack' once in a while.

Another source of community friendship in our new environment was the local church. Moncreiffe Church had been built as part of the development and was as raw and utilitarian as our houses! We had been members of the Wilson Church in Scott Street in the centre of Perth – a beautiful stately building that conjured up memories of dark glistening wood, red carpet and multi-coloured light coming through tall windows.

Moncreiffe Church had no such attributes, doubling as a community centre as well as a place of worship, but was soon the bustling hub of Boys' Brigade, Girl Guides, Brownies and many community based activities. I spent many happy hours there and made lifelong friends thanks in no small part to the wise counsel and support from Mr Mathers and Mr Leishman, the two ministers I had the good fortune to encounter there.

Life in 'the Glens' was not without its trials, mostly caused by inclement weather. The steep sloping roads could be treacherous in winter and, as few people had cars in those days, we had to rely on a bus service which wasn't the best but was essential. The houses were poorly insulated and relied on a coal fire to heat the whole house and also heat the water by means of a boiler at the back of the fireplace. Not a very safe arrangement as I understand. But, all things considered, it was a great place to grow up and gave me a solid sense of community and belonging. People were friendly and helpful in time of need, as I was to discover.

More changes were on the horizon. It was time to leave Craigie School and go to the Academy but at the same time my seriously ill mother passed away and another transition began.

Whilst serving overseas with the Royal Air Force during World War II and on hearing the call of a strange bird during the night, my late father, Donald M Paton, felt compelled to write the following nostalgic poem of the area around Buckie Braes:

The Call of a Bird

I heard the call of a bird in the night,
Startling, sudden, sharp with fright;

EATIN' TATTIES, CHIPS AND PEAS

I waited, listening, but heard no more
But the lapping waves on a sandy shore.

Alone in the dark it seemed to be
A voice of the past that spoke to me.
In fancy, I walked up the Buckie Braes,
That romantic spot of the olden days.

Passing the bridge, the track takes a turn
And skirts the edge of the Craigie Burn.
The old thatched cottages topped the hill,
The geranium pots on the window sill.

The scent of the broom on the evening air
Was wafted away, I know not where;
But I think as that scent comes back to me,
Perchance it was wafted across the sea.

Under the rowans the path dips down
To the gurgling burn all peaty and brown;
And there, in a dark mysterious dell,
I drank at Cock Robin's wishing well.

I saw again the cool retreats,
Rustic bridges and rustic seats;
The water tumbling o'er the falls,
The tallest tree where the blackbird calls.

Along the dyke where lovers stroll
To Callerfountain's wooded knoll;
Or further yet, from the haunts of men
Through the Cuddies Strip to Spinky Den.

I imagined I sat by the flagstaff tall
When again I heard that strange bird call;
Startling, sudden, I know not why,
But I'll hear that sound until I die.

Closing my eyelids, I tried to sleep,
But I found those eyes could only weep.
Oh memory! What thoughts were stirred
By the sudden call of an unknown bird.

Ian Macpherson who was born in one of the Craigie Place tenements in 1939 and has been a resident of Craigie for most of his life, recalled his boyhood days in the area with clear affection.

My first recollection of Craigie was playing in the Craigie Burn. In those days traffic was nothing like it is today and we had the freedom of playing in the streets and in the gutters. There was no danger, or very little danger, of being hit by a car or lorry and, more likely than not, it would have been by a horse and cart. Milk, bread, vegetables and fruit all came by horse and cart so playing in the gutters was a daily occurance, as was playing in the burn.

When our family of seven had outgrown the Craigie Place house we moved to a flat at Ainslie Gardens in Muirton where I had my first taste of school at Northern District. However, by the time I was seven or eight years old our family (now eight of us) moved back to Craigie to a bigger house for our growing family at 2 St Magdalene's Road. By then the main road, instead of coming along Priory Place and up Craigie Place, had been diverted by a new road, Glenearn Road. We still had the horses and carts and few more motorised vehicles but it was a great place in which to grow up.

While the houses were being built on one side of Glenearn Road, the other side of the road was the council yard at Craigie Haugh and a long stretch of woodland with mysterious places in which to play whatever games took your imagination . We played 'Cowboys and Indians', 'Battles', built gang huts and roamed these woods from morning until night, just coming out when we were hungry!

On moving to St Magdalene's Road I had recommenced my schooling at Western District (now Craigie School) and really enjoyed my time there. However, the town council decided in their wisdom that certain streets in Craigie, St Magdalene's Road being one of them, should have their primary school age pupils moved to Southern District School (known as 'the Shands') in Nelson Street and I finished my primary education there along with various others from 'the Glens'. I soon became accustomed to 'the Shands' and journeying to and from school I made a host of new friends as our route took us along the path at the side of the Craigie Burn and then through the South Inch towards Nelson Street. Two or three times we were late for class after having our attention diverted by something or other during our walk to school with the resulting punishment of having to stand in the corner following a lecture from the teacher!

But they were happy times. With Mum and Dad both working we became 'latch key kids' and, as I got older, I remember when we arrived home from school having to let ourselves into the house,. As a large family, we all had our jobs to do. My older brothers, Alistair and James, were away doing their National Service so along with my sisters, Betty and Ena, and younger brother Douglas we had the kitchen floor to clean, breakfast dishes to be washed and dried, the brass taps at the kitchen sink had to be polished, the kitchen table set for dinner, etc. We then had the usual homework to do before being allowed out to play. Looking back it wasn't such a bad thing and probably made us the adults we are today.

Craigie Cross was a thriving place at the start of the 1950s and I got my first job there at the age of twelve. Stirling the Bakers were looking for a couple of van boys to deliver their produce over the area, mainly Craigie. I applied along with my pal Dougie and we were lucky enough to get the jobs. Stirling's bakery was situated at the bottom of Croft Bank beside the railway line and they had two shops at Craigie Cross and one in Perth High Street. One of the Craigie shops was at the corner of Priory Place and Carrs Croft while the other was only a hundred yards away on the corner of the Cross. Doug and I had a lot of fun 'working' there! We had to keep the bakery tidy but on our deliveries we sat at the back of the van with the doors open and swinging our legs over the back. No health and safety in those days! As we approached our delivery, we would jump out while the van was still moving, run and deliver the bread or rolls, etc, and hop back on while Davy the driver and the van carried on down the road.

One incident I remember was at Christmas when the manageress, Chrissie Proudfoot, gave Doug and I a couple of bags saying 'there's a couple of cakes of shortbread and a bit of black bun for your Christmas. Don't let the boss see you'. Stuffing them down the front of our jackets, we proceeded along Priory Place only to see the boss, Iain Stirling, driving towards us in his car. Slowing down, he shouted out the car window 'I want to see you boys back at the shop'. Panic. Not knowing what was going to happen, we hid the bags of shortbread and black bun under the bushes at the side of the burn and slowly made our way back to the shop, only for the boss to hand us a couple of bags each, saying 'there's some shortbread and black bun for your Christmas'! We couldn't believe our luck.

The 1940s and 1950s were a great time for the railways. The situation of Perth meant that all the trains from London and the South, if they were heading to Inverness, Aberdeen and Dundee had to pass through Perth station. The railway provided a lot of jobs to the people of Perth and one of the things I loved was heading from my home in St Magdalene's Road and along Craigie Road to the marshalling yard – a large area of ground (now occupied by the Tesco Supermarket) where all railway rolling stock would wait until required. What I liked best was watching the train engines being turned around on the turntable – a big circular metal plate. If the engine was facing south it was driven onto the turntable which was manually turned until it faced north and the train driven off to its northern destination. It was an amazing thing to watch with all types of trains being seen up close and smoke and steam going in all directions. I loved watching them as an eleven year old.

In 1951, as my two elder brothers had now married and left home, our family downsized and we moved to 19a Darnhall Crescent. Darnhall was a different patch to St Magdalene's and, instead of the woods at Glenearn Road, we had the woods of Craigie Knowes and a little further away, Buckie Braes. There was also the grass park between Darnhall and Murray Crescent with its swings and, more importantly for me, room to play football. After school, it was a case of dropping the school bags, down to the park, jerseys as goal posts, and the game would begin. Loads of fun and laughs. Craigie Knowes was a small wood with lots of paths and trails and a flagpole at the top.

Although there was more traffic by the 1950s it was still light in comparison to today. Parents allowed a lot more freedom to explore and didn't worry if their kids didn't come home for tea or were late. It was a great time to be young. I was still young enough to enjoy the rough and tumble of the boys' games – football, Cowboys and

Indians and war games but eventually girls came on the scene. I remember a favourite game of mine was 'Chase, Catch and Kiss' with the girls and, as I was a pretty fast runner in these days, there were not many girls escaped me! There was also the Pitch and Putt course at the top of Glenlochay Road and many a Saturday and Sunday was spent trying to keep the ball in play.

When I was fourteen years old I changed jobs and became a message boy for the Co-operative in Bridgend. As well as delivering groceries all over the Bridgend area, I occasionally had to take deliveries to other Co-op branches, including Craigie. On one occasion, while on my way to the branch at Craigie, I had to drop off a delivery in Mill Street so I leaned my bike against the wall and proceeded up the close. I came down to find a crowd of onlookers standing talking and no bike! Perth at that time had an army barracks (located on the site of the present police station) and a soldier was being marched back, under escort, to the barracks when he escaped, grabbed my bike and made off. I then had to return to the shop and tell the boss that my bike and whatever I had to deliver to the Craigie branch had been nicked. On reporting after school the following day, the boss told me to pick up my bike from the police station in Tay Street as it had been dumped at the railway bridge. The deserter had obviously made his escape across the bridge's footpath to the Dundee Road.

I was now attending Perth High School in Gowans Terrace and, as my Dad had got me a bike, I was able to cycle there and back from Darnhall meeting up with two or three other pupils on the way. I wasn't a scholarly pupil but liked working with my hands and was lucky that my Dad knew a lot of tradesmen through his job as a part-time barman. This resulted in me getting a job as an apprentice joiner with Jimmy Moncrieff in Inchaffray Street. In those days, although there were five or six joiners working there, we had no van or vehicles and everything had to be transported on a barrow or on the bar of your bike. We used to cycle to our jobs with our tool bags balanced between our legs (again no Health and Safety) or walk with our bike laden with wood and other odds and ends. My job, among other things, was pushing the barrow and I particularly remember one occasion when I was returning down Viewlands Road after doing a job at Perth Academy. The barrow did not have brakes and the only way to stop or slow it was by rubbing the wheel against the kerb but coming down the steep hill the barrow gathered speed and I lost control. I could only stand and watch as the barrow gathered speed and careered down the hill on its own, cleared the main Glasgow Road and smashed into a hedge on the opposite side of the road. Fortune had favoured the brave. The barrow was fine and the only damage was to the hedge – and my pride!

By the early 1960s I was getting older and changing. We had now moved to Murray Crescent where living close to Orchard Place the tennis courts were another place to have fun although I was never really very good at tennis. Dancing had now come on the scene and Perth's City Hall was attracting all the big bands and big crowds. I remember Johnnie Dankworth, Kenny Ball and Ken MacIntosh although my favourite was a Scottish band – The Clyde Valley Stompers with their lead singer Mary McGowan.

Such wonderful memories of Craigie, a great place in which to stay and grow up.

Sheila Walker (formerly Sheila Annat) grew up in Gray Street and fondly remembers her Craigie years and particularly her connection with the Craigie Church Brownies.

It was an honour to be Tawny Owl alongside Mrs Bessie Donald the Brown Owl of the 4th Perthshire Brownies at Craigie Church. I still remember the happy faces of the Brownies while dancing in the grass outside Craigie Church. The day Jim and I married on 10th June 1961, I had a Guard of Honour of the 4th Perthshire Company and how proud we were to see them all standing outside the church.

I still remember playing rounders in the playing field at Needless Road in the evenings – with a stern warning from my parents before setting off – 'make sure that the ball does not go into Mr Lunan's garden'! Mr Lunan was our headmaster at Craigie School.

I also remember going to the chippie at Craigie on a Friday night with my 'threepenny bit' and making a great decision whether to buy a wee poke of chips or fritters! I usually bought the chips as I thought that I got better value and more in my 'wee pokie' than I got with the fritters!

Now resident in Melbourne, Australia, another former Craigie boy, John Annat (Sheila Walker's brother) was kind enough to send his youthful memories.

One of my earliest memories is of the 'Big Field'. Bordered between Cavendish Avenue and Pickletullum Road, it facilitated everything from sword fights with thistles to Guy Fawkes bonfires along with the occasional grass fire.

Cricket on the Craigie school playing field was wonderful and practicing my bowling against Mr Lunan's fence occupied a lot of my playtime. Mr Lunan was the retired headmaster of Craigie School. Cricket matches with the 'choosing of sides' approach were nightly thanks to daylight saving. Strangely, remembering the names and characteristics of some of the players comes back to me easily.

Alistair Cameron, Scott Miller, Ian Bailey, Andrew Webster, Arthur Jamieson, Brian Reid, Gordon Kirkwood, Clark Meldrum and Ally Rennie were all part of the group. Brian was always the wicketkeeper because he had all the gear and was very good! Arthur was the Usain Bolt and Dennis Lillee of the day – at football it was boot the ball up the pitch and Arthur at centre forward always got there first. Ally Rennie had the swing action bowling before Geoff Thomson! A good square drive was a four when it rolled into the top paddock of Hay's Mart!

Other friends around that time were John Cameron, Kevin Lynach, David Bousie, Dave Bertie, Ian Dougall and Russell Turnbull. Russell was the most experienced smoker when we experimented in the lane which ran between Needless Road and Abbot Crescent.

Looking back, Craigie had a lovely little shopping area around the St Leonard's Bridge. Most memorable for me was the popular 'chippie' and Joe Dow the fishmonger's shop where I worked as a message boy after school. There was a greengrocers owned by the Morrow family and their caption was 'Come To Morrow Today'.

Andrew, Ian and I were mad keen train spotters. Armed with our Ian Allen books we were always on the lookout for new engines. Perth engine sheds were 63A. In the Glover Street marshalling yards I used to see the pug 57345 every day. In frustration of not finding a new engine to cross off the list, I recall telling Ian Bailey I would remember that number for the rest of my life. Well, it has so far!

Darnhall Tennis Club was fun. There was a chap (I think his name was Dan) who ran the tennis and bowls hire and when we tried bowls for a laugh he would lecture us about belting bowls into the ditch at each end.

As a youngster, Sunday walks up through the Buckie Braes and Craigie Knowes with the family were fresh air adventures. Later 'the boys' would venture up to the Buckie Braes and invent team games.

Thinking back to Craigie School, we used to go to the Craigie Hall in Priory Place for gym and the whole school would attend church services at St Leonard's in the Fields Church in Marshall Place.

We did not have little boats but we did try to race sticks or other debris down the Craigie Burn to the South Inch which seemed a massive place. Even after all these years I can still remember the boating pond which was run by Davie Gannon. He would yell 'Come in Number 9. Your time's up' and the secret to getting more time on the boat and value for your money was to be at the far end of the pond around the time you were due to finish!

Gordon Hynd sent me his memories of living in Cherrybank. An area which he terms 'the salubrious suburb'!

We moved from Glendoick in the Carse of Gowrie to 28 Low Road, Cherrybank in November 1966, having bought the ground-floor flat (right) which formed part of Shepherd's Buildings (aka Burnside) erected by the Shepherds' Friendly Society in 1903 and to whom the rents originally would have been paid. The 1903 date stone (now slightly worn) can still be seen across the close door and incorporates a pair of shepherd's crooks. I think three of the flats were owner-occupied and one rented from Shepherds.

I only lived there from late 1966 until October 1970 and then again briefly for a few months in 1976/77. The flat comprised two bedrooms (one double, one single), living room, lobby with walk-in press and a very small kitchen off the living room with a sliding door. The shared toilet (with one other flat) was located downstairs but still within the cartilage of the building. The living room had good views up to Craigie Hill and the new clubhouse. The front of the house was north-facing and very cold in winter – there was no central heating or double glazing, only a coal fire in the living room and the double bedroom. In winter the small bedroom required an electric oil-filled radiator to prevent frostbite taking hold. I remember the frost patterns inside the windows – one didn't linger there of a morning!

Downstairs, facing towards Craigie Hill, was the large communal wash-house (with power),a communal drying green and individual cellars.The wash-house contained a deep double porcelain sink, wringer and a large solid fuel-fired 'copper' in the corner with its own chimney. Latterly we introduced a twin-tub Hoovermatic washing machine making the corner 'copper' effectively redundant. An interesting piece of social history was a small original wooden plaque on the rear of the wash-house door which instituted a rota by which each of the four households in the block could 'enjoy' a Monday as wash day. Originally the wash-house was locked after a day's effort there and the key was passed to the next household on the rota. Fridays appeared to be a free-for-all! This arrangement certainly wasn't strictly adhered to (even in the 1960s) and was abandoned soon after we arrived. It was understood that the close and the back stairs were to be swept every day and washed once a week. This was adhered to!

The small north-facing front gardens still have the large grids covering the cellar windows where coal would original have been delivered.

During the first half of the 1970s, the three tenement blocks (two of two storeys and one of three storeys) were the subject of a Council 'Housing Action Area' and inside bathrooms were installed with a re-arrangement of some of the kitchens.

The 'Auld Cherrybankers' called the suburb 'Chirry' and considered that they were not really a part of Perth itself.

The topography of Cherrybank is perhaps unusual in that it is split-level with three sets of steps leading to and from the Glasgow Road. One set is by the Cherrybank Inn; another by the flats which were built on the site of the former Burmah filling station; and a third set are beside the old toilet block above the road-sweeper's 'buckie'. Low Road was then two-way and Necessity Brae was a straight line as far as the wood at the top. The route of the Cherrybank bus (coming from the Perth direction) was up Oakbank Road from the Glasgow Road and down Oakbank Place to the current bus stop which then served as the terminus.

I well remember Drummond's Nurseries which were situated between Low Road and the Craigie Burn and accessed from a track between Numbers 16 and 18 Low Road.

The large open grassy space adjacent to the telephone box was referred to as 'The Metley' and l understand it was so called because of quantities of metal and machinery once stored there when it was a blacksmith's yard.

Pickembere Cottages are situated at the foot of Necessity Brae on the path leading up to the Buckie Braes and the allotments in front of them are managed bt Dupplin Estates. My father had one of the allotments and the dung provided by one of the Lamberkine farms made the soil extremely fertile and easy to dig. Not that I ever did any of the digging!

Bruno Bendinger owned a traditional grocery shop on the west side of the Glasgow Road and Oakbank Road junction. To those in the know, his Wiltshire bacon was considered the best in town.

The Cherrybank Post Office and Newsagents was run by Mr and Mrs Lindsay and I was a paper boy there between 1967 and 1970. My round took in the odd numbers of Glasgow Road along to Murray Place, then a few calls in Viewlands Place ending up at the Academy. The school library took the Glasgow Herald while Euan Fairbairn, one of the maths teachers, ordered the Daily Telegraph. Mondays were usually a light bag while Fridays were heaviest with lots of PA's.

Cherrybank Garage was the source of paraffin which was widely used in those days to take the chill off the rooms. I remember taking empty containers to be filled at the tank inside the garage.

The Last of the Summer Wine (or in this case the summer beer!) Left to right – the author, David Bertie, Stewart Bousie and Jim McNeill are pictured in the Cherrybank Inn in 2019 reminiscing about the old days. All lived in Needless Road during various stages of their lives .

EATIN' TATTIES, CHIPS AND PEAS

The Hill Farm of Pitheavlis (now the site of the Aviva offices) was accessed by a rough road opposite the Pitheavlis Cottages halfway up Necessity Brae and there was some skiing on the sloping fields when winter conditions were favourable.

Dae Ye Mind Lang Syne?

Dae ye mind lang syne
When the summer days were fine,
When the sun shone brighter far
Than it's ever done sin syne?
Dae ye mind the wood side turn
Whaur we guddled in the burn,
And were late for the schull in the morning?

Dae ye mind the sunny braes
Whaur we gaithered hips and slaes,
And fell among the bramble bushes
Tearin'a' oor claes?
And for fear we wid be seen
We went slippin hame at e'en,
But wid dae it ower again in the morning?

Dae ye mind the miller's dam
When the frosty winter cam?
We slid amongst the curlers' rinks
And made their game a sham;
When they chased us through the snaw
We took leg bail* yin and a'
But were feared for the tawse in the morning.

Where are a' these bright hearts noo
That were yince sae leal and true?
Some hae left life's troubled scene,
Some still are strugglin' through;
But some hae risen high
In life's changeful destiny,
For they rose wi' the lark in the morning.

NAE PLACE MAIR BRAW

Oh oor life's sweet spring is past
And the autumn's come at last;
Oor summer days hae passed away,
Life's winter's comin' fast;
But though lang the nicht may seem
We will sleep withoot a dream,
Till we wake on that bright summer's morning.

(Reverend George S Lawrie, 1800s)

*leg bail – escape by running.

MODERN TIMES

These are the times we shall dream about
And we'll call them the Good Old Days

(Scout Gang Show song by Ralph Reader, 1957)

In spite of all the changes of past generations, a Rip van Winkle could still recognise Craigie and Cherrybank and someone returning to the area after an absence of perhaps fifty or sixty years would find much of it in many ways unchanged.

The 'Lollipop clock' still stands on the Craigie Cross triangle, now surrounded by several fast food take-away shops which happily still include the Craigie chip shop of their youth. The wooden steps from St Leonard's Bridge to the railway station have long gone but they would have no trouble finding their way around their once familiar streets such as Priory Place, Abbot Street, Friar Street, Queen Street or Wilson Street. They might stroll along Young Street beside Craigie School and through the playing field, noting where the modern homes of Raeburn Park have replaced the once-thriving livestock mart, then wander up Needless Road past Pitheavlis Castle to Cherrybank.

At Cherrybank, our visitor would be glad to see that they could still have a drink in the Cherrybank Inn, have their car serviced at Cherrybank Garage, play a round of golf at Craigie Hill or simply saunter through the Buckie Braes and along the back of the golf course to Callerfountain Hill.

Going downhill towards Perth from these upper slopes they would find little changed in Upper or High Craigie although they would perhaps find Craigie Knowes a lot more overgrown than in their youth. The narrow lanes around Verena Terrace, Moredun Terrace and Moredun Square are still there, as are the Witches Steps down to the waterfall at Craigie Mill and Windsor Terrace. At Glenearn Road they might be fascinated by the number of new and thriving businesses but would be glad that they could still wander alongside the Craigie Burn and walk under the railway tunnel to the open space of the South Inch.

NAE PLACE MAIR BRAW

The Development of Cherrybank

It would be at Cherrybank that our Perth returnee might be amazed at the development that has taken place since the days when they may have taken the long climb up Necessity Brae. The trim cottages which once stood alone by the side of what was once a country road are still there but are now surrounded by the major housing development of Charlotte Gate which stretches almost to the top of the hill and westwards along the Glasgow Road towards Broxden.

As mentioned earlier, Cherrybank was originally a weaving hamlet situated within an agricultural community. It was not until the latter part of the twentieth century that companies saw the area as being viable for moving their businesses out of the city centre.

The first company to make the move to Cherrybank was the long established Perth firm of Bell's Whisky who, as a result of their product now being blended and bottled at East Mains in West Lothian, no longer required their Victoria Street premises. During the early 1970s, a striking office complex was built on Necessity Brae with a commanding view over the city.

The story of Arthur Bell & Sons Ltd is not dissimilar to that of their one time local rivals, Dewar's. Like John Dewar, Arthur Bell began in modest fashion in the early eighteenth century. Originally operating from premises in Perth's Kirkgate, the company moved to Victoria Street in 1909. Having established a successful business locally, Bell depended on the business acumen of his sons Robert Bell who, like Tommy Dewar, developed an overseas market and the better known

The offices of Arthur Bell & Sons Ltd at Cherrybank. (Photograph courtesy of Diagio Ltd).

Arthur Kinmond Bell who concentrated on home sales. A K Bell, recognised throughout Perth and beyond for his charitable and philanthropic deeds, died in 1942 and was succeeded by W G Farquharson who took the company to new heights and, like his predecessor A K Bell, received the freedom of Perth.

Farquharson was succeeded in turn by the dynamic and flamboyant Raymond C Miquel who moved the company from Victoria Street to Cherrybank where they continued to prosper.

New developments within the company saw sales of their whisky increase from eighteen million bottles in 1970 to forty five million bottles in 1974. Between 1970 and 1980 profits grew from just over £18 million to £159 million and by 1979 commanded twenty-five per cent of the home market. For many years, Bells had been the largest selling whisky in Scotland and was now among the leaders in several overseas markets.

In 1985, it was Raymond Miquel's misfortune to come up against the infamous Ernest Saunders in a hostile takeover bid from Saunders' company, Guinness. Despite a vigorous advertising campaign, Bell's sadly lost the takeover battle, the Guinness offer was accepted and Miquel resigned from the board.

Another nasty takeover took place in 1986 when Guinness acquired the Distillers Company of which Dewar's was then a part. Later, the aforementioned Guinness boss, Ernest Saunders, was found guilty of financial fraud and jailed and the one-time local rivals of Bell's and Dewar's became stable mates under a new company called Diageo.

In the early 1980s another of Perth's renowned employers made the dramatic move from their city centre headquarters.

The General Accident Fire and Life Assurance Corporation had been founded in 1885 by a group of Perthshire men which included several farmers, a lawyer, a banker and an estate agent. The Corporation came about as a direct result of the 1880 Employers Liability Act and premises were acquired in Perth at 44 Tay Street. The early development of the company was due to the drive and foresight of Francis Norie-Miller who was appointed Secretary in 1887 and Manager in

The General Accident complex at Pitheavlis under construction. (Courier & Advertiser photograph).

A 1986 view of the General Accident offices. The M90 motorway crosses the centre of the photograph and immediately above it are the trees of the Cuddies Strip. (Left) Her Majesty The Queen and the Duke of Edinburgh visited the new General Accident headquarters in 1985. (Photograph by D C Thomson & Co. Ltd).

1889.

From its modest beginnings the firm grew to become one of the leading names in insurance world-wide. As well as providing employment for generations of Perth people, it continued to retain its World Headquarters in Perth under the chairmanship of Sir Stanley Norie-Miller, the son of Sir Francis.

A few years after Sir Stanley stepped down in 1968, the company began to change. For a number of years the GA (as they were affectionately known) had outgrown their offices in High Street and other parts of the city and decided to base all the facilities of their world headquarters under one roof. Modern offices were constructed on the other side of Necessity Brae from the Bell's Whisky offices on the lands of the Pitheavlis Hill Farm and were soon to blend in perfectly with the contours of the surrounding hillside. Work on the new site commenced in 1980 and most of the staff moved themselves into the new building over a July weekend in 1983.

However, by 1991, it became clear that Perth was not going to continue to be the world headquarters of the company and reliable employment and company loyalty was not necessarily going to continue either as Bob Scott, the Chief Executive, came up with ideas for new development. In 1996 the UK investments work was transferred to London with only general insurance work left in Perth. A merger with Commercial Union in 1998 saw the company name changed to CGU with local people devastated that the familiar name of General Accident was now gone. A further merger in 2001 with Norwich Union saw the name changed to CGNU and a few years later to Aviva.

For a century General Accident had been an international company with its headquarters in the city of Perth and for many of its employees it had been looked upon as a family business. But during its life the GA changed in character. From having a local identity and being a reliable employer it became a remote part of a larger company with a name no longer synonymous with Perth.

Charlotte Gate and Broxden

In March 2008, plans to create a National Garden for Scotland on the Cherrybank Gardens site at Cherrybank ended when Scotland's Garden Trust failed to secure crucial £25 million backing from the National Lottery Fund. As it was clearly no longer viable for the Trust to continue with their £40 million project, named The Calyx, the ambitious scheme was sadly dropped. This also meant the closure of the Cherrybank Gardens and Scotland's National Heather Collection with the loss of fourteen jobs.

Four months later, a report in *The Courier and Advertiser* stated that Perth and Kinross Council were recommending that the local authority should deviate from its own local plan to facilitate a multi-million pound development over fifteen acres of brown field land

The Charlotte Gate development at Cherrybank. Necessity Brae is shown right of centre with Craigie Hill golf course, the Buckie Braes and the Aviva complex top right. (Photograph from Bellway Homes)

at Necessity Brae in Cherrybank. Despite initial objections from Dupplin Estates and neighbouring residents at Pitheavlis and Pickembere, permission was eventually granted for private housing. Initial development was by Persimmon Homes and in 2020, Bellway Homes were granted planning permission to build a further forty nine homes on the site. By the end of the second decade of the twenty first century the Charlotte Gate development was well established with streets

The Grouse sculpture at the Broxden roundabout. (Photograph by Mike Brocklebank).

bearing such names as Mailer Way, Brocks Road, Windyedge Drive, Robb Place, Scouring Burn Crescent, Weavers Well Crescent, Kirkton Road, Arthur Park, Kinmond Drive and Bell Gardens.

In recent years, the name of Broxden (once Brock's Den or Badger's Den) has become associated with travel in Scotland. The establishment of an interchange for long distance buses has led to the name appearing on destination boards at bus terminals throughout the country. The Broxden junction and roundabout being a central hub for the Scottish motorway network with roads leading to the cities of Aberdeen, Dundee, Edinburgh, Glasgow, Inverness and Stirling.

An excellent park and ride service from a four hundred space car park next to the bus interchange did provide quick communication to the centre of Perth but was discontinued in 2020. Over the years a multitude of business enterprises including a filling station, a travel lodge, fast food outlets, restaurants, a dental centre and a car showroom have become established beside the bus interchange and at the nearby Broxden Business Park.

From Broxden to Cherrybank the northern side between the Scouring Burn and the Glasgow Road is a modern housing development with streets such as Lamberkine Drive, Innerleithen Way, Coldstream Avenue and Tweed Place. The most recent homes are A & J Stephen's development at Woodlands between Berwick Brae and Colliers Way close to the old Weavers' Well.

A feature of the Broxden roundabout is the 'Red Grouse' – a thirty six feet tall wire frame sculpture which was erected in 2010 to mark the Perth 800 celebrations (the eight hundredth anniversary of the granting of the Charter of the City). Created by Ruaraig Maciver of Beltane Studios, the sculpture was gifted to the people of Perth by the Edrington Group – producers of The Famous Grouse whisky.

Romantic scene! Once more from thy proud steep,
I view the prospect far below;
Stirr'd with the memories of the past I weep,
As in my fancy boyhood's pleasures grow;
Even now I feel as I felt long ago.

(Francis Buchanan, 1890)

Recently I stood on a ridge of ground close to Callerfountain Hill, a place where I used to wander as a boy. From there I could see for miles across the M90 motorway, right across Cherrybank, Craigie and the city of Perth to the distant foothills of the Grampians. As I looked at the recent sprawl of housing stretching the length of Necessity Brae and out towards the Broxden roundabout and further north to the development at Bertha Park, I found myself wondering, as I often do when on a hill next to a city, what do all the people in all those houses do?

There was a time not all that long ago when the people of Perth worked, perhaps had a relative that worked, but certainly knew someone who worked in at least one of the city's long established and thriving

Broxden Farm in the old days. Taken from a painting by Malcolm Arthur, a Perth architect who specialised in the restoration of old listed buildings, including farms.

industries of whisky, dyeing and cleaning, insurance, the railway, printing, agriculture, etc. Firms which for decades had been a source of employment for thousands of school leavers. Now these industries and their associated buildings are virtually all gone and replaced by call centres, supermarkets and retail parks. What was once good farmland has become streets and houses. Leading local news stories are quite likely to be about another business or shop closure.

So I ask again. What do all the people in all those houses do and, more to the point, what will their children do?

PEOPLE AND PERSONALITIES

Motoring folk, sporting folk, married folk and courting folk;
Folk who came from Cherrybank and folk from Craigie View.
From Low Road, Craigie Road, St Magdalene's Road
and Needless Road,
Lots of local people and there's some you maybe knew!'

(Adapted by the author from a 'Scotland the What?'
song by kind permission of the late George Donald)

When casting our minds back over the romanticised history of bygone days, the forgotten squalor and the faded and perhaps tattered tapestry that is the backcloth to all our current affairs, let us not forget the more recent past.

The story of Craigie and Cherrybank is also the story of its people. Many of the area's inhabitants have made outstanding contributions to the city of Perth and some have achieved far beyond its environments.

Almost every trade and profession has been represented. There have been ministers of religion, politicians, headmasters and teachers, doctors, lawyers, musicians, actors, office workers, sportsmen, printers, railwaymen, policemen, members of the military and war heroes, butchers, bakers and, if we search deeply enough, candlestick makers.

It is impossible to mention everyone but I have selected a few people from over the years who, in my mind, are well deserving of recognition and I have listed them in alphabetical order.

Some may have lived in the area in their origin and some in their residence. Some for a short time, others for many years. Some are well-known, others less so, but each in their individual ways have stories which should be told in the context of the social history of Craigie and Cherrybank, thus of Perth and, indeed, of Scotland and further beyond.

ARTHUR KINMOND BELL (1868-1942)

One of Perth's leading philanthropists, Arthur Kinmond Bell was born and spent his early years in Craigie's Moncreiffe Terrace.

Arthur Kinmond Bell.

Following in the path of his father and grandfather, Arthur Bell joined the family business of Arthur Bell & Sons Ltd in 1895 and along with his brother Robert doubled the company's profits within five years. By the time he died in 1942, the company's profits were in excess of £100,000 per annum.

As a beneficiary of the booming Scotch whisky trade, Bell prospered and was able to use this prosperity for the benefit of Perth. His first major project was the building of the Gannochy housing estate between 1924 and 1932. This model housing scheme was intended to benefit the hardworking younger generation who had survived the harshness of World War I with many of the original tenancies being granted to workers of Arthur Bell & Sons.

Bell followed this project by establishing the Gannochy Trust in 1937, partly to maintain the Gannochy estate but also to ensure continuing improvements to his native city into the future.

A concern in post-war Perth was the supply of clean water as the River Tay was becoming increasingly polluted. In answer to this problem, Bell provided shares in Bell's Whisky to the Gannochy Trust for the purpose of establishing sewage treatment for Perth and the surrounding villages.

For his philanthropic activities and principally for his role in saving the Perth linen industry by financially backing the city's one remaining company, John Shields & Co. from closure and thus saving three hundred jobs, Arthur Bell was granted the Freedom of Perth in 1938. His modest approach to philanthropy was summed up in this quotation from his acceptance speech: 'After a man has a roof over his head and his bread and butter is fairly assured and has a surplus, I think you will agree with me that it is only common sense that he should spend part of that surplus for the benefit of his native city.'

In 1994, the decision was made to name Perth's new multi-million library the A K Bell Library in honour of the man whose legacy has had such a large impact on the city.

PEOPLE AND PERSONALITIES

MARK BOUSIE

Born and brought up in Needless Road, Mark Bousie is now one of the UK's leading musicians. Mark began learning the accordion at the age of eight, the piano at age thirteen and, while still at school, won the UK Junior Accordion Championship, performed as a soloist throughout Scotland and made several television appearances, including Grampian Television's popular Hogmanay show.

Mark went on to study at the Royal Academy of Music in London where he was elected Associate in 2007 and has been working in theatre in London since the early 2000s. Performing and conducting credits in the West End include *Miss Saigon, Crazy for You, Betty Blue Eyes, Oliver!, Carousel, Fiddler on the Roof, Evita* and *Jumpers*.

As a pianist, Mark recorded Stephen Warbeck's scores for *All of Us* at the National Theatre and *Uncle Vanya* and *Old Times* at the Harold Pinter Theatre. He has worked extensively in the National Theatre as musical director for numerous productions including *His Dark Materials* and *The Coast of Utopia*, performing scores by composers such as Jonathan Dove, Joby Talbot, Olly Fox, Michael Nyman, Steven Edis, Gary Yershon and Jeremy Sams.

Mark Bousie.
(Photograph courtesy of Mark Bousie).

For the Royal Shakespeare Company, Mark was a musical director at the 2011 Lincoln Center Festival in New York City as well as for many productions in Stratford-upon-Avon and London.

Performing credits include work with the CBSO in the UK premiere of Osvaldo Golijov's *Azul* at

Symphony Hall; the BBC Concert Orchestra in the *John William's Prom*, *Fiddler on the Roof Prom*, *Proms in the Park*, and Danny Elfman and Jerry Herman tribute concerts; the Joby Talbot Band in the Queen Elizabeth Hall; Budapest Café Orchestra; London Concertante; and Rambert.

Mark performed in the live BBC broadcasts *Liverpool Nativity* and *Manchester Passion* and has played on numerous soundtracks including *Beauty and the Beast*, *Whisky Galore* and *The Children Act* for which he was piano coach to Emma Thomson.

He is currently Associate Musical Director in the West End production of *Les Misérables*.

JAMES BUCHAN (1881-1949)

James Buchan, was a director of St. Johnstone FC and was also the club's honorary manager from 1920 till 1922. In 1920, St Johnstone became members of the Scottish Central League and the following year, with Jimmy as manager, were admitted to the Scottish Second Division for the first time. Jimmy Buchan had been a player with Fair City Athletic and St. Johnstone before moving to Hibs, Arsenal and Manchester City. He was also the proprietor of a popular billiard saloon in Perth.

James Buchan, honorary manager of St. Johnstone FC (1920-1922). (Perthshire Advertiser photograph).

JACK BUCHAN (1909-1975)

Jack Buchan, the son of James Buchan, was one of the 'old school' of journalists. Extrovert and unconventional, he was for many years one of Perth's great characters.

Jack began his career as a reporter with the *Perthshire Advertiser* before moving to the Perth office of the *Dundee Courier* as chief reporter. He later became a freelance journalist with his own *Perth News Agency* before starting a garage and motorcycle business in the Letham area.

He was a keen golfer and ice hockey player but his main passion was motorcycles. In 1972, at the age of sixty three, he set out to tackle the thirteen thousand mile road journey from the Magellan Straits at the southern-most tip of South America to Alaska and attempted the trip on a 175cc Honda. Unfortunately, he suffered a stroke in Mexico and spent six weeks in hospital before being flown home. It was always his intention to return and complete the journey but he never did and died three years later.

As a motorcycle racer, he won many honours including silver replicas in the Manx Grand Prix and gold medals in the international six-day trials in Italy and in the Scottish six-day trials.

JIMMY BUCHAN (1935-2016)

Jack Buchan's eldest son, Jimmy Buchan, was widely acclaimed as one of Scotland's best-ever motorcycle road racers.

In 1956 Jimmy celebrated a milestone triumph by winning both the junior and senior races at the Manx Grand Prix. In winning the senior race on the notoriously demanding Isle of Man circuit, Jimmy clocked up an average speed of 90mph over more than two and a half hours on the track. The previous year he had won the Clubman TT race on the island.

Jimmy's skills were first recognised in 1951 when, at the age of just sixteen, he rode sidecar passenger with his father at the International Six Days Trial in Italy, returning with the gold medal. As the 1950s drew to a close he continued to race at a variety of venues, including Errol Aerodrome.

In his younger days, Jimmy was a keen tennis player and golfer. He played football for Cherrybank City Boys and for the Perth Police in the Perth

Jimmy Buchan in action.
(Photograph from The Courier).

Half-Holiday League. His love of sport was reflected in his chosen career path and, after joining his father's news agency from school, he worked on national newspapers, firstly with the *Daily Record* and from 1961 to 1989 with the *Daily Express* whom he joined as night news editor and retired from as sports editor.

While always professional in his duties as a sports reporter, he particularly relished reporting on the fortunes of his beloved St Johnstone. While covering a League Cup semi-final with Rangers in 1961, he was nearly ejected from the press box for celebrating when Saints went two goals up! Sadly, Rangers eventually won the game 3-2 after extra time. What a shame Jimmy did not live to see Saints' famous victory over Rangers in the quarter final of the 2021 Scottish Cup on their way to that amazing cup double!

The Buchan family's association with motor cycles continued with Jimmy's younger brother, Donald (also a competitive motor cyclist), taking ownership of Buchan Motorcycles – the business founded by his father.

ARTHUR DEWAR (1934-2020)

During the 1980s and early 1990s there may have been some customers who, when purchasing their morning newspaper from the store at the corner of Glover Street and Needless Road, did not realise that they were being served by one of Perth's great sporting legends.

The achievements of Perthshire County Cricket Club from 1953 until the 1970s can only be described as phenomenal, with the club winning the Scottish Counties Championship nineteen times in twenty-four seasons. Much of this success can be attributed to the bowling skills of Arthur Dewar, who played for Perthshire for fifteen years and was capped six times for Scotland.

Arthur's international appearances were against Ireland in 1962 and 1963; the MCC in 1960 and 1961 and Warwickshire in 1961 and 1962. His best performance at international level was in one of the matches against Warwickshire at Edgebaston when he took seven wickets for seventy-one runs. He was described as having a flowing bowling style similar to the great Brian Statham and his action and delivery had enough lift and deviation to trouble the best batsmen.

An excellent all-round sportsman, Arthur was sports champion

Arthur Dewar.
(Perthshire Advertiser photograph).

at Robert Douglas Memorial School, Scone in 1945 and, as well as his prowess at cricket, was also a first-class lawn tennis player and golfer.

BARRIE DOUGLAS (1949-2018)

Barrie Douglas was one of the most popular figures across Scottish amateur golf and beyond, a man whose infectious enthusiasm and love of the sport rubbed off on many. A huge supporter of Scottish Golf Union and Scottish golf activities, Barrie performed various selection and captaincy roles at boys' level and played a close role in the career development of a host of young players over the years. A Great Britain and Ireland selector for the Royal and Ancient from 2009 until 2016, he worked with several generations of emerging young golfers and was well versed in identifying talented players as well as always being willing to give advice and guidance.

Barrie offered the same passion for the game locally and was a member of both Craigie Hill and Blairgowrie Golf Clubs. He was a multiple club champion at both clubs and was a Scottish Boys' internationalist. His involvement with county golf in Perth and Kinross was legendary and over a period of fifty five years, from his days as an under-fourteen junior and playing for the boys' and men's teams, he filled every role on the administrative side from team captain to president. His sporting activities away from golf included playing rugby for Perthshire Rugby FC and curling.

It was while acting as Scottish Golf's European Boys' captain at the team championship in La Manga, Spain in July, 2018 that Barrie took ill and was admitted to hospital where he was diagnosed with lung infections. Although he battled the illness with typical determination his condition steadily worsened and he died from heart failure.

In Barrie's memory the Barrie Douglas Foundation has been set up

Barrie Douglas. (Photograph from Scottish Golf).

to to encourage and help the young golfers of the future – a fitting legacy to a man who did so much for amateur golf.

CHARLIE GALLAGHER

Charlie Gallagher was one of Scotland's greatest badminton players and lived in Castle Terrace, Needless Road for a short time during the 1980s. Charlie was capped over fifty times for Scotland as a junior, youth or full international and was Scottish champion on twelve occasions at four different levels. He represented his country in European and World Championships, at the Commonwealth Games and at the All-England event.

Also a golfer of exceptional ability, being a plus-one player at Craigie Hill and Blairgowrie, he would have represented Scotland in this sport but for a bizarre decision by the Scottish Golf Union in 1996. Born in Donegal, Charlie moved to Perth with his parents when twelve years old and when deemed good enough to play badminton internationally, he chose Scotland as his country. However, the nationality rules of the SGU only allowed people born in Scotland, or with one or other of their parents born in Scotland, to enter their national amateur competitions. Charlie married Jane Ramsay, who lived at 69 Needless

Road and who was a prominent local, national and international lady curler.

ALAN GORRIE

Alan Gorrie is the founder and lead singer of the Average White Band – a group of internationally-known soul musicians. He started his musical career during the 1960s with a local group called The Vikings and one of their venues was the Blues Workshop held in Perth's County Hotel. It was as an offshoot of the type of music that they played there that resulted in the birth of the Average White Band. As well as The Vikings, the workshop also attracted musicians such as Roger Ball, Malcolm Duncan and Robbie McIntosh.

That was the common factor when they all found themselves in London during the 1970s. Alan managed to persuade them to give up their day jobs and the Average White Band was formed in 1972. In 1974 they stormed into the US charts with *White Album*, a blistering set of soul and funk masterpieces.

Frequent trips to the States followed and the band decided to base themselves there in 1975. They quickly established themselves and started to make a big impression in the charts. *Pick Up the Pieces* made No. 6 in the UK charts in February of that year and was quickly followed by *Cut The Cake* a few months later and *Queen Of My Soul* the following year. The band toured constantly and developed into one of the great live acts of the decade. They recorded frequently, releasing five successful albums during the next three years.

When the band broke up in 1982 (band member Hamish Stuart became guitarist for Paul McCartney and another, Steve Ferrone who had replaced McIntosh, joined Duran Duran) Alan Gorrie immediately recorded a solo album

Alan Gorrie.

Sleepless Nights.

In 1987, Alan formed a revamped Average White Band with 'Onnie' McIntyre, Ball and Duncan and recorded *After Shock* which was successful on the soul charts. The group has continued since then and still tour extensively across North America with appearances in the UK, Japan, South Africa and elsewhere,

Alan, who has retained the family home in Craigie, has also written a number of songs with Daryl Hall, many of which appeared on Hall's *Can't Stop Dreaming* solo album. In 2021 he released a reflective four song EP, *The Blues Workshop,* named after that jazz/blues/soul club of 1960's Perth where it all began.

EVE GRAHAM

It would not be surprising if a larger than usual number of Craigie residents were tuned into the BBC's *Eurovision Song Contest* on the evening of Saturday, 25th March, 1972. After all it was not every day that a Craigie girl featured in a live televised music spectacular.

Brought up in Craigie where her mother ran the Craigie Post Office for a number of years and her father was a member of the Perth Operatic Society, Evelyn Beatson began her singing at an early age. As a teenager she became the singer in the early 1960s with the popular Perth group The Cyclones until encouraged by her brother, who had spotted an advertisement in the *Musical Express,* she successfully attended an audition in London and became a singer with the famous Cyril Stapleton Orchestra and changed her name to Eve Graham. In the mid-1960s Eve became a founding member of The Nocturns before moving on in 1969 to be a founding part of The New Seekers for whom she was the lead singer for most of their hits.

By the early 1970s, The New Seekers had hit international fame and were the clean-cut super group on everybody's lips. Their song, 'I'd Like to Teach The World to Sing', made it to number one in the charts then hit stratospheric heights of success a second time when a re-recorded version was used in the Coca-Cola advertisements. Eve's three-octave range was showcased on several songs and most notably in the British and European hit, *Never Ending Song of Love,* which reached number six.

The 1972 *Eurovision Song Contest* mentioned earlier was held in the Usher Hall, Edinburgh with fans thronging Princes Street and a riot squad being called in to calm down the situation. With their song, 'Beg, Steal or Borrow', the group finished in second place. The New Seekers always had top quality songs from the best writers such as Neil Sedaka and Neil

Eve Graham (second right) with the New Seekers. (Photograph from the Daily Record).

Diamond and also worked with other artists such as Liza Minelli, Dionne Warwick and Andy Williams.

The group disbanded in 1974 and Eve moved onto solo cabaret work but rejoined a reconstituted New Seekers in 1976 singing lead on their hits 'It's So Nice To Have You Home' and 'I Wanna Go Back'. In 1978 she left the group, married ex-New Seeker Kevin Finn in 1979 and performed with him as a duo for many years releasing two singles and touring with Gene Pitney and Max Boyce.

On returning to live in Perthshire, a number of special projects brought Eve out of retirement, including two albums in 2005 and 2006 and a New Zealand tour in 2012.

GARRY HARVEY

Brought up in Cherrybank, Garry Harvey may have the most famous hands in golf.

Anyone who has watched the closing moments of the British Open has seen them for Garry is the man who engraves the winner's name on the base of the claret jug. It is a daunting task for as well as having a television camera focused on his work, he has only about ten minutes to complete the work from the time the winning putt is holed to the presentation of the trophy. Small wonder that he hopes that The Open champion will be one with a short name!

Garry's father, Alex Harvey, was the official engraver for thirty years before Garry took over the duties in 2004 after serving a seven year on-and-off apprenticeship while between times carving out a career as a professional golfer on the European Tour. In 1985 Garry won the Kenyan Open and qualified for the The Open in 1979.

As a young golfer at Craigie Hill, Garry won the British Boys Amateur Championship at Moortown in 1972 when he beat Robert Newsome by seven & five in the final. The previous year, when the tournament was played at Barassie in Ayrshire, Garry had also reached the final but lost to Howard Clark. For his 1972 achievement he was made an honorary member at Craigie Hill.

DAVID KAY (1900-1971)

David Kay lived in Needless Road for over ten years. Born in Blackford, where he worked as a mechanic in the family garage business, he thought up the idea of a free-rotor plane, the forerunner to the helicopter, when watching seed pods from sycamore trees spiralling to the ground in autumn.

Like many inventors, the inspired country lad discovered that raising cash for his project was a real problem. At that time, people had still to take conventional planes seriously, so who would sponsor an odd contrivance with rotors sprouting from its head? It looked daft. Who would confirm it would work?

One person to show faith in Kay was a Crieff businessman, William Taylor and the staggering sum of £20,000 was spoken of as getting the world's first gyroplane off the ground. Stewart Henderson, himself a flying pioneer, was persuaded to rent part of Shield's Garage, which he owned, in Perth's Dunkeld Road and a drawing board team was assembled. Kay and his co-designer, John Grieve of Scone, talked it over with the technical experts and Henderson's best men, all craftsmen to their fingertips, made the bits. By the mid 1930s, the tiny Kay Gyroplane was finally assembled.

David Kay's gyroplane was the first rotorcraft able to angle its blades to suit different flying conditions. It was powered by a 75 hp seven cylinder Pobjoy 'R' engine driving a four-bladed propeller.

Preliminary tests were carried out at Scone Aerodrome and suddenly the Air Ministry, who had earlier shown little interest in this seemingly zany venture, decided to arrange a full test programme at Farnborough.

Possibly because David Kay was a genius before his time, nothing transpired in terms of commercial development of the Kay Gyroplane although, as a result of the Air Ministry tests, the Kay-type 33/1 Gyroplane was built by Oddie, Bradbury & Cull and made its inauguration flight at Eastleigh Aerodrome, Southampton, in 1935. Meanwhile, a Polish firm, Sikorski, were pursuing the same idea with government support and are today still building helicopters.

David Kay spent the remainder of his working days living with his dream in the dying embers of ambition at Shield's Garage, working alongside Stewart Henderson's son, Bill.

The Kay type 33/1 Gyroplane G-ACVA. (Photographed by the author at the Museum of Flight, East Lothian).

The Kay-type 33/1 Gyroplane G-ACVA, the sole example of this type completed, can be seen today at the Museum of Flight at East Fortune in East Lothian. But what a pity that Perth itself did not find a place for what was a magnificent example of local enterprise and skill. After all, in Scone Aerodrome, Perth had Britain's first municipal aerodrome and also has the founder's badge in the Air Cadet movement.

WILLIAM LAIDLAW (1914-1941)

For many years Bill Laidlaw was regarded by those of his generation as the best golfer Perth has produced. Indeed there are many who believed that in the late 1930s he was an Open champion in waiting.

The son of a Perth High Street jeweller, Laidlaw learned his golf over the Craigie Hill course before becoming assistant professional at Gleneagles Hotel from 1932, at Malden from 1934 and then assistant to the great Henry Cotton at Ashbridge Golf Club in 1937. Early in 1939 he became the full professional at West Herts Golf Club.

In 1937, when The Open was played at Carnoustie, Bill Laidlaw tied for seventh place with a four-round score of 298 and finished eight strokes behind the winner who just happened to be Bill's boss, Henry Cotton! He also played in the 1934, 1935 and 1938 Opens.

Laidlaw's big win was in the 1938 Daily Mirror Assistants' Tournament at Blackpool North Shore when he scored 289 for the seventy two holes and won by nine strokes from Alan Waters and Geoff White. Later in 1938, he was second in the Czechoslovak Open although eleven strokes behind the winner who again just happened to be Henry Cotton.

Bill's golfing career then went on hold in September 1939 when he joined the RAF on the outbreak of the Second World War. On the night of 20/21 October, 1941, after leaving RAF Swinderby in a Handley Page Hampden, Pilot Officer Laidlaw was killed when his No. 50 Squadron was involved in a bombing raid on Bremen, Germany. He was survived by his wife Pamela Tanner, a singer, who he had married in 1940 and by his son, William, born in 1942 and whom he never saw.

PETER, EDITH and KATIE LOUDON

Whilst the Perthshire farming families of Hay, Smith and Muirhead will always be synonymous with international success in the sport of curling, the Loudon family from Cherrybank are right up there with them.

Peter Loudon was a member of the Scotland team which won the men's World Curling Championship held in Saint John, New Brunswick, Canada in 1999 and was also in the Great Britain men's team which competed at the 2002 Winter Olympics in Salt Lake City, USA. Peter also won gold medals as a member of the Scottish team at the 1996 and 1999 European championships along with silver and bronze medals from the same championships in 1995, 1997, 2002 and 2008. He has coached curling at the highest level and played a key role in organizing major curling events. A lifelong supporter of St Johnstone FC, for whom his grandfather Peter Gavigan played in the 1920s, Peter has a position on the St Johnstone board as a voluntary senior executive.

Edith and Katie are Peter's sisters and each have also had distinguished curling careers often playing together in the same Scotland and Great Britain ladies teams.

Like her brother, Edith is also a world curling champion and was a member of the Scotland ladies team which won the World Championship at Bismarck, North Dakota, USA in 2002 and, along with her sister Katie, represented her country at the 1995, 1996, 1998, 2001 and 2003 world championships. The girls also played together in the Scotland team at the 1988, 1990, 1991, 1994, 1995, 1997 and 2003 European Championships with Edith making an additional appearance at the 2002 championship.

Edith and Katie were both members of the ladies team which represented Great Britain at the 1998 Winter Olympics in Japan.

TOM McCREA (1913-1989)

Tom McCrea from Cherrybank was largely instrumental in the phenomenal success of Perth County Cricket Club during the 1950s and 1960s.

As a teacher at Perth Academy, he encouraged Perthshire's cricket professional Tommy Lodge (a former Yorkshire county player) to introduce cricket coaching classes at the school in the early 1950s. This resulted in the emergence of a new generation of talented young players such as Len Dudman, Scott Gardiner, Bob Young and Arthur Dewar.

He was a former club captain and his book on the history of Perth County Cricket Club from 1926 to 1976 was published in 1980.

A genial and popular character, Tom always enjoyed reminiscing over his cricketing days from his nightly spot in the Cherrybank Inn.

BILL MacDONALD (1934-2019)

For over thirty years, Craigie's Bill MacDonald had the best seat that money can't buy during the Wimbledon tennis fortnight. From his position in the umpire's chair, he was in the closest possible proximity to the superstars of world tennis.

Bill first officiated at Wimbledon in 1970 and, from 1981 until his retirement in 2000, was regularly umpiring matches on the famous Centre Court. He took charge of matches featuring most of the world's greatest tennis players such as Bjorn Borg, Boris Becker, Jimmy Connors, Stan Smith, John McEnroe, Ilie Nastase, Peter Fleming, Frew McMillan, Virginia Wade, Martina Navratilova, Hana Mandlikova, Pam Shriver, Steffi Graf, Jo Durie, Sue Barker, Kathy Jordan, Anne Smith and many more. Bill umpired three Wimbledon finals in the form of a men's doubles, a ladies' doubles and a mixed doubles and was in the umpire's chair for several semi-finals.

Bill held a special regard for Ilie Nastase once regarded as the 'Mr Nastie' of tennis and said that in his opinion the Rumanian was the most talented player that never won Wimbledon. He said that while Nastase could be temperamental and volatile on court he could be

Bill MacDonald umpiring on Wimbledon's Centre Court in 1981. Photograph by Russ Adams Production, Massachusetts, USA).

equally affable and friendly off-court and they held a mutual respect for each other. Bill recalled one particular incident during an indoor match at London's Royal Albert Hall when Nastase referred to him as 'an English pig umpire'. Bill promptly called Nastase over and said that, while he may be a pig umpire, he was a *Scottish* pig umpire and since then Nastase always referred to Bill as 'Sir'!

Bill first caught the eye of the Lawn Tennis Umpires Association through his performances as an official during the Dewar Cup. This was the first major indoor tennis event held in the United Kingdom and for its first two years was played at the Bells Sports Centre in Perth. During his thirty two years as a tennis umpire, Bill officiated at matches throughout the UK and in many overseas countries including South Africa, the USA, Dubai, France and Spain.

Bill was also a qualified football referee in both the junior and senior game and once was senior linesman at a European Cup quarter-final tie between Real Madrid and Ajax of Amsterdam, two of Europe's most famous and successful club sides.

He was president of Darnhall Tennis Club for over fifty years and latterly found time during the football season to be a commentator on Hospital Radio for St Johnstone FC's home games at McDiarmid Park.

ALLAN MACKINTOSH (1894-1982)

During the early 1920s it was not uncommon for the residents of Upper Craigie to be awakened from their early morning slumbers by the sound of a steam whistle! Two young lads, Allan Mackintosh and his brother Robert, had constructed a large sized model steamship in the garden of their parents' home at Mount Craigie in Verena Terrace and took great delight in letting the ship's whistle blow.

The fascination of steam-driven machinery followed Allan into his adult and working life and while employed by Perth Town Council he was the last man to drive the Council's steam lorry.

He was a founder member of the Perth Society of Model and Experimental Engineers and remained an active member of the society until his death.

Allan Mackintosh (second left) at a Bowerswell garden fete in the early 1960s when members of the Perth Society of Model and Experimental Engineers displayed a selection of their working steam models. (Photograph by the Courier and Advertiser).

JIMMY MACNAB (1937-2009)

Jimmy MacNab from Glover Street was once one of Craigie's great characters. After attending Craigie and Perth High Schools and doing some early work as a trainee auctioneer at Hay's Mart he embarked on a varied career working mainly with animals.

He worked as a keeper to the Marquis of Bute and naturalist Gerald Durrell before becoming head keeper for circus producer Billy Smart at Windsor Safari Park. It was at Windsor that Jimmy befriended an elephant, taking it along to the park's public bar most evenings where it would drink a pint of brandy and water, lifting the tumbler with its trunk and pouring the contents into its mouth. This near-nightly event became very popular with visitors to the park.

While working at Windsor, Jimmy met a Spaniard called Tony Pyatt who had inherited a zoo. Knowing very little about animal welfare, he asked Jimmy to run the zoo for him and, unable to resist the lure of sunshine, Jimmy moved to Andalusia. While there, Jimmy was bitten by both a lion and a chimpanzee but Jimmy's brother Peter, a police chief superintendent, reported that both lion and chimp had recovered fully from their ordeal!

During the 1970s, Jimmy returned to Scotland and to Strachur in Argyll where he worked for Sir Fitzroy MacLean as a gillie, driver, stalker, caddie and whatever else was required. Much of his time was spent at the family's Creggans Inn where Jimmy, once a fine entertainer and performer of bothy ballads around Perthshire (often travelling with Bill Wilkie's Band), coaxed many a local, guest or TV star to take part in impromptu ceilidhs. When Sir Fitzroy MacLean appeared on the popular television show *This Is Your Life,* Jimmy was one of the featured guests.

Jimmy's love of animals continued and he was a keen breeder of birds and won a supreme championship medal at the Royal Highland show in 1992.

After being best to rest in Strachur churchyard, over one hundred guests attended a funeral party at Strachur House hosted by Sir Charles and Lady Debbie MacLean. Remembering Jimmy's well-lived life, one local guest remarked: 'When Jimmy gets to heaven the angels will have smiles on their faces'.

JIM MALCOLM

Often described as the ultimate Scots troubadour and 'one of the finest singers in Scotland in any style', Jim Malcolm lived for a time at 113 Needless Road. Brought up in Perthshire, he was introduced to the traditional music of Scotland by his mother and by his early twenties was winning songwriting competitions and playing in folk clubs all over Scotland.

Jim's career took off when he hosted the open stage at an Edinburgh Folk Festival and through this secured a contract for his first solo album *Sconeward*. The album brought in bookings at folk clubs and festivals throughout Britain and abroad and established Jim as one of Scotland's leading traditional singers and songwriters and he was dubbed 'the new male voice of Scotland'.

His next album, *Rohallion*, consolidated his reputation as one of the country's most exciting young folk acts and brought repeated requests for television and radio appearances. In January 1999, he joined one of Scotland's most popular international folk bands, Old Blind Dogs from north-east Scotland, and worked with them all over the UK Europe, Canada and the USA for seven years. In 2004 the band were named Scottish folk band of the year and that same year Jim received the award of Scottish song-writer of the year.

In addition to the recordings already mentioned and the three recordings he made as the lead singer of Old Blind Dogs, Jim has released a number of solo CDs. One of them, *Live in Perth,* features his own song 'Blindness of My Youth' which mentions sledging near the golf course at Craigie Hill:

> As the winter hardened, we'd await a fall of snow,
> Up beside the golf course was the best place we could go.
> Though the sight of snowy Perth would soothe the sorest eye,
> I could only care that the snow would lie.

Jim maintains that his love of Perthshire has been the major inspiration for his music and his solo concerts are always highly entertaining, peppered with funny stories and observations, in the great tradition of Scottish artists through the ages.

Nowadays, Jim and his wife Susie often perform together as a duo and have travelled extensively doing gigs throughout the USA and the UK.

DONALD MAXWELL

In 1977, Donald MacAlpine, who had grown up in Murray Crescent, decided to forgo his five-year career as a teacher of geography to become a professional singer with Scottish Opera and, for equity purposes, changed his name to Donald Maxwell. Whilst teaching at Perth Academy, Donald had become well-known as a baritone with local amateur operatic groups and as a much sought after solo singer at concerts and ceilidhs so it was of little surprise that he decided to take this further step to make music his preferred career.

As an operatic baritone, director and teacher he has now sung with all the leading British opera companies as well as La Scala, Milan, Metropolitan Opera, Paris Opera, Vienna Staatsoper, Teatro Colon, Buenos Aires and Theatre Musical de Paris, among others. He has also sung on the concert stage in performances broadcast on radio and television.

In the early days of his professional singing career Donald regularly performed in the light entertainment trio Music Box with the singer Linda Ormiston and Perth's local piano virtuoso John Scrimger. Since then he has performed leading and character parts including major roles in several operas by the likes of Benjamin Britten, Arthur

Donald Maxwell.
(Perthshire Advertiser photograph).

Sullivan and Giuseppe Verdi. He was artistic director of the Buxton Festival, director of the National Opera Studio and head of opera studies at the Royal Welsh College of Music and Drama for several years and, since 1987, Donald has been a regular performer with The Royal Opera. He performs regularly with the National Gilbert & Sullivan Opera Company at the International Gilbert & Sullivan Festival and he is a patron of Somerset Opera.

Donald Maxwell's recordings include roles in *Amahl and the Night Visitors, The Marriage of Figaro, Noye's Fludde, Carmina Burana, A Midsummer Night's Dream, The Rape of Lucretia, Missa Sabrinensis, The Beggar's Opera, The Firebrand of Florence, Cox and Box, The Contrabandista, Trial by Jury, Patience, The Mikado, The Yeomen of the Guard, The Maid of the Mountains, Kismet, Bitter Sweet, The Student Prince* and *Sir John in Love*. He has also recorded an album of Scottish songs and played the title character in the Carl Rosa Opera Company's 2001 film of *The Mikado*.

Despite a hectic work schedule, Donald has never forgotten his Perth roots and, whenever possible, has returned to the Fair City to support various charitable, civic and private musical events ranging from Burns suppers to choral concerts.

SIR FRANCIS NORIE-MILLER (1859-1947)

Born in Cheshunt, Hertfordshire, Francis Norie-Miller began his insurance career in London then Glasgow but is best remembered for his role in developing the business base for the General Accident, Fire and Life Assurance Corporation in Perth. He is widely accepted as being the founder of the company which under his dynamic leadership built up a worldwide business. He has been described as being one of 'the great insurance autocrats of the late nineteenth and early twentieth centuries'.

Norie-Miller was intimately involved with the civic life of Perth for many years. For over fifty years he was a Justice of the Peace for the county of Perthshire and for over twenty years he was Chairman of the School Board of Perth or of Perth County Education Authority. He had a particular affinity for Craigie School and gifted the school playing field on the land between Young Street and Needless Road which is still in use today. He was also a director and later chairman of Perth Royal Infirmary. In 1933 he became a freeman of the city of Perth.

At the 1931 general election, Norie-Miller contested Perth as the Liberal candidate but was defeated by Lord Scone of the Conservative party. However, in 1935 when Lord Scone succeeded his father as Earl of Mansfield and went to the House of Lords, a by-election was called and the Perth Liberals invited Norie-Miller to fight the election as they learned that the Perth Conservatives were willing not to oppose him proving he stood as a Liberal National candidate. In a straight fight with the Labour candidate, Norie Miller won the by-election by a majority of 9,532 but his reign as the Member of Parliament for Perth was a short-lived one as he decided not to contest the general election which was held later that year.

Norie-Miller remained as chairman of General Accident until 1944 and as its honorary governor from 1938 until his death in 1947. He was succeeded in the baronetcy and as chairman of General Accident by his son Stanley who, in turn, ensured that the company retained its world headquarters in Perth throughout his lifetime.

Sir Francis Norie-Miller. (Photograph from the General Accident Archive).

Sir Francis Norie-Miller's family residence was in Cherrybank at Cleeve House and, when created a Baronet in the 1936 New Year's Honours List for political and public service in the County of Perth and for his local philanthropy, he chose the title of Norie-Miller of Cleeve.

NAE PLACE MAIR BRAW

JACK NORWELL (1917-2003)

Regular customers at the Cherrybank Inn during the 1960s and 1970s were well acquainted with Jack Norwell, the genial and popular 'Mine Host' of that era. Affectionately known to his regulars as 'the duke', Jack was a member of the Norwell family who owned quality shoe shops in Perth for many years but he was also one of 'the few' of the Battle of Britain.

As the war clouds loomed over Europe in the late 1930s, Jack did advanced flying training with the Royal Air Force Voluntary Reserve and on the outbreak of war in September 1939 he was posted to the RAF's 54 Squadron at Hornchurch. Over Dunkirk on 24th May 1940 he destroyed a Me109 and on the 25th shared in destroying another. He shared in damaging a Do17 on 3rd July, shared a Me110 and damaged two others on 18th August, destroyed a Me109 on the 22nd, probably another on the 28th and shared one on the 31st. Jack then joined 41 Squadron at Hornchurch around 11th September and flew his first sortie on the 16th. On the 17th of that month he damaged two Me109s and destroyed two more on the 27th and 30th.

In October 1940, he volunteered for service in Malta and joined the aircraft carrier HMS Argus which was destined for the Mediterranean. On 17th November, he was in the first flight of six Hurricanes to take off. Two were lost when their fuel gave out but Jack landed with only gallons remaining. After joining 261 Squadron at Ta Kali, Malta, further postings took him to the Middle East and to Greece.

On leaving the RAF in 1946 with the rank of Flight Lieutenant, Jack re-joined the Voluntary Reserve. After retiring in 1954 he took over ownership of the Cherrybank Inn where for a number of years his wartime fighter pilot exploits were remembered by a framed drawing of Jack and his Spitfire.

DONALD M PATON (1904-1988)

My father, Donald M Paton, lived in Needless Road for almost fifty years. Born in Stenhousemuir, he came with his family to settle in the Balbeggie and Scone areas at an early age. As the eldest son of a large family, social and economic times saw him, at the age of fourteen, employed as a conductor on the old Perth trams and later the bus company. He became a well-known figure on the Scone to Cherrybank route and it was during this time that he started to write plays and became involved in amateur dramatics. His daily work of interaction afforded him the opportunity to observe the local people and formed the characters and colouring for his plays.

He was the founder of the Scone Scottish Players (later to become the Perth Scottish Players) regular performers in the village halls of Perthshire, Angus and Fife and often the plays performed were both written and produced by him. In addition to this, he was also known as an excellent character actor in his own right. Each November, until the early 1950s, the Perth Scottish Players performed for one week in Perth Theatre playing to capacity audiences and it was not unusual for 'House Full' notices to be posted outside. The enthusiasm of these amateur players, encouraged by a supportive public, eventually provided sufficient funds to build a cottage for the Bowerswell Memorial Homes in Perth.

As a recognised playwright he wrote several three-act plays, some in collaboration with Ella S Boswell and also Fred J Forbes who lived in Craigie's Abbot Street. In addition, he wrote many one-act plays which are still available for performance today. Plays bearing such names as *His Ain Folk, The Call o' the Glen, Guests at Glentaggart, Mistress of The Manse, Glencraig Comes Home, The Incomer, Hamespun and Tinsel* and *The Tinker's Warning* were mainly a comment on the Scottish rural life of the 1920s and 1930s.

In 1949 he was a principal organiser and producer of a Perth Historical Pageant which took place at the old Muirton Park football ground. This unique event, which took place over an entire week, attracted many leading show-business personalities to the city, including film stars Anna Neagle and Danny Kaye.

During war service with the RAF in

The Perth Historical Pageant held at Muirton Park in 1949. Left to right: Bill Chalmers, Donald Paton, film producer Herbert Wilcox, film star Anna Neagle, Lord Provost Sir John Ure Primrose, David Band, Stanley MacDonald and Philip James. (Perthshire Advertiser photograph).

Donald and Janie Paton in their garden at Needless Road in 1952 with the famous Scottish actor Duncan MacRae. (Photograph by A C Cowper & Co., Perth).

Palestine and the Middle East, these talents were again utilised in providing morale-boosting entertainment for the forces. Further postings based him in the north-east of Scotland and the Outer Hebrides where he ran drama groups and concert parties which were instrumental in raising for charity, notably the Red Cross, the sum of over £11,000. His prolific outpouring of plays continued upon returning to civilian life, firstly with the old-established High Street grocery firm of J & D Gowans and later with the General Accident Insurance Company.

A passion for the works of Robert Burns made him a much-in-demand speaker at Burns Nights throughout the United Kingdom. In 1975, despite it still being the time of 'the cold war', he travelled to Moscow for what was described in the press as 'the Burns Supper of the century' and was invited to recite a few lines of the Bard's works in Russian on Moscow Radio. His enthusiasm was instrumental in the revival of The Perth Burns Club in the year 1977 and he was president of the club from 1977 to 1979.

PEOPLE AND PERSONALITIES

RACHEL PENNYCUICK (1850-1926)

From 1835 until 1921 the council-owned Perth Fire Brigade operated from 13 Tay Street in a pend below the city chambers. During this time much of the apparatus was fairly primitive and had been of little use in several major and severe fires which had occurred in the city – notably those in 1919 at the Bell's whisky bond in Canal Street (when news reports of the time mentioned the local streets running as rivers of whisky) and at the St Catherine's Road dyeworks of P & P Campbell.

It was the gift to the city of two motor fire engines by Miss Rachel Pennycuick of Murrayfield House in Craigie which prompted the council to proceed with the modernisation of the service and to transfer their operations from Tay Street to new city centre premises in King Edward Street. The fire engines gifted by Miss Pennycuick were two of the latest Dennis sixty five horsepower units with thirty five feet scale ladders. Each fire engine had twenty four lengths of one hundred foot hose and was capable of delivering five hundred gallons of water per minute.

For over sixty years a prominent feature in Perth's city centre was the fire station's sixty foot hose tower and this was erected as the result.

When she opened the new King Edward Street fire station in 1921 Miss Pennycuick was warmly thanked for 'the most unique gift ever given to the municipality' and presented with a golden key.

Although a native of Morayshire, Rachel Pennycuick evinced

Rachel Pennycuick's gifts to the city of two fire engines are shown in this photograph taken at the opening of Perth Fire Brigade's new fire station in King Edward Street in 1921. (Photograph from Perth & Kinross Libraries).

much public spirit for her adopted city and this was recognised on 21ˢᵗ June 1921 when she was presented with the Freedom of the City.

ERIC M RAITT (1912-2007)

For many years a kenspeckle figure in Craigie and Cherrybank with his push bike and golden retriever dog, Eric Raitt always maintained that golf is the top male social game. A most affable character, Eric who spent his working life with the General Accident Insurance Company, was for many years a pillar of the Craigie Hill Golf Club.

What a lot of people don't realise is that Eric invented golf's Winter League. It began at Craigie Hill in 1932 with only seventeen members taking part but within a few years that number had swelled dramatically and today the Winter League is a vital and integral part of almost every golf club in Britain. His contribution towards organising fifty years of Winter League golf was recognised in 1982 by Craigie Hill and he was made an honorary life member of the club.

I am not sure if it has yet been done, but if ever anyone gets round to compiling a definitive history of the game of golf then the name of Eric M Raitt should figure prominently in it.

HARRY C ROBERTSON (1913-1974)

Well known throughout the city and county as a press photographer with the *Perthshire Advertiser*, Harry Robertson was one of Perth's best all-round sportsmen. He was a graceful and purposeful golfer, a stylish footballer, had positively devastating speed at table tennis and in his later years showed great skill on the bowling green. He epitomised what has always been regarded as the epic British sportsman – the natural ball player.

But sport was only one of his many talents. An accomplished pianist, he played with various dance bands and was also greatly in demand as a solo performer. In 1963, when two young lads called the Alexander Brothers were starting to make their mark on Scottish show business and were doing a summer season at Perth Theatre, Harry wrote the musical accompaniment for a new song, 'The Hill of Kinnoull', which the duo eventually recorded. The lyrics of the song were written by a Craigie lady, Elizabeth Brazier.

PEOPLE AND PERSONALITIES

INNES RUSSELL (1919-1971)

Innes Russell, who lived in Needless Road, was one of several Perth men who were captured at St Valery-en-Caux in France on 12th June 1940, shortly after the evacuation of the British Expeditionary Force from Dunkirk during the Second World War.

The 51st Highland Division, made up of men from mainly Central and North East Scotland, had resolutely fought a rearguard action after the evacuation but were overwhelmed by German armoured forces and formally surrendered to General Rommel. As the men were marched across France to the prison camps of Eastern Germany, the sound of their 'tackety boots' on the French cobblestones provided Innes and his fellow prisoners with background rhythm for the creation of new Scottish country dances during their five long years in captivity.

Many of these dances such as 'The Reel of the 51st Division' are still performed today and one of them, 'The St Johnstoun Reel', was devised by Innes and another Perth man, John Williamson, leading figures in the Scottish country dance scene.

JOHN SCRIMGER, MBE

Affectionately known for years as 'Perth's Mr Music', John Scrimger from Gray Street can trace his musical background to age six when he sang as a boy soprano in the St John's Kirk choir.

While still at school John played a small foot pedal harmonica in the Brotherhood Mission Hall in 1945 and at age seventeen became the organist at Scone's West Church. For fifty years he was organist and choirmaster at St Andrew's Church in Atholl Street and when that church closed he became organist at St Leonard's in the Field's Church, a position which he held until retiring in 2020, thus ending seventy years in Perth as a church organist.

Before giving up a career with the Perth County Council to become Perth Theatre's musical director, he was the founder of the popular John Scrimger Singers, was a member of Bill Wilkie's Concert Party and was instrumental in the formation of *The Music Box* with Donald Maxwell and Linda Ormiston. John also found time to assist with Perth Drama Club productions as well as giving solo performances and accompanying local singers.

John Scrimger.
(Perthshire Advertiser photograph).

As a professional musician he has been a familiar face for many years at musical shows, concerts, pantomimes and cabaret events at Perth Theatre, Pitlochry Festival Theatre, Dundee Repertory Theatre and further afield.

WILLIAM SOUTAR (1898-1943)

William Soutar was born on 28th April 1898 at 4 South Inch Terrace, Perth, the only son of John and Margaret Soutar, a master joiner. He attended Southern District School from 1903 to 1912 and Perth Academy (then situated in Rose Terrace) until 1916 where he distinguished himself in sports and academic subjects. In 1913, the Soutar family moved to number 22 Kinfauns Crescent in Craigie's Needless Road.

It was while living in Kinfauns Crescent that William Soutar began to write poetry at the age of fifteen. Buckie Braes, Craigie Knowes and Callerfountain Hill became the inspiration for many of his poems and one can almost imagine the youthful Soutar walking past Pitheavlis Castle pondering one of his latest poetic gems.

On leaving school, William initially studied medicine at Edinburgh University but after a year transferred to the arts faculty. He spent two years from 1916 to 1918 doing war service with the Royal Navy, serving mainly in the North Atlantic and it was in 1918 that he contracted a mysterious ailment which affected his legs and feet and led to him leaving the navy. He went back to his studies and left university in June 1923 intending to try for a career in journalism or teaching but his health had now worsened and he returned to his parents' home in Perth for medical treatment. It is said that, while walking in Edinburgh one evening, he stopped under the pillars of St George's West Church, saying to himself 'now I can be a poet.'

The Soutar family moved from Kinfauns Crescent in May 1924 to a rented house at 28 Wilson Street. There, along with his business partner Tom McQueen, John Soutar designed and built a new semi-detached bungalow across the street at Number 27, both the Soutar and McQueen families occupying separate halves of the property. It was Willie who gave his new home the name of Inglelowe

William Soutar. (Photograph from Perth and Kinross Libraries).

but he was by now a weak man. In 1929 he contracted pneumonia and pleurisy and, despite lengthy spells in hospital and extensive periods of convalescence, his condition, now diagnosed as ankylosing spondylitis, led to him being completely bedridden by 1930.

William Soutar spent the remaining thirteen years of his life writing a prolific stream of poetry, journals and diaries but his great contribution to Scots literature was as a poet. He wrote in English but, most notably, in Scots and often about Perth and its people. During his illness, William's room was extended and adapted with strategically placed mirrors to widen the field of vision available to the increasingly immobilised poet. Hugh McDiarmid, Alexander Scott, Helen Cruickshank and almost all of Scotland's great literary figures of that era were regular visitors to his bedside until his death in 1943.

The former Wilson Street home of William Soutar is now preserved by Perth & Kinross Council as a tribute to his memory and between 1989 and 2010 was used by the following leading authors and poets during their time as the council's Writer in Residence: Raymond Vettese; John Herdman; Donald Campbell; Robert Alan Jamieson; Carl MacDougall; Brian McCabe and Ajay Close.

NAE PLACE MAIR BRAW

The Soutar house in Wilson Street.

JEAN VALENTINE (1924-2019)

Jean Millar Valentine (later Jean Rooke) grew up in Wilson Street in Craigie and was the sister-in-law of the golfer Jessie Valentine. At the age of eighteen and after doing some local fire watching on the outbreak of World War II, she decided to become more involved in the defense of her country and in 1943 joined the Women's Royal Naval Service ('the Wrens'). During training she did an intelligence test and her scores were so high that she was sent to work at the Government Code and Cypher School (GCCS) at Bletchley Park.

The main objective of the GCCS at Bletchley Park was to break the code of the German Enigma Machine and Jean became an operator of the bombe decryption device which was designed by Alan Turing and others to help translate the Enigma messages. As Jean was only five feet tall, a special stool was made to that she could reach the drums on the deciphering machine!

The work was highly secretive and no one ever talked about what they were doing or would be doing when outside of Bletchley Park. Jean remained quiet about her work until the mid-1970s but eventually became involved with the reconstruction of the bombe at Bletchley Park Museum which was completed in 2006. Jean then led tours at the Museum and also demonstrated the working of the reconstructed bombe.

During the final years of World War II, Jean was sent to work in Colombo, Sri Lanka, travelling by sea and braving the danger of German U-boats. She remained in Colombo until the end of the war helping to break the Japanese meteorological code.

She latterly lived in Henley, Oxfordshire where she died at the age of 94.

PEOPLE AND PERSONALITIES

JESSIE VALENTINE (1915-2006)

Jessie Valentine (formerly Jessie Anderson) was arguably the best and most competitive female Scottish golfer for much of the twentieth century. A member of the Craigie Hill club and daughter of the Craigie Hill professional Joe Anderson, she started playing golf at the age of five and won the Girls Amateur Championship in 1933.

In 1935, Jessie became the New Zealand Ladies Champion and the following year the French Ladies Champion. She was a member of the Great Britain and Ireland Curtis Cup team in 1936, holing a sixty foot putt on the eighteenth green at Gleneagles to secure a win and help the team tie with the United States. She represented Great Britain and Ireland seven times in the Curtis Cup between 1936 and 1958.

Jessie Valentine won the British Ladies Open Amateur Championship three times. The first as a twenty two-year-old at Turnberry in 1937 when she beat Doris Park (daughter of the famous Willie Park Jnr. of Musselburgh) by six and four in the final. Further victories were achieved at Royal Portrush, Northern Ireland in 1955 and at Hunstanton, Norfolk in 1958. She won the Scottish Ladies Championship on six occasions between 1938 and 1956.

Following these successes, Jessie relinquished her amateur status to join the professional ranks. In 1959 she was awarded the MBE

Jessie Valentine with both the British Ladies and Scottish Ladies Championship trophies in 1955. (Perthshire Advertiser photograph).

for services to golf and was inducted into the Scottish Sports Hall of Fame in 2003. She was married to the Perth garage owner and St Johnstone FC director George Valentine.

PETE WISHART MP

Resident in Craigie, Pete Wishart has been the Member of Parliament for Perth and North Perthshire since 2005. He is the longest-serving Scottish National Party MP having previously served as the MP for North Tayside from 2001 until that seat was abolished for the 2005 general election.

Prior to becoming a Member of Parliament at Westminster, for fifteen years Pete Wishart was a member of the popular Scottish Celtic rock band Runrig in which he played keyboard. In the early 1980s and prior to joining Runrig, Pete played with another famous Scottish band, Big Country. At Westminster, he is a founder member of the parliamentary rock group MP4.

As a politician, he has served as the SNP's Chief Whip and is currently the SNP Shadow Leader of the House in the House of Commons and the chair of the Scottish Affairs Select Committee.

This chapter has only scratched the surface of some of the prominent residents of Craigie and Cherrybank and there will probably be readers of this book with their own selection of personalities which differ from mine. Those selected are simply my own personal choice but there are many others well worthy of mention from all walks of life so let us briefly name a few more.

From the world of football, there have been St Johnstone players such as Johnny Welsh, Johnny Cameron, Allan Whyte, Doug Copland, Jim Donaldson (goalkeeper in the successful team of the late 1960s/ early 1970s), Billy Beatson, Billy McManus and Alan McKillop all of whom had connections with the Craigie and Cherrybank area at some point. There was also Hamish Watt from Glamis Place who played for East Fife. Donald Mackay, The Dundee United goalkeeper of the 1960s and later the manager of Dundee FC, was a former Craigie Cub. Kenny Cameron, a centre forward with Dundee, played in the 1964 Scottish Cup final and scored his side's only goal in their 3-1 defeat from Rangers but honed his goal scoring prowess ten years earlier in the Craigie School team. Scott Findlay, now 'Mine-Host' at the Cherrybank Inn, was a goalkeeper with several senior Scottish teams including St Johnstone, Livingston and Dundee.

The acting profession has been represented with the notable Scottish stage and television character actors of Alec Heggie and Marjory Thomson. There has also been Alex McCrindle who appeared in the first *Star Wars* film and Malcolm Jamieson who some will remember for his roles in *Victor Victoria, The Last Days of Pompeii* and as Frenchman Claude Dupont in the 1980s television series, *Howard's Way.*

Brought up in Craigie, Bruce Fummey is one of Scotland's leading stand-up comedians and in 2014 was declared Scottish Comedian of the Year. His comedy routines are known for their irreverent presentations of traditional Scottish culture with shows themed around topics such as The Jacobite Rising, Robert Burns' 'Tam o' Shanter' or Robert the Bruce. The son of a Ghanaian father and a Scottish mother (also from Craigie), Bruce describes himself as 'the finest comedian on the Afro-Celtic circuit'!

Let us not forget Sheena Macleod whose beautifully crafted Highland character dolls had reached a world-wide market and gained success in Scottish Design Council awards before her untimely death in a road accident at St Andrews in 1998.

Following a career as an award-winning journalist, Ajay Close came to Perth in 2000 as Writer in Residence at the William Soutar House in Wilson Street and when her tenure expired in 2010 decided to settle in Craigie. A dramatist and writer of literary fiction, her novels explore the emotional flashpoints of place, politics and family.

Kay McKay, a writer of children's books, lived in Needless Road. Her first book, *The Potion Maker*, was published in 2004 and featured the fictitious village of Pickletullum, obviously named after the street near her home.

Ian Spring came to live in Needless Road in 2019 and founded Rymour Books, a publisher of Scottish-themed books in 2020. He has published on Scottish cultural history and folk song and writes literary fiction and also detective fiction under the name Simpson Grears.

Former Caledonian Road School primary teacher Rhoda Fothergill from Pitheavlis Crescent will be remembered as being a leading authority on Perth's local history.

As we have read, the area has been home over the years to some outstanding musical talent. In addition to those already featured there

Martin and Marion Neilson performing in the Salutation Hotel at an annual dinner of The Perth Burns Club. Martin was the music accompanist at this popular event for thirty four consecutive years between 1978 and 2011. (Photograph by Elliott Boyle).

was George Findlay and his broadcasting Fair City Dance Band who were a popular attraction when Friday and Saturday night dances filled the village halls of Scotland during the 1950s and early 1960s.

Perth Academy music teachers Martin and Marion Neilson lived in Murray Crescent for over thirty years and during this time contributed greatly to Perth's musical scene – Martin as a highly accomplished pianist and Marion with her soprano singing voice. As well as being regular performers at concerts in the city, they are fondly remembered for forming The Fair City Singers who reached national and international acclaim. Their daughter, Helen Neilson, is now a freelance cellist and double bass player based in London.

Pete Chan, owner of the China China takeaway at Craigie Cross is well known for his charitable work in the area. In 2020 during the Covid-19 lockdowns he initiated free takeaways to the elderly and those in isolation. On another occasion, following severe flooding around Craigie, he delivered free meals to people who had been flooded out of their homes or who had lost the use of their kitchen.

Across the road, Michael Clark is the genial owner of The Fish and Chip Company. Known for years as the 'Craigie Chippy', the shop has been a Craigie fixture since the 1940s, being run first by the Giulianotti family and later the Lawrie family. Michael started working there as a small boy but over a period of seventeen years worked his way up to become the all-important fryer. He bought the business in 2000 and is popularly known as 'the memory man' due to his uncanny ability to remember a customer's order no matter how busy the shop may be. Indeed, Mike's wife, Charlene, maintains that that he still takes orders in his sleep as she has heard him muttering phrases such as 'two fish

Michael and Charlene Clark outside the Fish and Chip Co. (Photograph courtesy of Michael Clark).

suppers for the gentleman' or 'single fish and a haggis supper for the lady at the end'!

Chic and Peggy Doogan have run Craigie's local pub, The Abbotsford, for nearly twenty years. It remains a treasured meeting place and resource for the community.

This staged photograph of the Abbotsford Lounge Bar was actually taken in 2014. Featured are Chic Doogan and Steven Harper.

POSTSCRIPT

Writers tell me that the wrap-up of a book is very important. But how does one finish the ongoing, ever-changing pattern of events that have been recorded on the previous pages?

As we approach the end of the first quarter of the twenty first century it is a difficult, if not impossible, challenge to forecast the future of Craigie and Cherrybank. What is certain is that recent growth has ensured that, even after a period of two hundred years, it is still regarded as a popular and desirable place in which to live. It has always been and continues to be a very special community and one with which I have been proud to have been a part of over my lifetime.

Social history books are intended to provide personal and unique insights into the character of the places in which we live. There exists in all of us a nostalgia to remember and document the people and events of the past. But this book is also a thank you to those who came before us and gave their time, labour and often their names and their lives to create the Craigie and Cherrybank of today.

I would like to think that the book is timeless and will be read by our children and grandchildren and help them appreciate how our community and families have changed over the years.

BIBLIOGRAPHY

Aitken, William R (editor). *Poems of William Soutar: A New Selection.* (Edinburgh: Scottish Academic Press, 1988)

Baxter, Peter. *Perth Past and Present.* (Perth: John McKinlay, 1928)

Baxter, Peter. Perth and Sir Walter Scott. (Perth. Thomas Hunter & Son Ltd, 1932)

Brotchie, A.W. *Perth's Trams and Early Buses.* (Catrine: Stenlake Publishing Ltd, 2019)

Bruce, Kenneth. *Where Sky and Summit Meet.* (Perth: Tippermuir Books Limited, 2019)

Cocker, W D Poems *Scots and English.* (Glasgow: Brown, Son & Ferguson, Ltd., 1932)

Cowan, Samuel. *The Ancient Capital of Scotland.* (London: Simpkin, Marshall, Hamilton, Kent & Co., 1904)

Duncan, Jeremy. *Perth: A Century of Change. The Fair City 1900-2000.* (Derby: The Breedon Books Publishing Company, 2008)

Duncan, Jeremy. *Lost Perth.* (Edinburgh: Birlinn Limited, 2011)

Findlay, William H. *Heritage of Perth.* (Perth: Photolog Press, 1984)

Fittis, Robert Scott. *Ecclesiastical Annals of Perth.* (Perth: S Cowan & Co.,1885)

Fittis, Robert Scott. *Chronicles of Perthshire.* (Perth: The Perthshire Constitutional, 1877)

Ford, Robert. *Harp of Perthshire.* (Paisley: Alexander Gardner, 1893)

Fothergill, Rhoda. *A Short History of Craigie Primary School.* (Perth: Munro & Scott Ltd, 1982)

Hendry, Joy. *The Diary of a Dying Man.* (Edinburgh: Chapman Publications, 1991)

House, Jack. *Pride of Perth.* (London: Hutchinson Benham Ltd, 1976)

Hulbert, John. *Perth. A Comprehensive Guide for Locals and Visitors.* (Edinburgh: Luath Press Ltd, 2015)

Hutton, Guthrie. *Bygone Perth.* (Catrine: Stenlake Publishing Ltd, 2005)

McCormack, David. Memories of Perth in Verse and Prose. (Perth: D. Leslie, 1956)

McCrea, T H. *Perth County Cricket Club 1926-1976.* (Perth: John McKinlay, 1980)

McFadden, David W. *An Innocent in Scotland.* (Toronto: McLelland & Stewart Inc., 1999)

McFarland, Elaine W. *Building the Promised Land: The Church of Scotland's Church Extension Movement, 1944-61*. (Glasgow: Glasgow Caledonian University, 2011)

McLeish, Alexander. *Songs of St Johnston*. (Perth: Wood and Son,1899)

Macmillan, J E. *Know Your Perth. Volumes 1 and 2*. (Perth: The Perthshire Advertiser, 1983 and 1984)

Martine, Roddy. *Scotland – The Land and the Whisky*. (Beaconsfield: The Keepers of the Quaich, 1994)

Munro, Denis. *A Vision of Perth*. (Perth: Perth and Kinross Libraries, 2000)

Ogilvy, Graham. *The River Tay And Its People*. (Edinburgh: Mainstream Publishing, 1993)

Paton, Donald N M. *'Twixt Castle and Mart: A History of Needless Road*. (Perth: Perth & Kinross Libraries, 2005)

Paton, Donald N M. *Perth: As Others Saw Us*. (Perth: Tippermuir Books Limited, 2014)

Paton, William. *Hame Links*. (Perth: Milne, Tannahill & Methven, 1930)

Peacock, David. Perth: *Its Annals and Its Archives*. (Perth: Thomas Richardson, MDCCCXLIX)

Penny, George. *Traditions of Perth*. (Perth: Dewar, Sidey, Morison, Peat & Drummond, 1836)

Philippou, Paul and Antoniewicz, Roben. *Perth Street by Street*. (Perth: Tippermuir Books, 2012)

Scott, Tom (editor). *The Penguin Book of Scottish Verse*. (London: Penguin Books, 1970)

Smith, Jess. *Way of the Wanderers*. (Edinburgh: Birlinn Ltd, 2012)

Strachan, David. *Perth: A Place in History*. (Perth: Perth and Kinross Heritage Trust, 2011)

Roughead, William. *Mainly Murder*. (London: Cassell & Company Ltd, 1937)

Torrance, Margaret. *The First Hundred Years of Craigie Parish Church 1895-1995*. (Perth: Danscot Print, 1995)

Tranter Nigel. The Queen's Scotland: The Heartland. (London: Hodder & Stoughton Ltd., 1971)

Urquhart, Alexander Reid. *Auld Perth*. (Perth: John MacGregor & Co., 1906)

Young, Peter. *A Premium Business. A History of General Accident*. (Cambridge: Granta Editions, 1999)

INDEX